To Mr. John Cockerell
President John Cockerell Inc.,
with very best wishes,

Joseph Darrow

September 14-1959.

THE CLASSIC FRENCH CUISINE

DECORATIONS BY

WARREN CHAPPELL

JOSEPH DONON

THE CLASSIC FRENCH CUISINE

New York: Alfred · A · Knopf

1 9 5 9

L. C. Catalog card number: 59–8837

© *Joseph Donon, 1959*

THIS IS A BORZOI BOOK,

PUBLISHED BY ALFRED A. KNOPF, INC.

FIRST EDITION

FOREWORD

This volume is the culmination of my lifetime experience as a wearer of *la toque blanche,* the tall white cap that is the badge of office and the mark of honor of the professional chef who, in the words of the great Escoffier, my master, earns the right to wear it by his perfect workmanship.

In these pages I propose to guide the student cook and gourmet to an appreciation of the art of fine dining, to help him develop a keen sense of gastronomic discrimination, and, above all, to instruct him in the science of fine cookery.

The precepts and techniques which I present are those of *la haute cuisine française,* a cuisine deservedly called classic because it has endured for centuries and continues to stand the test of time. Over the years French cuisine has successfully crossed national boundaries, borrowing from and lending to the cuisine of other countries for mutual enrichment, and finding acceptance wherever it goes. The classic rules apply equally to *la haute cuisine* and to "home cooking." The recipes in this volume encompass the elaborate dishes served at world-famed restaurants and in elegant private establishments, as well as simple, delicious foods that have contributed to the day-to-day pleasure of modest homes.

I beg the student to follow the recipes exactly, and to take advantage of the ample information given on methods of handling and combining ingredients, timing, and cooking temperatures. Wherever it seemed necessary, advice on marketing has been included. *Most of the recipes are designed to serve six, unless otherwise noted.*

The problem of nutrition as such does not concern us here, but it has not been overlooked. I believe that the problem solves itself when foods chosen from the widely publicized "Daily Seven" are prepared in a variety of ways so that they tempt the appetite and make a genuine pleasure of good eating for good health.

WINE WITH FOOD

Appetite may be encouraged by a pre-dinner *apéritif,* preferably a glass of flavored aromatic wine, or by a cocktail made of strong spirits. Most connoisseurs restrict themselves to a single *apéritif* and prefer not to blunt the palate with even one cocktail when fine wine is to be served with dinner.

Wine, on the other hand, is in the opinion of many indispensable to the full enjoyment of a good dinner, and the habit of taking wine with meals is one worth cultivating.

The tradition of centuries suggests that certain wines go best with certain foods; for example, a light, dry white Chablis is a better companion to the delicate flavor of fillet of sole than the richly red, full-bodied Burgundy an expert might choose to drink with venison. When more than one wine is served with a meal, the preferred order is light wines before heavy wines, white wines before red, dry wines before sweet. If the main dish has been cooked with wine, one should drink with it more of the same wine. Or one may prefer to drink a versatile wine such as a rosé or champagne with everything.

In the end, however, the wine one drinks is a matter of personal preference developed by education and experience. A friendly wine merchant will help the novice by suggesting the proper wine for a particular menu, just as the wine steward in a fine restaurant makes his recommendation when you choose your meal. There are fine domestic wines and fine imported varieties; one should buy the best he can afford.

To enjoy wine fully, drink it from thin, clear glasses of generous size, no more than one third full. A tulip-shaped glass will serve adequately for most purposes.

Champagnes should be iced, white wines and rosés chilled for an hour or so before serving. Red wines are drunk at "room temperature," by which is meant about 65°f. Because red wines tend to cast a sediment, they are placed upright and opened an hour before serving, so that the sediment will settle to the bottom of the bottle and the clear wine can be decanted. Not many modern homes have provision for wine storage, which requires that the bottles be arranged on racks on their sides in a dark, not too dry place in which the temperature remains at a constant 55°f. Constancy is of greater importance than exact temperature, and the humidity in the air helps to keep the corks from drying and shrinking.

KITCHEN EQUIPMENT

A WELL-EQUIPPED KITCHEN is of equal importance to the professional chef and to the lady whose proficiency at the stove has earned her the enviable sobriquet of *cordon bleu*. The *cordon bleu*, or blue ribbon, was once the insigne of a *chevalier* of the

Order of the Holy Spirit, the highest honor awarded by the French monarchy. I think it loses no prestige by being used to describe a good cook.

Pots and Pans

A cook is only as good as his—or her—tools; for this reason, it pays to invest in the best. Instead of buying "sets" of the same material, buy pots and pans a few at a time as they are needed, selecting items for various uses in the material best suited for that use. For instance, a Dutch oven in cast iron or aluminum is heavy, durable, and particularly adapted for long, slow cooking of pot roasts and the like. A large enameled pot is indispensable for preserving, and will be used for boiling pasta and some soups. The many dishes started on the stove and finished in the oven require pans made of material that is both heat- and oven-proof. I make frequent use of a "sauté pan," a wide, fairly shallow, heavy-bottomed pan. Its shape and size make it possible for most of the food to be in direct contact with the bottom. A small saucepan with a heavy bottom and, preferably, rounded corners is essential for sauces; larger versions of this pan can be used for many purposes. Skillets of two sizes are essential. I use a small, flaring-sided skillet for preparing omelettes and *crêpes,* and a larger skillet for cooking quickly such items as calf's liver and minute steak. These may be made of any material, but they should be heavy enough to heat slowly and distribute heat evenly. Earthenware casseroles that can be used on top of the stove and in the oven, besides being attractive enough to be brought to the table, are also useful, and a large earthenware stockpot will serve to make stocks or soup or to cook large quantities of meat or fish.

Glass is very popular for baking, as it allows the cook to observe the degree of browning of the bottom crust of cakes and pies. Baking-sheets are usually made of aluminum or of tin, which darkens with use and imparts a good brown crust to cookies and pastries.

Foreword

The list of materials used for pots and pans now ranges from aluminum through enameled cast iron and copper-clad stainless steel to glass; all have advantages and disadvantages that should be considered before making a purchase.

Utensils and Appliances

I think that if I had to choose but one major kitchen appliance, I should select the electric mixer and its attachments for beating and grinding. I also appreciate the convenience of an electric frying-kettle with thermostatic controls and of the electric blender that takes the place of the *tamis,* or fine sieve; and of course we take for granted such equipment as electric waffle irons and toasters.

As for utensils, every kitchen should have two or three strainers of different sizes and mesh, as well as a large-holed colander. Only wooden spoons should be used for stirring at the stove; the wire sauce whisk is the exception to this rule. A roast-meat thermometer is invaluable to the novice cook; a candy thermometer helps to make preserves failure-proof; and a deep-fat thermometer ensures accuracy. Every kitchen should boast an assortment of good-quality French knives for various purposes, as well as spatulas, a ladle, a skimmer, and a perforated spoon. Scissors, kitchen needles, larding-needles, and skewers have special functions. For baking, a flour-sifter, measuring spoons and cups, a scale, and a pastry bag and tube are required. Such items as the floating knife peeler, the pastry wheel, ball-cutters, and pastry-cutters will be purchased as the cook's repertoire grows, as will many other gadgets that may or may not prove to be worth the space they occupy!

CONTENTS

Contents

I

STOCKS, SAUCES, *and* SOUPS

STOCKS

If any single preparation can be called the essential base of *la cuisine française,* that preparation is stock, which serves as the foundation for numerous soups and many all-important sauces. The secret of this rich broth is the long, slow cooking that extracts every vestige of flavor and strength from bones, vegetables, and seasonings.

Because the recipes in this volume frequently call for stock, formulas for the various kinds are given here for easy reference.

Fond Blanc
(*White Stock*)

3 peppercorns
2 teaspoons salt
5 quarts water

1 fowl, 4 pounds, or 4 pounds shin beef
1 pound veal knuckle bones
2 carrots
1 onion, stuck with a clove
1 bouquet made of 1 stalk of celery, 1 sprig each of thyme and parsley, and a bit of bay leaf

COMBINE all the ingredients in a 2-gallon stock pot. Bring the water to a boil, skim off the solids that rise to the surface in the form of scum, and reduce the heat. Cook slowly for 3 hours. Remove the fat from the surface. Strain the stock through a fine cloth; cool. This makes about 3 quarts, which will keep for a week or longer in the refrigerator.

Chicken Broth
(*Chicken Stock*)

MAKE the *fond blanc,* or white stock, using a fowl instead of beef.

Fond Brun
(*Brown Stock, or Foundation Stock*)

2 pounds beef shin
2 pounds veal knuckle
¼ pound lean raw ham with the bone
2 carrots
2 onions
5 quarts water
1 bouquet of celery, parsley, thyme, and bay leaf

SPREAD the meat and bones all in fairly small pieces, on a flat pan, sprinkle them with a little fat, and brown them well in a moderate oven or on top of the stove, stirring occasionally. Slice the carrots and onions and brown them with the meat for a few minutes. Transfer all to a 2-gallon stock pot and add the water, the bouquet, and 2 teaspoons salt. Bring the water to a boil, skim well, reduce the heat, and cook for about 3 hours. Cool the stock, remove the fat, and strain the stock through a fine cloth. This makes 3 quarts of stock, which may be stored in the refrigerator for a week or more.

Fond de Poissons Blanc
(*White Fish Stock*)

2 pounds bones and trimmings of white-fleshed fish
2 onions, sliced
3 sprigs parsley
3 peppercorns
juice of ½ lemon

COMBINE the ingredients in a 4-quart saucepan with 2½ quarts water, a little salt, and some mushroom peelings, if available. Bring the liquid to a boil, skim, and simmer for 30 minutes. Strain the stock through a fine cloth, cool, and store in the refrigerator. Makes about 2 quarts.

SAUCES

The true purpose of a sauce is to emphasize and enhance the good natural taste of the food with which it is served. Therefore, the ideal sauce is light, smooth, perfectly blended, and discreetly seasoned to complement or contrast with the flavor of the dish. No one knows better than an expert *cuisinier* that the richer the cooking, the more speedily one tires of it. You will find that in *la haute cuisine* sauces are carefully chosen to maintain a healthful balance of richness and simplicity.

Sauce making demands the cook's exclusive attention and vigilance, for many sauces must be stirred almost constantly to insure perfect blending and prevent scorching; but the time of preparation is generally relatively short, and the results well worth the trouble.

A small, heavy-bottomed saucepan, preferably with rounded corners, is essential equipment for the *saucier,* as are a small wire whisk and a wooden spoon.

Most sauces are thickened with a *roux* of butter and flour (I deal elsewhere in this volume with dessert sauces and pan sauces, made by lightly thickening the cooking liquid of fish, fowl, or meat), and this *roux* must be thoroughly cooked to eliminate the taste of raw flour. Some sauces are further enriched with an egg yolk; they must not be allowed to boil after the egg yolk is added. If necessary, any

5

sauce may be strained through a fine sieve or several thicknesses of cheesecloth.

White Sauces

IN MAKING WHITE SAUCES, the *roux* is not allowed to color, although it must cook for at least one minute, and preferably for two minutes.

Sauce Velouté

1 cup white stock
1 tablespoon butter
2 tablespoons flour
1 tablespoon cream

MELT the butter in a small, heavy-bottomed saucepan and stir in the flour. Cook, stirring constantly with a wooden spoon, for about 2 minutes without letting the *roux* discolor. Add the stock gradually, stirring now with a sauce whisk. Cook, still stirring, until the sauce thickens and is smooth. If the sauce seems too thin, cook it a little longer; if it is too thick, add a little more stock. Finish the sauce with the cream, and add salt and white pepper to taste.

Sauce Suprême

ENRICH *sauce velouté* with 1 more tablespoon of cream and swirl in 1 tablespoon sweet butter just before serving.

Sauce Chaud-Froid
(*Jellied White Sauce*)

2 tablespoons butter
3 tablespoons flour
4 cups chicken stock
2 egg yolks
CONTINUED

MAKE the *roux* and stir in the stock as for *sauce velouté*. Cook, stirring, for a few minutes and add the gelatin, softened in ¼ cup cold water. Cook the sauce gently for a few minutes longer and stir in the egg yolks beaten with the cream.

6

Heat, but do not allow the sauce to boil again. Strain the sauce through a fine cloth and stir it. *Sauce chaud-froid* is used to coat cold chicken dishes. It jells with a handsome shine, and makes an excellent background for cut-out truffles and other garnishings.

½ cup cream
1 envelope gelatin

Sauce Paprika pour Chaud-Froid

TINT and flavor white *chaud-froid* sauce with paprika: allow 1 teaspoon paprika to each cup of sauce.

Sauce Poulette

MELT the butter in a heavy-bottomed saucepan, add the flour, and cook, stirring, for 2 minutes. Do not allow the *roux* to brown. Gradually add the boiling hot stock and cook, stirring with a wire whisk, until the sauce is thickened and smooth. Clean and slice the mushrooms and chop the shallot. Combine these with the wine, bring the mixture to a boil, and simmer for 10 minutes. Stir this mixture into the thickened sauce and bring to the boil. Adjust the seasoning. Beat the egg yolks with the cream, warm them with a little of the hot sauce, and stir them into the sauce. Heat, stirring constantly, without allowing the sauce to boil. Add the lemon juice and parsley.

2 tablespoons butter
2 tablespoons flour
2 cups white stock
½ pound mushrooms
1 shallot
1 cup white wine
2 egg yolks
1 cup cream
1 teaspoon lemon juice
1 teaspoon chopped parsley

Sauce au Curry
(*Curry Cream Sauce*)

MELT the butter in a heavy-bottomed saucepan and in it cook the onion, chopped, until it is soft, but not brown. Sprinkle with the flour and

2 tablespoons butter
1 medium onion
CONTINUED

7

2 tablespoons flour
1 tablespoon curry powder
¼ bay leaf
pinch of powdered thyme
2 cups white stock
½ cup cream

cook, stirring with a wooden spoon, for 2 minutes. Add the seasonings and cook for 1 minute longer. Gradually add the boiling hot stock and cook, stirring constantly with a sauce whisk until the sauce is smooth and thickened. Simmer the sauce for 10 minutes to marry the flavors, stirring occasionally to prevent scorching. Add the cream, reheat the sauce without allowing it to boil, and strain it through a fine sieve.

Sauces Made with Fish Stock

Fish Velouté

Follow the recipe for *sauce velouté* substituting fish stock for the white stock specified in the recipe.

Sauce Vénitienne

1 cup white wine
1 cup tarragon vinegar
2 cups *fish velouté*
1 tablespoon sweet butter, or
1 cup *sauce Hollandaise*
½ teaspoon mixed chopped
  chervil and tarragon

Over high heat reduce the wine and vinegar to half its original volume. Stir in the fish *velouté* and cook, stirring, until the sauce is smooth. Remove the pan from the heat and swirl in the butter. Or fold in the *sauce Hollandaise,* to make a richer sauce. Add the chopped herbs and adjust the seasoning with salt and pepper.

Sauces Made without Stock

Louis XIV's *maître d'hôtel,* Béchamel, was a former financier whose experience undoubtedly made him a very valuable steward; but Béchamel goes down in history not as a financial genius, but as the creator of a basic sauce.

Sauce Béchamel
(Cream Sauce)

MELT the butter in a small, heavy-bottomed saucepan, stir in the flour, and cook the *roux,* stirring, for a few minutes without allowing it to color. Scald the milk with the onion and parsley and strain it into the *roux,* stirring briskly with a sauce whisk. Bring the sauce to a boil and cook it slowly for a few minutes. If the sauce seems too thick, add a little more milk. Add the cream, bring the sauce again to the boil, and season it with salt, pepper, and a dash of freshly grated nutmeg.

1 tablespoon butter
2 tablespoons flour
1 cup milk
1 thin slice of onion
1 sprig of parsley
1 tablespoon cream

PHILIPPE MORNAY (1549–1623) was a great friend of Henri IV, and shared that royal gourmet's enthusiasm for fine foods. Joseph Voiron, chef to Herbornez au Grand Vefour, named this sauce in Mornay's honor, according to the practice of the day.

Sauce Mornay

To THE hot Béchamel sauce add the cheese and the egg yolk beaten with a little cream. Warm the egg yolk with a little of the hot sauce before stirring it into the pan, and be careful not to allow the sauce to boil again. Finish the sauce with 1 tablespoon butter.

1 cup Béchamel sauce
2 teaspoons grated Swiss or
  Parmesan cheese
1 egg yolk
1 tablespoon butter

Sauce Moutarde
(Mustard Sauce)

MELT the butter, stir in the flour, and cook the *roux* over low heat for a minute or two, stirring

½ tablespoon butter
CONTINUED

9

½ tablespoon flour
½ cup scalded milk
½ cup light cream
½ tablespoon dry mustard

constantly, without allowing it to color. Stir in the hot milk and the cream and cook for 5 minutes. Blend the dry mustard to a paste with a little water and stir it into the sauce. Adjust the seasoning with salt and cayenne pepper.

Sauce Soubise
(*Onion Sauce*)

1 cup sliced onions
2 tablespoons butter
2 tablespoons flour
1 cup milk

POUR boiling water over the onions, drain them well, and cook them in the butter until they are soft, but not at all browned. Stir in the flour and cook, stirring, for 2 minutes. Add the hot milk, season with salt and pepper to taste, and cook, stirring, for 5 minutes. Force the sauce through a sieve or purée it in an electric blender and enrich it with a little cream, if desired.

Brown Sauces

THE *roux* for a brown sauce is made of equal parts of flour and butter, and it must be cooked from 2 to 4 minutes. It should be allowed to brown lightly, but it must not be allowed to burn and thus impart a bitter flavor to the sauce.

Sauce Brune
(*Brown Sauce*)

2 cups brown stock
2 tablespoons butter
2 tablespoons flour
2 tablespoons tomato juice
1 tablespoon diced carrots
1 tablespoon diced onion
1 tablespoon diced salt pork
CONTINUED

MELT the butter in a heavy-bottomed saucepan, stir in the flour, and cook the *roux,* stirring constantly with a wooden spoon, until it is golden brown. Add the brown stock and bring the sauce to a boil, stirring constantly with a sauce whisk. Reduce the heat and simmer slowly.

Brown the salt pork dice lightly in a skillet, add the onions and carrots, and continue to cook, stirring occasionally, until all are brown. Pour off the fat. Add the white wine, bring the liquid to the boil, and add the tomato juice, the thyme, and the bay leaf. Add this mixture to the brown sauce and simmer all together for 1 hour, stirring from time to time. Skim off the fat that rises to the surface and adjust the seasoning. Put the sauce through a fine sieve or purée it in an electric blender, reheat it, and add ½ cup Madeira or sherry.

The brown sauce should be thick enough to coat a spoon; if it is too thin, cook it a little longer. Or it may be thinned by adding a little brown stock.

Brown sauce will keep well in the refrigerator in a covered jar.

a bit of bay leaf
a small sprig of thyme
1 cup dry white wine

Sauce Piquante

1 tablespoon flour
1 tablespoon vinegar
2 tablespoons chopped pickles

2 cups brown stock
1 tablespoon butter
1 carrot
1 onion
1 shallot
1 sprig of thyme
a bit of bay leaf
1 sprig of parsley
6 crushed peppercorns

COOK the carrots, onion, shallot, all diced, with the bay leaf, thyme, and parsley, in the butter, stirring constantly. Stir in the flour and cook, stirring, until the flour browns. Add the stock gradually and cook, stirring, for a few minutes. Add the peppercorns and the vinegar and cook for 1 hour, stirring from time to time. Strain the sauce, adjust the seasoning with salt, and finish with the pickles.

Sauce Bordelaise

COOK the shallots and wine until the liquid is reduced by half. Add the brown sauce and cook until the liquid measures about ¾ cup.

2 teaspoons finely chopped
  shallots
CONTINUED

11

1 cup red Bordeaux wine
1 cup brown sauce
2 tablespoons beef marrow
1 teaspoon chopped parsley

Poach the beef marrow in salted water, cut it in small dice, and add it to the sauce. Finish the sauce with the parsley. Serve with calf's liver, steak, and other meats.

Sauce Robert

1 tablespoon butter
2 onions
1 tablespoon flour
½ cup white wine
1 cup brown stock
1 tablespoon wine vinegar
1 tablespoon dry mustard

MELT the butter in a heavy-bottomed saucepan and brown the onions, finely chopped. Add the flour and brown it well. Stir in the brown stock and the white wine. Bring the sauce to a boil, stirring, and cook it for 10 minutes. Stir in the mustard, blended with the vinegar and a pinch of sugar. Adjust the seasoning and serve. Do not boil the sauce after the mustard has been added.

Sauce Madère
(*Madeira Sauce*)

1 tablespoon chopped ham
1 small onion
1 small carrot
1 stalk celery
1 sprig parsley
½ sprig of thyme
1 garlic clove
2 tomatoes
a bit of bay leaf
2 tablespoons butter
2 tablespoons flour
2 cups brown stock

3 peppercorns
1 cup Madeira

COOK the chopped ham in the butter for a few minutes. Add the carrots, onions, and celery, all chopped, and cook briskly, stirring constantly, until the vegetables are brown. Stir in the flour and brown it. Add the brown stock and the remaining vegetables and herbs and cook, stirring, until the sauce thickens. Cook slowly for 20 minutes. Remove the fat that rises to the surface during the cooking. Strain the sauce and discard the vegetables. The sauce will be thick as cream. Finish the sauce with the Madeira, and heat it without boiling. Adjust the seasoning with salt and pepper and serve.

Butter Sauces

THE MOST WIDELY KNOWN and best liked of butter sauces is Hollandaise. The tart, refreshing flavor of Hollandaise and its lightness make it especially suitable for vegetables and for fish.

Sauce Hollandaise

COMBINE the egg yolks and cream in a small saucepan and stir them together with a sauce whisk. Put the saucepan in a pan containing hot but not boiling water and continue to stir until the mixture is thick as heavy cream. Melt the butter and skim the surface carefully. Add the hot butter gradually to the egg and cream, stirring briskly to incorporate each spoonful of butter before adding the next. Finish the sauce with the lemon juice; adjust the seasoning to taste with salt and a little red pepper.

3 egg yolks
1 tablespoon cream
1 cup sweet butter
juice of ¼ lemon

Sauce Mousseline

TO THE completed *sauce Hollandaise* add 1 tablespoon whipped cream.

MANY RECIPES have been dedicated to Henri IV, but perhaps the most famous of these is this one for *sauce Béarnaise*. Béarn was the original name of the Basses-Pyrenées region in southwest France. Because in this part of France much oil is used in cookery, it is possible that, as some culinarians argue, the first *sauce Béarnaise* was a cooked mayonnaise. If so, we owe our greatest debt not to the originator of the sauce, but to the genius who first substituted butter for oil in the recipe.

Sauce Béarnaise

¼ cup dry white wine
½ cup tarragon vinegar
2 shallots
2 sprigs of tarragon
2 sprigs of chervil
4 crushed peppercorns
3 egg yolks
½ tablespoon cream
1 cup butter, clarified

COMBINE in a small saucepan the vinegar, white wine, and peppercorns. Add the shallots, chopped, and the chopped stems of the chervil and tarragon. Reserve the herb leaves for later use. Cook this mixture over high heat until it is nearly dry. Cool it and stir in the egg yolks beaten with the cream. Set the saucepan in a pan containing hot but not boiling water and continue to stir with a whisk until the sauce is creamy. Melt 1 cup butter, skim it, and pour it off the milky sediment that settles to the bottom of the pan. Add this clarified butter to the sauce gradually, stirring to incorporate each spoonful before adding the next. Strain the sauce through a fine cloth. If it seems too thick, add a few drops of cold water to prevent curdling. Adjust the seasoning with salt and cayenne pepper and finish the sauce with the chopped tarragon and chervil leaves.

Sauce au Beurre
(*Butter Sauce*)

1 ½ tablespoons butter
1 tablespoon flour
1 cup hot water
1 egg yolk
2 tablespoons sweet butter
juice of ¼ lemon

MELT the butter, add the flour, and cook the *roux* for a minute or two, stirring constantly, without letting it take on color. Remove the pan from the stove and let the *roux* cool. Add the boiling water gradually, stirring briskly with a whisk to keep the sauce smooth. Add a little salt and bring the sauce to the boiling point, stirring constantly. Stir in the egg yolk, which has been blended with cream and warmed with a little of the sauce, and add the sweet butter, bit by bit. Finish with the lemon juice, and adjust the seasoning. This sauce is used like Hollandaise. Although it is not as rich, it will not curdle, and is equally delicious.

Clarified Butter

MELT as much butter as is required, skim it, and pour the clear oil carefully off the milky sediment that will settle to the bottom of the pan. In addition to its use as a sauce and as an ingredient in other sauces, clarified butter is good for sautéing because it has a higher burning point than ordinary butter.

Sauce Maître d'Hôtel

CREAM the butter in a small bowl and work in the other ingredients, blending thoroughly. Season to taste with salt and white pepper.

2 tablespoons sweet butter
1 teaspoon chopped parsley
juice of ½ lemon

Miscellaneous Sauces

Sauce au Pain
(*Bread Sauce*)

1 cup fine fresh bread crumbs
¼ cup cream.

2 ½ cups milk
1 small onion
1 small stalk celery
2 cloves
1 sprig of parsley
6 peppercorns

COMBINE all ingredients except bread crumbs and cream in the top of a double boiler and cook over hot water for 20 minutes. Strain the milk and return it to the pan. Add the bread crumbs and cook for 5 minutes longer. Add the cream and adjust the seasoning with salt and cayenne pepper.

Sauce Cumberland

6 tablespoons currant jelly
1 orange
1 lemon
4 shallots
6 tablespoons port wine
½ teaspoon powdered sugar
red pepper, ginger, dry
  mustard

SQUEEZE the currant jelly through a fine cheese-cloth. Peel the orange and lemon very thinly, cut the zest into small shreds, and parboil the shreds for 10 minutes in water to cover. Drain well. Add the peel to the jelly. Add also the juice of the orange and of half the lemon. Chop the shallots and parboil them in water to cover for 4 minutes. Drain them, cool, and add them to the sauce. With a small wire whisk, stir in gently the wine, sugar, and seasonings to taste. Serve cold, with cold venison or other meats.

Sauce Raifort Froide
(*Cold Horse-radish Sauce*)

½ cup freshly grated
  horse-radish
½ teaspoon dry mustard
1 tablespoon powdered sugar
2 tablespoons white wine
  vinegar

1 cup fresh bread crumbs
1 cup heavy cream

DRAIN the horse-radish and mix it with the seasonings and vinegar. Soak the bread crumbs in milk and press them well to dry. Toss all together and store in a cool place until serving time. Whip the cream and gently but thoroughly fold the horse-radish into it. Adjust the seasoning with salt.

Sauce Tomate
(*Tomato Sauce*)

1 tablespoon diced lean salt
  pork
1 tablespoon diced carrots
1 crushed garlic clove
CONTINUED

BROWN the salt pork lightly in a saucepan. Add the carrots and onion and simmer all together for 10 minutes. Stir in the flour and cook for a few minutes, stirring constantly. Add the fresh tomatoes, peeled and seeded, or 1 quart canned

16

tomatoes, the garlic, and the herb bouquet, and salt, pepper, and sugar to taste. Cover the pan and cook very slowly until the vegetables are thoroughly cooked. Or put the covered pan in a moderate oven. Put the sauce through a fine sieve or purée it in an electric blender, and finish it with 1 tablespoon butter. Makes 1 quart.

6 large, ripe tomatoes
1 teaspoon flour
bouquet of 1 sprig of parsley, 1 stalk of celery, ½ sprig of thyme, and a bit of bay leaf

Cold Sauces

THE MOST POPULAR and most versatile of the cold sauces is mayonnaise, which has many variations and is used for many different foods. Mayonnaise salad dressings will be found in the chapter on salads.

Mayonnaise

AN ELECTRIC MIXER, set at low speed, is very useful in making mayonnaise. Lacking the mixer, use a sauce whisk.

Combine in a mixing-bowl all the ingredients except the oil. Beat well with a sauce whisk. Beat in the oil very slowly, almost drop by drop at first, then in a thin stream, until all has been incorporated and the sauce is thick and light.

If the sauce becomes too thick, add a little water. Do not over-beat the mayonnaise, as it may make it curdle. Mayonnaise should be kept at a temperature of from 45 to 50 degrees; below this point it may curdle. If it does, start the curdled sauce all over again, beginning with one tablespoon of hot water. Avoid adding salt after the sauce is finished, as this might make it curdle.

4 egg yolks
½ teaspoon salt
1 teaspoon dry mustard
⅛ teaspoon pepper
1 tablespoon wine vinegar
1 tablespoon tarragon vinegar
juice of ¼ lemon
2 cups olive oil

Sauce Moutarde Froide
(*Cold Mustard Sauce*)

2 cups mayonnaise
1 tablespoon French dressing

2 tablespoons prepared French
  style mustard

COMBINE well and adjust the seasoning to taste
with salt and pepper.

Sauce Verte
(*Green Mayonnaise*)

1 cup mayonnaise
1 tablespoon chopped chervil
½ tablespoon chopped cooked
  spinach
1 tablespoon chopped tarragon
  leaves

1 tablespoon chopped
  watercress leaves

COMBINE well and adjust the seasoning to taste
with salt and pepper.

Sauce Tartare
(*Tartar Sauce*)

1 cup mayonnaise
1 hard-cooked egg
1 teaspoon chopped chives

CHOP the egg and combine it with the mayonnaise and chives. Adjust the seasoning to taste
with salt and pepper.

Oil and Vinegar Sauces

THE *sauce vinaigrette,* also called French dressing, is
used for many foods in addition to salads. The salad dressings are listed in the salad chapter.

Sauce Vinaigrette

2 sprigs of chives
1 tablespoon capers

2 tablespoons wine vinegar
½ teaspoon dry mustard
4 tablespoons olive oil
2 sprigs of parsley
2 sprigs of chervil
2 sprigs of tarragon
1 teaspoon onion
1 tablespoon chopped
  hard-cooked egg

IN A small mixing-bowl stir the vinegar and mustard together, using a wire whisk. Add salt and a little freshly ground black pepper. Add the herbs, all finely chopped, and gradually stir in the olive oil. Add the capers and chopped egg, and adjust the seasoning to taste.

Sauce Vinaigrette avec Moutarde
(*Mustard French Dressing*)

¼ teaspoon freshly ground
  black pepper

3 tablespoons olive oil
1 tablespoon wine vinegar, or
  juice of 1 lemon
1 teaspoon dry mustard
½ teaspoon salt

MIX the mustard, vinegar, and seasonings in a small bowl, using a wire whisk, and stir in the oil. This dressing may be made in advance and stored in a bottle in the refrigerator. It should be shaken well before serving.

Sauce Gribiche

FORCE the egg yolks through a fine sieve and cut the whites in very small julienne strips. In a small mixing-bowl combine the sieved egg yolks with the vinegar. Very slowly beat in the olive oil. Finish the sauce with the chopped mixture and with the egg whites julienne, and adjust the seasoning with salt and freshly ground pepper.

3 hard-cooked eggs
3 tablespoons wine vinegar
1 cup olive oil
1 tablespoon mixed chopped
  gherkins, capers, parsley,
  chervil, and tarragon leaves

SOUPS

Soup has many functions in the meal; it may serve to sharpen the appetite at the beginning of an elaborate dinner, or to bolster a rather light entrée, or as a meal in itself. Many soups begin with stock (you will note that the words stock, broth, and bouillon are used interchangeably in the recipes that follow); others are made with meat and fowl that are then served with the soup; still others have milk or even water as their liquid.

Consommés are made with beef, chicken, fish, or game stock; their distinguishing characteristics are richness of flavor and crystal clarity of appearance.

Consommé

Consommé
(Clear Soup)

3 quarts white stock
1 pound chopped beef
1 carrot
1 leek
1 small onion
1 stalk of celery
3 egg whites
4 peppercorns
2 cloves
1 fresh crushed tomato

COMBINE the cold stock, sliced vegetables, and egg whites in a soup kettle and bring the mixture slowly to a boil, stirring constantly with a wooden spoon. The egg whites attract the floating particles of solid matter in the soup, thus unifying and clarifying it. Simmer one hour, then strain the consommé through a flannel cloth. Garnish to taste with rice, fine noodles, vegetables, or croutons.

Consommé Velours
(*Velvet Consommé*)

½ cup cream
1 pony glass dry sherry

1 ½ quarts chicken or beef
consommé
⅓ cup minute tapioca
1 egg yolk

BRING the consommé to the boil and gradually add the minute tapioca. Boil the soup for 10 minutes. At serving time, stir in the egg yolk, cream, and sherry, beaten together, and reheat without boiling.

Consommé au Fumet de Céleri
(*Celery Consommé*)

the leaves of 1 head of celery, chopped
½ onion, stuck with a clove
4 peppercorns

2 quarts chicken stock
1 pound chopped beef
some chicken bones, if available
2 egg whites
1 leek
1 carrot
1 tomato

COMBINE the ingredients in a stock pot and bring the liquid to a boil, stirring constantly. Simmer for 1½ hours. Strain the consommé through flannel cloth; it will be very clear and of a rich golden color. Season to taste and garnish each serving with a few julienne strips of celery.

Consommé Madrilène
(*Tomato Consommé*)

PEEL and slice the tomatoes and clean and slice the pepper. Combine the tomatoes and the pepper with the consommé and simmer all together for 1 hour. Strain the consommé and add a little red coloring, if necessary. Serve hot, with a few strips of ripe tomato in each cup.

2 quarts clarified consommé
6 ripe tomatoes
1 green pepper

21

Consommé Madrilène may be served jellied;
if necessary, add ½ envelope gelatin, softened
in cold water, to the hot soup (see Jellied Soup,
which follows).

Jellied Soup

A CONSOMMÉ MADE WITH BEEF, veal, and chicken bones
in sufficient quantity should jelly naturally. Test a little of
the consommé in a saucer. If after a stay in the refrigerator
it thickens slightly but does not stiffen, add to the hot soup
½ envelope gelatin softened in ¼ cup cold water.

To serve jellied soups, stir them with a fork and pile into
chilled consommé cups. Or, if desired, the soup may be
poured into the cups and put in the refrigerator to set.

Gelée de Volaille
(Chicken Aspic Jelly)

4 cups chicken broth in jelly
1 teaspoon chopped tarragon
12 peppercorns
1 envelope gelatin
2 egg whites

BRING 1 cup of the chicken broth and the tarragon and peppercorns to a boil, then cook rapidly until the mixture is reduced one-half. Add
the remaining chicken broth, bring the liquid
to a boil, and stir in the gelatin softened in ¼
cup of cold water. Stir in the egg whites lightly
beaten and bring to a boil again, stirring briskly
with a whisk. Cook very slowly for 10 to 15
minutes, correct the seasoning with salt and
cayenne pepper, and strain the jelly through a
fine cloth.

Gelée de Porto
(Port Wine Aspic)

1 ½ cups port wine
CONTINUED

BRING 1 cup of the wine and the seasonings to a
boil, then cook rapidly until the mixture is

thick and syrupy. Add the chicken broth, bring the liquid to a boil, and stir in the gelatin, softened in ¼ cup cold water. Stir in the egg whites, lightly beaten, and bring to the boil again, stirring briskly with a whisk. Cook very slowly for 5 to 10 minutes, correct the seasoning with salt and cayenne pepper, and strain the jelly through a fine cloth. Cool it and add the remaining ½ cup port wine.

1 teaspoon chopped chervil
1 teaspoon chopped tarragon
12 peppercorns
4 cups chicken or beef stock
1 envelope gelatin
2 egg whites

Soups Made with Beef Stock

Potage Julienne

1 small onion
2 quarts beef stock

1 tablespoon clarified butter
3 small carrots
1 small white turnip
1 leek
1 small head of celery
2 leaves of cabbage

PEEL the vegetables and cut them into thin julienne or matchsticks. Cook the julienne in the butter until the strips are soft, stirring from time to time with a wooden spoon. Add the boiling beef stock, a little salt, and a pinch of sugar. Simmer the soup slowly for 1 hour. Skim off the butter that rises to the surface.

Soupe à l'Oignon
(*Onion Soup*)

SLICE the onions thin and cook them in the butter, stirring from time to time with a wooden spoon, until they are thoroughly cooked, soft, and lightly golden in color. Sprinkle with the flour and continue to cook, stirring, for a few minutes. Add the beef broth and salt and freshly ground pepper to taste. Simmer the soup for 10 to 15 minutes.

Toast French bread on both sides and put the

6 small onions
1 tablespoon butter
1 teaspoon flour
6 cups beef broth
3 tablespoons grated Parmesan cheese
6 slices toast

toast in a soup tureen or in individual casseroles. Pour the soup over the toast, sprinkle with grated cheese, and put the tureen in a moderate oven or under the broiler to melt and brown the cheese. Serve very hot.

Crème Portugaise
(*Tomato Soup*)

1 carrot
1 onion
1 stalk of celery
1 tablespoon butter
1 tablespoon flour
1 garlic clove
1 small sprig of thyme
3 cups canned tomatoes
2 quarts bouillon

DICE the carrot, onion, and celery and cook them in butter for 10 minutes. Sprinkle with flour and cook for a few minutes longer. Add the bouillon, a pinch of sugar, the thyme, and the garlic and cook slowly for 1 hour. Force the soup through a sieve or purée it in an electric blender. Add salt and pepper to taste and finish the soup with a little more butter or ½ cup cream, if desired.

Soupe au Fromage Suisse
(*Swiss Cheese Soup*)

4 slices white bread
2 tablespoons clarified butter
1 small white onion
4 cups beef or chicken stock
1 cup hot heavy cream
2 egg yolks
½ cup grated Swiss cheese

CUT the bread in small cubes and brown the croutons on all sides in butter. Mince the onion and brown it in the clarified butter. Add the croutons and the stock and cook for 10 minutes. Force the soup through a sieve or purée it in an electric blender, and bring it to the boiling point. Stir in the egg yolks beaten with the cream and the grated cheese. Adjust the seasoning with salt and white pepper to taste. Serves 6.

Soups Made with Chicken Stock

Potage de Légumes Davenport
(*Vegetable Soup Davenport*)

SLICE the onion, leek, and garlic and cook them slowly in the butter until they are soft, but not brown. Add the stock, the potatoes, sliced, the

1 tomato
1 tablespoon grated cheese

½ onion
½ leek
½ garlic clove
1 tablespoon butter
1 quart chicken stock
1 potato
½ cup sliced winter squash
1 cup chopped spinach leaves
1 cup shredded lettuce

squash, spinach, and lettuce, and the tomatoes, peeled, seeded, and coarsely chopped. Cook slowly for about 45 minutes. A little vermicelli or fine noodles may be added 10 minutes before the soup is done. Adjust the seasoning with salt and pepper and stir in the grated cheese and, if desired, a little cream.

Potage Germiny
(*Sorrel Soup*)

SHRED the sorrel and stew it in the butter until the leaves are soft. Add the hot chicken broth and cook for 15 minutes. At serving time, beat the egg yolks with the cream, add them to the soup, and heat without boiling. Add salt and white pepper to taste and serve at once. Serves 3.

¼ pound sorrel leaves
1 tablespoon sweet butter
2 cups chicken broth
3 egg yolks
½ cup cream

Vichyssoise
(*Cold Cream of Potato and Leek Soup*)

SLICE the leeks and onions thin and cook them slowly in the butter for from 10 to 15 minutes, stirring occasionally with a wooden spoon, until they are soft, but not browned. Add the chicken broth and the potatoes, diced, and cook for 15 minutes longer. Add the scalded milk and bring the soup to the boiling point. Season well with salt and white pepper and put the soup through a fine sieve or purée it in an electric blender. Chill thoroughly, add the cream, and serve in chilled cups with a sprinkling of chopped chives on each portion. Serves 8.

6 leeks, white parts only
2 small onions
2 tablespoons sweet butter
5 potatoes
4 cups chicken broth
1 teaspoon salt
2 cups scalded milk
1 cup cream

25

Soups Made with Stock or Water

Potage Crécy
(*Cream of Carrot Soup*)

½ pound carrots
1 onion
4 cups chicken stock or water
½ cup butter
½ cup rice
½ cup cream
1 teaspoon sugar

CHOP the onion and cook it in half the butter without allowing it to take on color. Add the carrots, scraped and sliced thin, and stew gently for about 10 minutes. Add the liquid, the rice, the sugar, and a little salt. Cook slowly until the rice and vegetables are very tender. Rub the soup through a sieve or purée it in an electric blender, add the hot cream and the remaining butter, and adjust the seasoning. Serves from 4 to 6.

Potage Santé Froid
(*Cold Health Soup*)

1 leek
1 potato
2 teaspoons butter
2 cups water or chicken broth
5 leaves sorrel
1 cup scalded milk

SLICE the leeks and simmer them in the butter for about 10 minutes. Add the water or chicken broth, the potato, sliced, and a little salt and pepper. Cook, covered, for 45 minutes. Force the soup through a fine sieve or purée it in an electric blender and return it to the saucepan. Add the sorrel, shredded, cook the soup for 2 minutes, and add the hot milk. Correct the seasoning and let the soup cool. Skim off the butter that will rise to the surface. Chill the soup and serve it very cold in chilled cups. If desired, the soup may be enriched by the addition of a little cream. Serves 4.

Potage Garbure Paysanne
(*Thick Soup*)

3 stalks of celery
1 leek
CONTINUED

MINCE the vegetables and stew them in the butter for 30 minutes. Add the chicken broth or water and cook for 1 hour. Force the soup through a fine sieve or purée it in an electric blender, bring it to a rolling boil, and adjust the seasoning with salt and white pepper. Serve with slices of French bread that have been toasted, spread with butter, sprinkled with grated Parmesan cheese, and browned under the broiler. Serves from 4 to 6.

1 onion
1 white turnip
2 carrots
¼ small cabbage
1 tablespoon butter
1 quart chicken broth or water

Crème de Champignons
(Cream of Mushroom Soup)

WASH the mushrooms, trim off the tough stem ends, and slice caps and stems thin. Simmer the mushrooms, covered, with half the butter, 1 tablespoon broth, and the lemon juice. Add a little salt and pepper and the remaining broth; bring the liquid to a boil. Melt the rest of the butter in another pan, stir in the flour, and cook the *roux* for 1 minute. Gradually add the mushroom broth and cook, stirring, for a few minutes. Add 2 tablespoons cream and adjust the seasoning. If desired, this soup may be forced through a fine sieve, or puréed in an electric blender. Serves 2 or 3.

½ pound mushrooms
1 tablespoon butter
2 teaspoons flour
½ teaspoon lemon juice
2 cups chicken broth or water
2 tablespoons cream

Meat Soups

THE most famous of all French soups, *Le Pot au Feu,* is more than a soup. It is a meal in itself, and usually provides leftovers for another day as well.

Le Pot au Feu

PUT the meat (a fowl may be added) in a stock pot. Add 4 quarts cold water and bring the water to the boiling point, removing the scum,

2 pounds beef shank
3 pounds beef plate
CONTINUED

27

6 carrots

2 parsnips

2 onions, each stuck with a
  clove

4 leeks, white parts only

1 head of celery

1 sprig of parsley

2 tablespoons salt

½ head of cabbage

which consists of indissoluble solids, as it forms. Add a little cold water from time to time to slow down the boiling and encourage the scum to rise (the clearness of the completed broth depends upon this operation). Add the vegetables, except the cabbage, and bring the liquid again to the boil. Skim often and wipe the top of the pot with a damp cloth to keep it free from scum. Add the salt and simmer the broth slowly for 3–4 hours.

About 1 hour before serving, cut out the core of the cabbage, cut it into wedges, and put the wedges in a small saucepan. Cover with boiling water, drain well, and add ½ cup of the broth and ½ cup of the fat that will have risen to the surface of the stock pot. Cook the cabbage in this mixture until it is very soft.

Remove the stock pot from the heat and add 1 cup cold water to the contents. In a few minutes the fat will rise to the surface and can be readily removed.

To serve the *pot au feu,* strain the bouillon into a large soup tureen. Arrange the meat on a large platter with the vegetables around it and the cabbage at each end. Serve the broth and meat together. A dish of coarsely ground salt and mustard usually accompanies the *pot au feu,* or horse-radish or mustard sauce may be served with it. Serve also a dish of boiled potatoes. Serves from 6 to 8.

PIERRE BAGRATION (1765–1812) was a Georgian prince and a famous gourmet. One of his favorite dishes was the elaborate veal *potage* that bears his name.

Potage Bagration
(*Veal Soup*)

CUT the veal cutlet into small cubes and brown the meat in the butter over high heat. Add the *velouté*, which should be made from veal stock and only lightly thickened, and cook slowly for 1½ hours, until the veal is very tender. Force the soup through a fine sieve or purée it in an electric blender. Thicken the soup with the egg yolks beaten with the cream, and finish it with 2 tablespoons butter. Garnish with the macaroni, cut in small pieces, and pass grated Parmesan cheese separately. Serves 12.

1 pound veal cutlet
3 tablespoons clarified butter
3 quarts *sauce velouté*
4 egg yolks
1 cup cream
2 tablespoons butter
1 cup cooked macaroni

Potage aux Abats
(*Turkey Giblet Soup*)

DICE the vegetables and cook them in the butter for 10 to 15 minutes. Cover the giblets with cold water, bring the water to a boil, and drain and rinse the meat. Add the giblets to the soup pot with the water and a little salt. Cook slowly for ½ hour, or until the meat is tender. Cut the meat into dice and return it to the soup. Discard the bones. Adjust the seasoning with salt and pepper and sprinkle with a little chopped parsley.

2 onions
3 stalks of celery
2 carrots
1 leek
1 tablespoon butter
3 tablespoons barley
the turkey giblets, wing tips, and neck
3 quarts of water

THE Creoles of Louisiana, part French, part Spanish in heritage, have made many notable contributions to American cuisine, not the least among them their characteristic soup, the gumbo. The first gumbos were thickened with

29

filé, powdered sassafras leaves; later okra was also used for the same purpose. *Filé* is obtainable in specialty grocery shops.

Gumbo Filé
(*Chicken Gumbo*)

1 3½-pound chicken
1 pound raw ham
2 onions
1 small sweet red pepper
2 tomatoes
2 tablespoons clarified butter
1 tablespoon filé powder
4 tablespoons cooked rice

DISJOINT the chicken and brown the pieces on all sides in the clarified butter. Add the ham, cut in pieces, and simmer for a few minutes. Add the onions, coarsely chopped, stir well, season with a little salt and pepper, and cover the pan. Cook for 10 minutes. Add sufficient water generously to cover the meat, the red pepper, free of pith and seeds and cut in dice, and the tomatoes, peeled and cut in dice. Cook slowly, covered, until the chicken is very tender.

Remove the chicken and ham. Cut some of each into small dice and return it to the soup; the rest may be served separately or at another meal. Skim off any fat that rises to the surface of the soup and bring the soup to the boil. Adjust the seasoning, remove the pan from the fire, and stir in 1 to 2 tablespoons *filé* powder to attain the desired thickness. Add 4 generous tablespoons cooked rice and serve in soup plates. Serves from 4 to 6.

Soups Made with Water or Milk

Potage aux Herbes
(*Herb Soup*)

1 cup sorrel leaves
1 cup watercress leaves
½ cup chervil
CONTINUED

SHRED the herb leaves and cook them in 2 tablespoons butter for a few minutes. Add the water, the potatoes, peeled and quartered, and a little salt. Cook slowly for about 1 hour. Force the soup through a fine sieve or purée it in an electric blender. Add 2 tablespoons sweet butter, adjust the seasoning with salt and white pepper, and serve hot. Serves from 4 to 6.

Potage aux Pois Cassés
(*Split Pea Soup*)

PICK over the peas and soak them in cold water for 1 hour. Drain them and put them in a soup kettle with the onion, leeks, lettuce, salt pork, and water. Simmer gently for from 1 to 2 hours, until the peas are thoroughly cooked. Force the soup through a fine sieve or purée it in an electric blender. If the soup seems too thick, it may be thinned with a little stock or water. Reheat the soup, adjust the seasoning, and stir in 2 tablespoons butter.

2 tablespoons butter
1 quart water
5 potatoes

1 ½ cups dried split peas
1 ½ quarts water
2 onions
2 leeks
a few lettuce leaves
¼ pound lean salt pork
2 tablespoons butter

Shellfish Soups

Manhattan Clam Chowder

2 tablespoons butter
1 cup diced potatoes
3 cups boiling water
2 cups tomato juice

1 pint freshly opened clams
1 onion
1 clove of garlic
1 teaspoon coarsely chopped parsley
½ cup finely minced celery
3 to 4 soda crackers
1 tablespoon finely minced green pepper

SIMMER the onions, celery, green pepper, and garlic in the butter for 20 minutes. Add the potatoes, the water, and a little salt. Cook until the potatoes are tender and add the tomato juice, the clams, minced, and their juice, and salt, pepper, thyme, sage, and cayenne to taste. Bring the chowder to the boil, add the chopped parsley, and pour the soup into a tureen over the coarsely crumbled crackers. Serves 6.

31

New England Clam Chowder

1 quart freshly opened clams
¼ pound salt pork
1 onion
3 cups diced potatoes
3 cups boiling water
2 tablespoons butter
1 tablespoon flour
1 quart scalded milk
6 water crackers

HEAT the clam juice to the boiling point and strain it. Separate the hard part of the clams from the soft. Chop the hard portions finely. Cut the salt pork in small dice and fry it, stirring, for a few minutes. Add the onion, sliced thin, and cook until the onion is lightly golden.

Parboil the potatoes for 5 minutes in boiling salted water and drain them. Combine the potatoes, the pork and onion, the chopped clams, and the boiling water. Add a little salt and pepper and cook for from 10 to 15 minutes or until the potatoes are very tender. Add the hot milk, the crackers, crushed and soaked in milk, and the soft portions of the clams. Bring the mixture to a boil.

Reheat the clam juice and thicken it with the butter and flour, rubbed to a paste. Combine the two mixtures, adjust the seasoning with salt and pepper, and serve hot. Serves from 10 to 12.

Soupe aux Clams
(*Cream of Clam Soup*)

8 freshly opened hard clams
2 cups milk
1 sprig parsley
½ stalk of celery
½ small onion
5 peppercorns
1 egg yolk
1 tablespoon cream

IN THE top of a double boiler over hot water cook together for 10 to 15 minutes the milk, parsley, celery, onion, peppercorns, and a little salt. Strain the milk and return it to the double boiler.

Put the clams through the food chopper and put them with their juice in a small saucepan. Add enough water barely to cover and cook for a few minutes, removing the scum that rises. Blend the egg yolk with the cream and stir it into the milk. Cook the milk, stirring, for 2 minutes. Do not allow it to boil. Strain the clam broth into the milk and adjust the seasoning with salt and white pepper. Serves 2.

Bisque de Homard
(Lobster Bisque)

SPLIT a live lobster in half and cut each section of the tail into 4 pieces. Break the claws. Remove and discard the intestinal vein and the stomach. Heat the butter in a large pan and toss the lobster pieces over high heat until they turn red. Add the carrot and onion, both diced, and the herbs. Season with salt and pepper and simmer, covered, for 10 minutes, shaking the pan from time to time. Sprinkle with brandy, blaze the spirit, and, before the flame dies out completely, add the wine. Cover the pan and simmer for 15 minutes. Add the quart of white stock.

While the lobster is cooking, cook the rice in the remaining stock until it is very soft. Add the rice to the pan and cook all together, covered, for 15 minutes. Remove the pieces of lobster from the pan. Discard the shells and dice the meat. Rub the bisque through a very fine sieve and reheat it, stirring with a whisk. The bisque should be thick as light cream; if necessary, add a little more white stock. Add the lobster. Adjust the seasoning, adding a dash of cayenne pepper, and finish the bisque with 1 tablespoon sweet butter and ½ cup cream, if desired. Serve separately small croutons of bread browned in butter.

1 2-pound lobster
2 tablespoons butter
1 carrot
1 onion
2 sprigs parsley
1 sprig thyme
bit of bay leaf
¼ cup brandy
1 cup dry white wine
1 quart white stock
¼ cup rice
2 cups white stock

Potage Boula Boula Gratiné
(Green Pea and Turtle Soup)

COOK the green peas until tender in a little boiling salted water. Drain off any surplus liquid and mash the peas with the green turtle soup.

2 cups freshly shelled green peas
CONTINUED

33

2 cups canned green turtle
  soup
1 tablespoon sweet butter
1 cup sherry

Strain the mixture through a fine sieve or purée it in an electric blender, and reheat it. Add 1 tablespoon sweet butter and salt and white pepper to taste. Add 1 cup sherry, heated to just under the boiling point, and pour the soup into serving cups. Cover each cup with a spoonful of unsweetened whipped cream and put the cups under the broiler to brown the topping. Serve at once. Serves 4.

II

HORS D'OEUVRE AND CANAPÉS

HORS D'OEUVRE

[*Appetizers*]

There are, strictly speaking, two sorts of hors d'oeuvre: the tidbits served with the pre-dinner *apéritif* or cocktail, and, in France, the appetizing first course that is always part of the luncheon menu. As the French are thrifty housekeepers, this course is likely to consist of the odds and ends left from the previous day, served with a tangy sauce, and perhaps supplemented by sardines, anchovies, sausages, *pâté,* or another savory food. Small portions of well-seasoned dishes that would otherwise make a luncheon or supper entrée are also served as hors d'oeuvre; the menu-planner is at liberty to choose these from the recipes given under the separate categories.

The following recipes are particularly suited to be first-course hors d'oeuvre.

Cold Hors d'oeuvre

Caviar

ONE of the most highly prized of hors d'oeuvre is caviar, and of the three types of caviar generally available, the gray, the black, and the red, the first is choice.

Gray caviar, made from the roe of sturgeon,

is lightly salted and packed in oil for canning. It is served either in the can, bedded in cracked ice, or in a glass bowl. Dishes of finely chopped onion and hard-cooked eggs accompany the caviar, along with buttered toast or tiny buttered rolls. Or make *blinis* (tiny buckwheat pancakes) and put a little caviar and a dab of sour cream on each hot pancake.

Black caviar is made from the roe of fish other than the sturgeon, and is artificially colored. The excess color may be removed by draining the caviar briefly on absorbent paper toweling before serving it; if desired, the excess oil and salt may be washed off by putting the caviar in a fine meshed sieve under running cold water for a moment.

Red caviar is the least expensive of all; it is made from salmon roe, large, brightly colored eggs.

Harengs Marinés
(*Marinated Herring*)

12 ½-pound herring
1 quart white wine
2 cups vinegar
2 tablespoons salt
2 carrots
2 onions
4 shallots
1 sprig thyme
½ bay leaf

3 sprigs parsley
12 peppercorns
basil, sage

CLEAN the herring, wash them, and fillet them or not, as desired. Lay them side by side in a flat pan. Bring the wine and vinegar to the boil with the seasonings and sliced vegetables, add a pinch each of dried basil and sage, and cook slowly for 30 minutes. Pour the hot *court-bouillon* over the herring and cook them for 10 minutes. Remove the fish and the marinade to a serving dish. Serve cold.

Filets de Maquereaux au Vin Blanc
(*Fillets of Mackerel in White Wine*)

LAY the fish fillets side by side in a flat pan and sprinkle them with salt and freshly ground black pepper. Spread over them the onion, sliced very thin, and the herbs. Add the wine and lemon juice. Cover the pan, bring the liquid to a boil, and cook for 4 minutes. Adjust the seasoning with more salt and pepper and let the fish cool in the marinade, covered. Arrange the fillets in a serving dish. Strain the cooking liquor over them. Pick out the onion slices and add them to the dish. Discard the herbs. Chill in the refrigerator overnight before serving.

1½ pounds small mackerel fillets
1 onion
1 spring of parsley
a bit of bay leaf
1 small sprig thyme
1 cup dry white wine
juice of ½ lemon

Filets de Merlan Orientale
(*Whiting Oriental*)

LAY the whiting fillets side by side in a shallow pan and season them with salt and pepper. Chop the onion, shallots, garlic, and saffron, and simmer them in a little olive oil without letting them take on color. Add the tomatoes, peeled, seeded, and coarsely chopped, and simmer for 15 minutes. Add the white wine and bring it to a boil. Pour the mixture over the fish, add the bouquet, cover the pan, and cook the fish slowly for 10 minutes. Add salt and pepper to taste and cool the fish in the sauce. To serve, discard the bouquet and arrange the fish in a glass hors-d'oeuvre dish. Pour the sauce over the fish and chill thoroughly.

6 fillets of whiting
olive oil
1 small onion
2 shallots
2 garlic cloves
½ teaspoon saffron
6 tomatoes
2 cups dry white wine
a bouquet of 2 sprigs of parsley, ½ sprig thyme, ½ bay leaf

Escargots Bourguignonne
(*Snails Burgundy Style*)

THE snails, imported from France, may be purchased in cans. The shells are packed separately. Cook the wine, shallots, and garlic for 10 min-

3 dozen canned snails
1½ cups white wine
CONTINUED

1 teaspoon chopped shallots
½ teaspoon chopped garlic
¾ cup butter
3 teaspoons chopped parsley
juice of ½ lemon
1½ tablespoons fresh bread
  crumbs

utes, add the juice from the can of snails, and continue to cook until the mixture is greatly reduced in volume. Add salt and pepper to taste. Heat the snails in this sauce for a few minutes, let cool, then put one snail, coated with sauce, in each shell. Fill the shells with a butter made by combining into a paste the butter, parsley, lemon juice, and bread crumbs. Sprinkle with more bread crumbs. Arrange the shells in a baking dish on a bed of rock salt to hold them upright. (There are also special baking dishes with small indentations for the snails.) Bake in a hot oven (400°f.) until the crumbs brown. Serve piping hot. The snails can be prepared in advance and refrigerated until 30 minutes or so before serving time.

Crevettes Cocktail
(*Shrimp Cocktail*)

½ cup tomato ketchup
1 tablespoon chili sauce
1 tablespoon mayonnaise
juice of ½ lemon
6 drops Tabasco

BLEND the ingredients and force them through a fine sieve or purée them in an electric blender. Let the sauce ripen for 1 hour in the refrigerator. Allow 5 medium shrimp for each serving. Cook them in *court-bouillon* and shell and devein them. Arrange the shrimp on crushed ice and put a small bowl in the center of the dish to hold the cocktail sauce. Each shrimp may be pierced with a wooden pick, if desired.

Cooked lobster or crab meat may be prepared in the same way. Cut the lobster into thick slices and put the picked-over crab meat in a small glass dish that can be embedded in the crushed ice.

Saumon Fumé
(*Smoked Salmon*)

SERVE very thin slices of smoked salmon on lettuce leaves. Garnish with lemon. Thin slices

40

of dark bread, spread with sweet butter, are the usual accompaniment.

Oysters Mignonnette
(Oysters with Pepper Sauce)

ARRANGE the oysters on their deep shells on individual serving plates, 6 to a portion. Combine the remaining ingredients, add salt to taste, and spread the sauce over the oysters. Serve at once. Mignonnette pepper is a white variety; it should be freshly and rather coarsely ground for best flavor.

36 oysters, freshly opened
3 tablespoons mignonnette pepper
6 shallots
3 tablespoons chopped parsley
3 tablespoons wine vinegar

Cervelles de Mouton à la Robert
(Lamb Brains for Hors d'oeuvre)

WASH the brains thoroughly under running water and remove the membranes. Soak the brains in cold water for 1 hour and cook them in salted water acidulated with a little vinegar, or in the *court-bouillon* for calf's brains 10 to 15 minutes. Cool the brains and slice them. Arrange the uniform slices in an hors-d'oeuvre dish and force the end pieces and odd bits through a fine sieve. Combine this purée with the mustard sauce and the celery. Adjust the seasoning of the sauce and pour it over the sliced brains. Thin the sauce with a little tarragon vinegar if it seems too thick. Serve chilled.

6 lamb's brains
½ cup mustard sauce
½ cup julienne of celery

Pâté de Foie de Porc
(Pork Liver Pâté)

USE 2 thin slices of fat pork to line the loaf pan in which the *pâté* will be baked. Put the rest of the fat through the finest blade of the food

1 pound pork liver
½ pound fat pork
CONTINUED

41

2 teaspoons flour

1 egg

1 pinch thyme

¼ bay leaf

1 teaspoon finely chopped
  parsley

½ teaspoon salt

¼ teaspoon freshly ground
  pepper

1 shallot

1 small onion

chopper with the pork liver. Put the meat in the bowl of the electric mixer. Beat in slowly the flour, the egg, and the seasonings. Chop the shallot and onion and cook them in a little butter. Add them to the *pâté* and continue to mix for about 10 minutes longer, until the mixture is very light and fluffy. Adjust the seasoning with more salt and pepper and turn the mixture into the loaf pan. Bake the *pâté* in a moderately hot oven (400°f.) for about 1 hour. Test it by inserting a small knife; when the knife comes out dry, the *pâté* is done. Cool the *pâté* before unmolding it. The mold may be filled with aspic jelly if desired. To facilitate the unmolding, dip the pan quickly into very hot water.

Oeufs Farci

(*Stuffed Eggs*)

HARD-COOKED eggs may be stuffed with almost any desired mixture, usually based on the puréed egg yolks. Such seasonings as curry powder, mustard, Worcestershire sauce, and Tabasco may be used, and fish and meat pastes, cheese, olives, caviar, and chopped herbs offer possible variations. The imagination may be given free rein.

In cooking eggs for stuffing, turn them frequently during the first minutes of cooking to insure the yolk's remaining at dead center. Cool the eggs rapidly in cold water—this prevents the formation of an unsightly green ring. The eggs may be split vertically or horizontally; if vertically, cut a small slice from the end to provide a firm base. Force the egg yolks through a fine sieve and whip them with enough light cream or mayonnaise to make a fluffy mixture.

Season to taste and, using a pastry bag fitted with a fancy tube, refill the whites. The garnish may be as simple as a dash of paprika, or it may be a slice of olive, a small cocktail onion, a caper, or anything else fancy suggests.

Vegetable Hors d'oeuvre

Such cold, cooked vegetables as celery, asparagus, leeks, or beets make appetizing hors d'oeuvre. They are usually dressed with a spicy *vinaigrette* sauce or other salad dressing that disguises the fact that the vegetables were probably left over from the previous day. Of course, vegetable hors d'oeuvre are also specially prepared, often in the manner called *à la grecque*, in a Greek marinade.

Marinade Grecque
(*Greek Marinade*)

a cheesecloth bag containing 3 fennel leaves, 12 coriander seeds, 1 sprig thyme, 1 bay leaf, and 12 peppercorns

2 cups water
½ cup olive oil
½ teaspoon salt
juice of 3 lemons

Combine all the ingredients in a saucepan and bring the liquid slowly to the boil.

Légumes à la Grecque
(*Vegetables in Greek Marinade*)

Bring the Greek marinade to the boiling point, and cook in it such vegetables as parboiled celery or artichoke hearts, cauliflower buds, asparagus tips, small white onions, sliced cu-

43

cumbers, or mushrooms. Add boiling water, if necessary, to cover the vegetables, and cook them until they are tender, but still crisp. Do not overcook. Drain the vegetables and chill them. Reduce the marinade over high heat to half its original quantity and cool it. Pour the marinade over the vegetables and store in the refrigerator until serving time.

Champignons en Marinade
(Marinated Mushrooms)

1½ pounds small button mushrooms
2 tablespoons olive oil
2 cups Greek marinade

HEAT the oil in a skillet and cook the mushrooms quickly, over high heat until they just begin to brown. Pour the Greek marinade over them and chill thoroughly before serving.

Coeurs d'Artichauts à la Diable
(Deviled Artichoke Hearts)

12 small artichokes, cooked or canned
1 tablespoon mayonnaise
1 tablespoon wine vinegar
1 tablespoon "Escoffier Sauce Diable" (bottled)

ARRANGE the artichokes on a serving dish and chill them thoroughly. Combine the remaining ingredients, spread the dressing over the artichokes, and serve cold.

Céleri-rave
(Celeriac Salad)

3 celeriac
2 cups mustard dressing

CELERIAC, or celery root, is a variety of celery of which only the root is used. Peel the roots and cut them into thin, match-like julienne strips. Parboil the strips in boiling salted water until tender but still crisp. Do not overcook. Cool the celeriac and toss it with mustard dressing. Serve cold.

Aubergines en Hors d'oeuvre
(*Eggplant Appetizer*)

PEEL the eggplants and cut them into small cubes. Heat the olive oil in a skillet, add the thyme, bay leaf, and crushed garlic, and let the oil infuse for 5 minutes. Discard the seasonings and cook the eggplant in the seasoned oil until the cubes are tender and brown on all sides. Sprinkle with salt and pepper and put aside.

Chop the onion and cook it lightly in a little olive oil. Peel the tomatoes and add them to the pan. Cover the pan and cook the mixture in a moderate oven (350°f.) for about 1 hour, until the tomatoes are mushy. Combine the tomatoes and eggplant, adjust the seasoning with salt and freshly ground black pepper, and chill thoroughly before serving.

2 eggplants
½ cup olive oil
1 sprig thyme
1 bay leaf
3 garlic cloves
1 large onion
8 tomatoes

Tomates Ravigote
(*Tomatoes with Ravigote Sauce*)

PEEL the tomatoes, slice them, and remove the seeds. Lay the slices on the bottom of a shallow glass dish. Chop the hard-cooked eggs and mix them with the mayonnaise and herbs. Adjust the seasoning of the sauce and pour it over the tomatoes. Serve cold.

6 ripe tomatoes
3 hard-cooked eggs
¾ cup mayonnaise
1 generous teaspoon mixed chopped chives, chervil, and parsley

Tomates Antiboise
(*Stuffed Tomatoes*)

CUT a thin slice from the stem end of the tomatoes and scoop out the seeds with a teaspoon. Mix the tuna fish and herbs with the chopped

2 tomatoes
½ cup tuna fish
CONTINUED

45

1 hard-cooked egg
1 tablespoon capers
1 teaspoon mixed chopped
  parsley, chervil, and tarragon
½ cup mayonnaise
1 teaspoon anchovy paste.

egg white. Blend the mayonnaise with the anchovy paste and combine the two mixtures. Adjust the seasoning and stuff the tomatoes, mounding the stuffing high. Force the egg yolk through a sieve and sprinkle it on the stuffing. Chill thoroughly before serving. Serves 2.

Fresh Fruit as a First Course

Coupe de Fruits Rafraîchis
(*Chilled Fruit Cup*)

CUT up and combine as desired any of the following: melon balls, grapefruit sections, peaches, pears, raspberries, pineapple cubes, and strawberries. The fruit may be garnished with fresh mint leaves, or a little rum, Kirsch, or cognac may be poured over it. Serve very cold.

Pamplemousse à l'Orange Rafraîchie
(*Grapefruit and Orange Cup*)

CUT the grapefruit in half crosswise and remove the seeds with a fork. With a sharp pointed knife, separate the pulp from the skin all around the grapefruit and separate the sections from the membranes on both sides. Remove the center membranes with a scissors or a knife, leaving a hollow in the middle of the fruit. Fill this hollow with peeled orange wedges free of pith and membrane. Sprinkle with sugar and serve cold. Allow ½ grapefruit and ½ orange for each serving.

Pamplemousse Flambée
(Flaming Grapefruit)

Prepare ½ grapefruit for each serving, removing the seeds and separating the pulp from the skin and membrane with a sharp knife. Garnish each half with 3 strawberries, sprinkle generously with powdered sugar, and bake in a hot oven (450°f.) until the fruit begins to brown. Warm 1 teaspoon rum for each serving, pour the rum over the hot grapefruit, and set it ablaze. Serve flaming.

Pamplemousse au Marasquin
(Grapefruit Maraschino)

Prepare ½ grapefruit for each serving, sweeten it lightly, and put a Maraschino cherry in the center. Pour over all 1 teaspoon Maraschino liqueur. Serve very cold.

Suprême de Melon à l'Orange

Cut the melon open, discard the seeds and fibers, and scoop out the flesh with a ball cutter. Half fill 6 glass fruit dishes with sliced oranges, pile the melon balls on the oranges, and pour the orange juice over the fruit. Sprinkle with orange rind cut into very fine julienne strips or coarsely grated. Serve very cold.

1 large honeydew melon or canteloupe
2 oranges
juice and grated rind of 1 orange

Hot Hors d'oeuvre

Beignets de Truffes
(Truffle Fritters)

Cut 1 or 2 medium truffles in thick slices and marinate for 1 hour in cognac seasoned with

salt, pepper, thyme, and bay leaf. Dip the slices
in beer fritter batter and fry them until light
brown in hot deep fat (370°f.). Drain on paper
toweling and serve hot.

Croustades aux Truffes
(*Tart Shell with Truffles*)

FILL baked tart shells with diced truffles mixed
with enough Madeira sauce or cream sauce to
moisten. Sprinkle with grated Swiss cheese
and brown the topping under the broiler.

Canapés de Truffes
(*Truffles on Toast*)

CUT large truffles into thick slices and sprinkle
them with salt, pepper, and melted butter. Cut
as many rounds of breads as truffle slices, trim
them to fit, and brown the croutons on both
sides in clarified butter. Put a truffle on each
crouton, sprinkle with grated Parmesan cheese,
and brown under the broiler. Serve very hot.

Croûte aux Champignons
(*Mushrooms in a Crust*)

1 8-inch pie shell, baked
1 pound mushrooms
2 tablespoons clarified butter
2 shallots
1 cup *velouté* sauce
2 egg yolks
1 teaspoon cream
1 tablespoon grated Swiss
   cheese

SLICE the mushrooms and brown them lightly
in clarified butter over high heat. Add the
shallots, chopped, and cook all together until
the shallots are lightly browned. Pour off the
butter and add the *velouté* sauce. Beat the
egg yolks with the cream, warm the mixture
with a little of the hot sauce, and stir it into the
pan. Heat all together without letting the sauce
boil, adjust the seasoning with salt and pepper,

48

and pour the mixture into the prepared pie shell. Sprinkle with the grated cheese and brown the topping in a moderate oven (350°f.). Serve hot.

Rôties des Epicures
(*Epicures' Toast*)

MELT the butter and in it brown the bread slices on both sides. Remove the toast and add to the pan the mushrooms, pimientos, and green pepper. Cook this mixture, stirring, until the vegetables are soft and most of the moisture has evaporated. Add the anchovies and the Worcestershire sauce and season with salt, pepper, and cayenne to taste. Spread the mixture on the toast and serve hot.

2 tablespoons sweet butter
6 slices white bread
2 tablespoons chopped fresh mushrooms
2 tablespoons red pimientos
2 tablespoons green pepper
2 tablespoons anchovies
½ teaspoon Worcestershire sauce

Croûtes au Fromage
(*Cheese Toast*)

MELT the butter, stir in the flour, and cook, stirring for 1 or 2 minutes without allowing the *roux* to take on color. Stir in the milk and cook, stirring with a sauce whisk until the mixture is smooth and thickened. Warm the egg yolk with a little of the sauce and return it to the pan. Stir the sauce over the heat for a minute or so without allowing it to boil. Remove the pan from the heat and season the sauce with salt, pepper, and cayenne to taste. Cool the sauce for a few minutes. Stir in the grated cheese and fold in the egg white, beaten stiff. Spread this mixture on freshly made slices of toast and put the toast in a very hot oven or under the broiler to brown the topping lightly. Sprinkle with paprika and serve hot. Serves 4.

1 tablespoon butter
1½ tablespoons flour
½ cup scalded milk
1 egg
½ cup grated Swiss cheese
4 slices toast

Gougère Bourguignonne
(Cheese Puff)

1 cup milk
¼ cup butter
½ teaspoon salt
dash of freshly ground black
  pepper
⅞ cup flour
4 eggs
3 ounces Swiss cheese, diced
1 tablespoon cream

BRING the milk to a boil in a saucepan with the butter, salt, and pepper. Remove the pan from the heat and beat in the flour, all at once. Put the pan over the heat and stir the paste with a wooden spoon for a minute or two, until it cleans the sides of the pan and forms a ball. Remove the pan from the heat and beat in the eggs, one at a time, and the diced cheese and cream. Beat well to blend the batter thoroughly and pour it into a buttered pie plate. Sprinkle with a few Swiss cheese dice and bake in a moderate oven (325°f.) for about 40 minutes, until the *gougère* is well puffed and golden brown.

Tartelettes au Fromage
(Cheese Tarts)

2 cups light cream or milk
3 eggs
1 cup grated Swiss cheese
⅔ cup diced Swiss cheese
1 tablespoon melted butter
12 partly baked tart shells

BEAT the eggs and cream together, season with salt, pepper, and cayenne to taste, and strain. Add the grated cheese and the melted butter. In the bottom of each partly baked tart shell— they should be three-fourths done, firm but not at all colored—put a spoonful of the diced cheese. Fill the shell with the custard mixture and bake in a moderate oven (350°f.) for about 15 minutes, until the custard is set and lightly browned. Serve warm.

Quiche Lorraine
(Cheese Tart with Bacon)

LINE a 9-inch pie plate with pie dough and sprinkle over it 6 slices bacon, fried crisp and crumbled. Proceed as for *tartelettes au fromage,* substituting the bacon, or the same amount of ham, cut in small dice, for the diced Swiss cheese. Bake the pie in a moderately hot oven (375°f.) for about 45 minutes, until the filling is set and the crust browned. Serve warm, as hors d'oeuvre.

CANAPÉS

Every cook should have his own repertoire of canapés, for the creation of a canapé is certainly the expression of the individual's artistic talents as well as of his gastronomic tastes. There are, however, certain basic rules which the amateur of canapés can use as a guide. The wise beginner will confine his efforts to the simpler effects at first, and broaden his attack with elaborate garnishings and fanciful designs as he achieves confidence.

A canapé is basically a tasty morsel of food presented on a couch or base, usually bread or a cracker, which permits it to be eaten in the fingers. The bread should be of the firm, dry sort that will not grow limp and soggy. White bread may be toasted or browned in butter to make it crisp and resistant to moisture.

The compound butters that follow are the foundation of the canapé. These flavorful mixtures, chilled and spread on bread or crackers, can be garnished as fancy dictates with such items as rolled anchovy fillets, olives stuffed with everything from pimientos to nuts, tiny shrimp, capers, and red and black caviar. Flowers and geometric designs may be cut from olives, hard-cooked egg white, and truffles. A pastry bag permits the use of decorative whorls and stars and rosettes of mayonnaise or cream cheese or butter. Chopped parsley or other green herbs and riced egg yolk make colorful borders.

Compound Butters for Canapés

Anchovy Butter: Wash and dry 12 fillets of anchovy and force them through a sieve with 2 tablespoons butter. Blend well.

Caviar Butter: Pound 3 ounces caviar in a mortar with ½ cup butter and rub through a fine sieve.

Curry Butter: Chop finely 1 small white onion and cook it in a little butter without letting it brown. Add 1 teaspoon curry powder and simmer for 2 minutes. Cool and blend with 1 cup butter. Force the butter through a fine sieve.

Horse-radish Butter: Pound in a mortar 4 tablespoons drained, grated horse-radish. Blend with 1 cup butter, force through a fine sieve, and add salt and pepper to taste.

Montpellier Butter: Blanch 3 sprigs each of water cress, parsley, chervil, chives, and tarragon, 1 sliced shallot, and 6 spinach leaves. Drain the leaves and press them dry in a towel. Pound in a mortar with ½ tablespoon drained capers, 1 gherkin, 1 garlic clove, and 4 washed and dried fillets of anchovy, all chopped. Blend with 1 cup butter and force the whole through a fine sieve. Season with salt and cayenne to taste.

Paprika Butter: Chop finely 1 small yellow onion and cook it in a little butter without letting it color. Add 1 tablespoon paprika and simmer for 1 minute. Cool, blend with 1 cup butter, and force through a fine sieve.

Pimiento Butter: Pound together in a mortar equal quantities of canned red pimientos and butter. Rub the mixture through a fine sieve and season it with salt and cayenne pepper.

Smoked Salmon Butter: Pound in a mortar equal weights of smoked salmon and butter. Force the mixture through a fine sieve and season it with pepper.

Canapés de Caviar

TRIM 2 dozen slices of firm white bread and toast them. Spread with sweet butter and cut each slice into 3 fingers. Put a spoonful of caviar on each toast finger and garnish with a very thin slice of lemon. Dip the edges in finely chopped hard-cooked egg white or yolk. Or chop an onion fine, wrap in cheesecloth, wash in cold water, and dry thoroughly: use this onion as a border. Allow about 1 pound caviar for 72 finger canapés.

Rillettes d'Angers
(Pork Spread)

½ pound fresh fat pork
2 pounds fresh lean pork
1 cup water
1 tablespoon salt
1 teaspoon ground allspice

CUT the fat into small cubes and brown slowly in a skillet. Add the lean pork, also cut into cubes, and brown slowly. Add the water and seasonings, cover the pan, and cook in a moderately slow oven (300°f.) for about 3 hours, until the moisture has entirely evaporated. Cool the meat to lukewarm and beat it to a paste, using a wooden spoon or the electric mixer. Season highly with salt and pepper and pack the paste into small jars. Serve very cold, as a spread with French bread or toast.

Hot Cocktail Appetizers

ONE OR TWO hot cocktail appetizers are always welcome at a cocktail party.

Rissoles à la Reine
(Chicken Turnovers)

½ pound puff paste
1 cup *velouté* sauce
CONTINUED

HEAT the *velouté* sauce and stir in the egg yolks. Do not allow the sauce to boil after the egg yolks are added. Add the chicken, mush-

54

rooms, and truffles and season highly with salt and pepper to taste. Set the mixture aside to cool.

Roll the puff paste out ⅛ inch thick and cut it into from 12 to 14 fluted 4-inch rounds. Put 1 tablespoon of the prepared mixture on half of each round and fold the pastry over to cover the filling. Pinch the edges to seal them and to allow for the escape of steam prick the turnover or cut a design with a sharp pointed knife. Brush the turnovers with egg beaten with a little milk and bake the *rissoles* in a moderately hot oven (400°f.) until the pastry is golden brown. Serve hot, as hors d'œuvre for cocktails.

2 egg yolks
1 cup diced cooked chicken
½ cup diced cooked
  mushrooms
¼ cup diced truffles
1 egg

Paillettes aux Anchois
(*Anchovy Sticks*)

WASH the anchovy fillets and dry them with a towel.

Roll puff paste out on a lightly floured board into a rectangle ⅛ inch thick. Cut the rectangle into long strips 2 inches wide. Moisten the edges of alternate strips with milk, water, or beaten egg, lay a line of anchovy fillets down the center, and cover each with a second strip of dough. Press the edges to seal. Brush the top with the egg beaten with the cream and cut the strips into ½-inch pieces. Bake in a moderately hot oven (400°f.) and serve hot, as a cocktail appetizer.

canned anchovy fillets
puff paste
1 egg
1 tablespoon cream

Sablés au Fromage
(*Cheese Crackers*)

CREAM the butter and combine it with the other ingredients, blending gently but thoroughly. On a lightly floured pastry board roll

½ cup salted butter
¼ cup grated Swiss or
CONTINUED

55

Cheddar cheese
1 tablespoon grated Parmesan
cheese
½ cup flour
1 egg yolk

the dough out into rectangles ¼ inch thick.
Cut the dough into 2-inch squares, sprinkle
lightly with cayenne and generously with paprika, and bake in a moderate oven (350°f.)
until the squares are firm and begin to color.
Serve hot, with cocktails.

Cigarettes de Fromage
(*Cheese Cigarettes*)

1 cup Béchamel sauce
2 egg yolks
1 tablespoon cream
1 cup grated Parmesan cheese
thinly sliced white bread

ADD the egg yolks, beaten with cream, to the
Béchamel sauce and heat, stirring with a
whisk, without allowing the sauce to boil. Season with salt, pepper, and cayenne to taste. Cool
the mixture slightly and gently stir in the Parmesan cheese. Spread thinly on very thin slices
of bread. Trim off the crusts and cut each slice
of bread in 3 parts. Fold and roll with the cheese
inside, as a cigarette. Trim the ends evenly and
arrange in a frying-basket. Just before serving,
dip the basket in hot fat (400°f.). The cigarettes
will brown almost immediately. Serve as cocktail appetizers.

Croquettes de Fromage
(*Cheese Croquettes*)

1 tablespoon butter
2 tablespoons flour
1 cup scalded milk
3 egg yolks
1 cup cubed Swiss cheese
1 egg

MELT the butter, stir in the flour, and cook the
roux for a minute without letting it take on
color. Stir in the scalded milk and cook, stirring,
until the sauce comes to the boil. Beat in the
egg yolks and beat well. Season to taste with
salt, pepper, and cayenne. Cool the mixture for
10 minutes and stir in the cheese. Spread the
paste on a flat platter to cool. Mold it into balls
the size of walnuts, roll the balls in flour, dip
them in beaten egg and in fresh bread crumbs,

and fry them in hot deep fat (370°f.) to a golden brown. Serve hot, pierced with a cocktail pick.

Or cut the cooled paste into sticks 1 inch wide, 2 inches long, and ½ inch thick, fry them as indicated, and serve them, 3 or 4 to a portion, as hors d'oeuvre, with a sauceboat of tomato sauce. These croquettes are called *délices de Gruyère,* or Swiss cheese delights.

Fondue de Fromage sur Biscuits
(Melted Cheese Appetizers)

½ pound Cheddar cheese
½ cup beer
¼ teaspoon dry mustard
½ teaspoon cornstarch
2 egg yolks
1 tablespoon cream
24 round crackers

THE cheese should be at room temperature. Melt it slowly over hot water and stir in the beer, the mustard mixed to a paste with a few drops of water, and a dash each of cayenne pepper and salt. Stir the mixture until it is smooth and well blended. Mix the cornstarch to a paste with a little water and mix it with the beaten egg yolks and cream. Add this mixture to the cheese and cook, stirring, until the fondue is smooth and creamy. Spoon some of the fondue onto the crackers and put the crackers into a hot oven (450°f.) or under the broiler to brown the topping. Sprinkle with paprika and serve hot, as an appetizer with cocktails.

Olives au Bacon
(Olive-Bacon Rolls)

18 large stuffed green olives
6 slices of bacon

CUT each slice of bacon in 3 pieces and wrap the squares around the olives, fastening them in place with wooden picks. Broil, browning the bacon on all sides. Drain on absorbent paper and serve hot.

57

III

FISH *and* SHELLFISH

FISH AND SHELLFISH

For purposes of classic cookery, fish are divided first according to their fat content and then according to their size and shape—i.e., whether they are cooked whole, cut into steaks, or filleted. Your dealer will recommend the fish that are in season and therefore at the peak of their flavor and least expensive. Ask him to tell you whether the fish is a fat or a lean one. Or for this information you can consult the charts that appear in general cook books.

The recipes given here were chosen to represent all the preparations that apply to different kinds of fish. To achieve infinite variety, simply substitute the fillets of one fat fish for another, one lean white-fleshed fish steak for another, and so on. All shellfish are lean, and any of the crustaceans —lobster, shrimp, crab, and the like—may replace each other in most recipes. This is also true of the bivalves, such as oysters, clams, and mussels.

Anyone who has had the pleasure of eating fish cooked directly after it came from the water does not need to be reminded of the importance of freshness in fish. Look for firm flesh, red gills, bright eyes, and the absence of any unpleasant odor. Shellfish should always be cooked alive. Dead uncooked shellfish are not only unpalatable, but also poisonous.

61

Court-Bouillon

FISH AND SHELLFISH gain in flavor when cooked in a seasoned liquid rather than in plain water. The white wine *court-bouillon,* or short-broth, may be used for poaching or boiling any fish or shellfish.

Court-Bouillon pour Poissons
(Court-Bouillon for Fish and Shellfish)

2 quarts water
1 cup white wine or cider
  vinegar
8 peppercorns
3 sprigs of parsley
½ bay leaf

½ sprig of thyme
1 onion
1 stalk of celery
1 teaspoon salt

BRING all the ingredients to a boil and cook for 20 minutes. Strain and cool the *court-bouillon* before using it for fish. Shellfish should be plunged into boiling *court-bouillon.*

Court-Bouillon for White Fish

1½ quarts water
2 cups milk
juice of ½ lemon
1 teaspoon salt

COMBINE the ingredients and bring them to a boil. Add the fish—sole or cod, for instance—and cook over very gentle heat until the fish flakes readily at the touch of a fork.

Fish

Filets de Sea Bass St. Germain
(Sea Bass Sauté)

6 fillets of sea bass
½ cup flour
1 egg
CONTINUED

WASH and dry the fillets, dredge them in the flour, dip them in lightly beaten egg, and roll them in bread crumbs. Heat the clarified butter in a skillet and brown the fillets quickly on both sides. Season with salt and pepper and serve with *sauce Béarnaise*.

½ cup fresh bread crumbs
½ cup clarified butter

Filets de Sea Bass à l'Estragon
(Sea Bass Sauté with Tarragon)

POUR the milk into a pie plate and spread the flour on a second pie plate. Wash and dry the fillets and dip them first in the milk and then in the flour. Brown the fillets quickly on both sides in clarified butter. Arrange them on a serving dish, sprinkle with lemon juice, and spread with the blended butter and tarragon. Pour over all the hot cooking butter.

6 fillets of sea bass
½ cup milk
½ cup flour
½ cup clarified butter
juice of 1 lemon
1 tablespoon coarsely chopped tarragon
3 tablespoons butter

Bass Rayée Grillée, Maître d'Hôtel
(Broiled Striped Bass Maître d'Hôtel)

HAVE the bass cleaned and split for broiling. Brush both sides with clarified butter and season with salt and pepper. Arrange the fish, flesh side up, on a pre-heated broiling pan. Broil slowly for from 15 to 20 minutes, depending upon the thickness of the fish. Do not overcook. If the broiling pan is sufficiently hot, it will cook the underside of the fish and eliminate the necessity of turning and perhaps breaking it. Spread with a generous amount of *sauce maître d'hôtel* and serve hot. Serves from 8 to 10.

1 striped bass, 5 to 6 pounds
½ cup clarified butter

Filets de Bass Rayée Fermière
(Poached Striped Bass)

HAVE the dealer fillet the bass, removing head, bones, and skin. Put the fish trimmings in a saucepan with water to cover and a little salt and pepper, and cook for 30 minutes. Strain the stock. There should be 1 cup.

striped bass, 3 pounds
2 shallots
½ pound mushrooms
½ cup red wine

Arrange the fillets on a shallow buttered pan and sprinkle them with the shallots, finely chopped, the mushrooms, sliced, and a little salt and pepper. Add the wine and 1 cup fish stock. Cover the fish with a buttered paper and put the pan in a moderate oven (350°f.) for 20 minutes, until the fish flakes readily at the touch of a fork. Remove the fish to a serving dish and reduce the cooking liquid over high heat to one fourth its original volume. Thicken the sauce by stirring in 1 teaspoon butter kneaded with 1 teaspoon flour, add a little chopped parsley, and pour it over the fish.

Bluefish à la Diable
(*Deviled Bluefish*)

1 bluefish, 4 pounds
2 tablespoons dry mustard
2 shallots
1 tablespoon wine vinegar
1 garlic clove
½ cup brown sauce
1 teaspoon chopped parsley

HAVE the fish cleaned and split without separating the halves. Season with salt and pepper and sprinkle with olive oil. Put the fish flesh side up on a hot, oiled broiling pan and broil for about 10 minutes. Brush with the mustard mixed to a paste with a little water and sprinkle with fresh bread crumbs. Return the broiling pan to the heat and broil the fish slowly until the crumbs are brown and the fish tests done.

Make the sauce by cooking the vinegar, chopped shallots, and garlic with a little freshly ground black pepper until the mixture is almost dry. Add the brown sauce, bring it to a boil, and stir in the parsley. Pour the sauce over the fish and serve hot.

DUGLÉRÉ, one of the great chefs of the early nineteenth century, was instrumental in saving from oblivion the Café Anglais, for generations a rendezvous of gourmets. The restaurant was about to close its doors in 1814, for the political disturbances of the time had all but ruined business. A wine merchant of Paris invited sixteen well-known epicures to have dinner at the Café Anglais and sample his wines. The dinner was such a success that word of Dugléré's skill spread like wildfire throughout the city; the next day all Paris wanted to dine at the Café Anglais and sample *potage Germiny* and *Turbotin à la Dugléré*.

Turbotin à la Dugléré
(Halibut Dugléré)

THE chicken halibut is the approximate American equivalent of the turbotin, a fish of great delicacy caught only on European shores.

Have the fish cleaned and trimmed. The backbone should be removed. Lay the fish in a buttered baking dish and cover it with the onion, tomatoes, and wine. Add salt and pepper to taste, cover the fish with buttered paper, and set the dish in a moderate oven (350°f.) to poach for about 20 minutes, until the flesh flakes readily at the touch of a fork. Transfer the fish carefully to a serving platter and remove the skin.

Over high heat, reduce the cooking liquid in the baking dish to a thick purée. Stir in gradually the sweet butter, or use fish *velouté* if desired, for a less rich sauce. Adjust the seasoning and pour the sauce over the fish. Garnish the platter with crescents of puff paste.

1 turbotin, or chicken halibut, 4 to 6 pounds
1 teaspoon chopped onion
2 cups peeled, seeded, chopped tomatoes
1 cup dry white wine
1 cup sweet butter

Harengs Frais Bordelaise
(Baked Fresh Herring, Bordelaise)

HAVE the herring cleaned and the backbones removed without separating the halves. Season

2 herrings
CONTINUED

1 tablespoon olive oil
1 teaspoon chopped parsley
1 teaspoon chopped chervil
1 teaspoon chopped shallots
1 teaspoon chopped chives
2 garlic cloves

with salt and pepper and sprinkle with a little oil. Broil on an oiled, pre-heated pan for about 8 minutes. Transfer the fish to a baking dish and pour over them the herbs mixed with the chopped garlic and the remaining oil. Bake in a hot oven (450°f.) for about 10 minutes, basting frequently with the pan juices. Serves 2.

Alose à l'Angevine
(*Baked Stuffed Shad*)

1 shad, 3 pounds
1 pair shad roe
1 cup fresh bread crumbs
½ pound mushrooms
1 small onion
1 small shallot
2 eggs
1 teaspoon chopped chives
½ tablespoon chopped parsley
1 clove garlic
2 cups light cream

HAVE the fish cleaned, split, and boned. Parboil the roe for 5 minutes in salted water to cover; drain; and chop. Soak the bread crumbs in warm milk and press them dry. Chop the mushrooms, onions, and shallot and cook them in a little butter for 5 minutes. Cool. Combine the roe, vegetables, bread, eggs, chives, parsley, and chopped garlic to make a stuffing. Season with salt, pepper, and nutmeg to taste. Stuff the shad with this mixture and sew the opening with kitchen string.

Butter an oval baking dish or platter that can be brought to the table. Cover the bottom with a layer of shredded young cabbage mixed with leek and a little sorrel. Lay the fish on the vegetables. Cut 3 diagonal slashes on each side to help the fish to retain its shape during the baking. Scald the cream and pour it over the fish. Bake the fish in a moderately hot over (375°f.) for about 1 hour, until the fish flakes readily at the touch of a fork. Baste frequently with the pan juices. Serve in the baking dish.

Red Snapper Niçoise
(*Baked Red Snapper with Tomatoes*)

1 red snapper, 3 pounds
CONTINUED

HAVE the fish cleaned. Sprinkle it with salt and pepper and lay it on an oiled, oven-proof oval dish or platter that can be brought to the table. Pour the tomatoes and wine over the fish. Brown the bread crumbs lightly in butter and dust the fish with them. Sprinkle with olive oil or melted butter and bake, uncovered, in a moderately hot oven (400°f.) for about 45 minutes, until the fish flakes readily at the touch of a fork. Baste every 10 minutes with the pan juices. Sprinkle with lemon juice and with washed and dried capers, and serve in the baking dish.

2 cups stewed tomatoes
1 cup dry white wine
½ cup bread crumbs
juice of ½ lemon
2 tablespoons caper

Brochet Rôti au Chablis
(*Roast Pickerel in Chablis*)

CLEAN the fish without splitting them. With a sharp knife, make several diagonal slashes on each fish. Season with salt and freshly ground black pepper and lay the fish side by side on a generously buttered baking dish. Sprinkle with the shallots, chopped, and the tomatoes, peeled, seeded, and coarsely chopped. Add the wine and bake in a hot oven (400°f.) for about 15 minutes or until the fish tests done, basting frequently. Adjust the seasoning of the sauce and serve sprinkled with parsley.

6 pickerel, ¾ pound each
6 shallots
6 tomatoes
2 cups Chablis
¼ cup butter
juice of 1 lemon
2 teaspoons chopped parsley

Filets de Pompano Bercy

SPRINKLE the parsley and the shallots, chopped, on a buttered shallow baking dish. Season the pompano fillets with salt and pepper and lay them side by side on the herbs. Add the wine and the lemon juice and cover the fish with a piece of buttered paper. Bake in a moderate oven (350°f.) for about 15 minutes, until the fish tests done.

6 pompano fillets
2 shallots
1 teaspoon chopped parsley
2 cups dry white wine
juice of ½ lemon
2 tablespoons butter

Pour the cooking liquid into a small saucepan and reduce it over high heat to one fourth its original volume. Remove the pan from the heat and swirl in the butter, bit by bit. Adjust the seasoning and pour the sauce over the fish in the baking dish. Put the dish under the broiler for a minute or two to glaze the sauce.

Quenelles de Brochet
(Pike Dumplings)

1 pound pike fillet
2 egg whites
2 cups light cream

CUT the pike, which should be completely free of skin and bones, into small pieces and pound it to a paste in a mortar. Force the fish through a fine sieve or put it in an electric blender to make a smooth purée. Set the bowl containing the fish in a pan of ice. Slowly work in the egg whites with a wooden spoon. Add gradually, stirring constantly, about half the cream. Season lightly with salt, white pepper, nutmeg, and cayenne, and stir in more of the cream. Test the mixture by poaching ½ teaspoon in hot but not boiling salted water. The *quenelles* should just hold their shape. The lighter the mixture, the better the *quenelles,* and frequent testing is the best way to determine how much cream may be added to the forcemeat.

Heap a tablespoon with the forcemeat, and with a second spoon shape an oval form. Dip the second spoon in hot water and scoop the *mousseline* or *quenelle* onto a buttered, flat pan. Shape all the mixture in this fashion. Pour into the pan enough boiling water or fish stock to come halfway up the *quenelles.* Cover the pan and simmer the *quenelles* gently for from 15 to 20 minutes. Drain the *quenelles* on a napkin and serve with *sauce Venitienne.*

Vol au Vent aux Quenelles de Brochet

MAKE *quenelles de brochet* (above). Fill patty shells or a large puff paste shell with alternate layers of *quenelles* and mushrooms cooked for a few minutes in water acidulated with lemon juice. Cover with fish *velouté* mixed with the mushroom liquor, and garnish with slices of truffle.

Chaboisseau, Southern Style
(*Rosefish or Ocean Perch*)

LAY the fillets side by side in a flat pan, sprinkle them with olive oil, and season them with salt and freshly ground black pepper. Cover the fish with the tomatoes, peeled and cut into thick slices, the olives, sliced thin, the garlic, crushed, and the herbs. Add the wine, cover the pan, bring the liquid to a boil, and cook over high heat for from 10 to 15 minutes, until the fish is done. Adjust the seasoning of the sauce and serve hot.

12 fillets of rosefish (or ocean perch)
1 tablespoon olive oil
6 tomatoes
12 stuffed olives
½ bay leaf
3 sprigs parsley
1 sprig thyme
3 garlic cloves
½ cup dry white wine

Saumon au Court-Bouillon
(*Poached Salmon*)

SALMON steaks and whole fish may be prepared in this fashion. Whole fish require an oval fish kettle, long enough to hold the fish with head and tail intact. The fish may be wrapped in cheesecloth for easy removal from the kettle. Add sufficient fish *court-bouillon* to cover the fish, and bring the liquid slowly to the boiling point. Reduce the heat and simmer, covered, for from 15 to 20 minutes. Drain well on a towel and serve hot with *sauce Hollandaise* or cold with mayonnaise. If the fish is to be served cold, it should cool in the *court-bouillon*.

Saumon Grillé
(*Grilled Salmon Steaks*)

THE salmon steaks should be cut about 1 inch thick. Season with salt and brush with melted butter. Broil the steaks on a pre-heated oiled broiling pan until they flake at the touch of a fork. Reduce the heat during the last part of the cooking period.

Eperlans à l'Anglaise
(*Pan-fried Smelts*)

12 small smelts
1 egg
1 cup bread crumbs
4 tablespoons clarified butter

CLEAN the smelts, split them down the back, and remove the backbones. Roll the fish in beaten egg and then in fresh bread crumbs. Sauté the fish in the hot clarified butter until they are nicely browned on all sides. Pour *sauce maître d'hôtel* over them and serve at once. Serves 2.

Raie au Beurre Noir
(*Skate with Brown Butter*)

3 pounds skate meat
1 cup cider vinegar
½ cup capers
1 tablespoon chopped parsley
2 tablespoons sweet butter
juice of 1 lemon

HAVE the fish dealer clean the skate and cut the meat into portions weighing ¼ pound each. Wash well. Put the fish in a flat pan and add water to cover, the vinegar, and a generous amount of salt. Cover the pan and bring the liquid to a boil. Reduce the heat and simmer for 30 minutes.

Drain the fish on a towel and remove and

discard the skin and the bones. Arrange the fish on a hot platter and sprinkle it with the capers, parsley, and lemon juice. Cook the butter in a small skillet until it begins to brown, and pour it at once over the skate. Serve with boiled new potatoes.

The scrod is a young codfish; its flesh is white, tender, and of excellent flavor.

Cabillaud, Nouvelle Angleterre
(*New England Scrod*)

Have the scrod cleaned and the backbone removed without separating the halves. Season the fish well with salt and pepper and let it stand overnight in the refrigerator. Arrange the fish, flesh side up, on a pre-heated broiling pan. Sprinkle with olive oil and broil for from 12 to 15 minutes. Arrange the fish on a serving dish and pour over it the butter mixed with the parsley and lemon juice. Fresh tarragon makes a delicious substitute for parsley.

1 scrod, 3 to 3½ pounds
olive oil
juice of ½ lemon
1 teaspoon chopped parsley or tarragon
1 tablespoon butter

One of the simplest, and most satisfactory ways of cooking such fish as fillet of sole and trout is that called *à la meunière,* in the manner of the miller's wife. As the mill was located on a stream, and the stream was a source of fish, what was more natural than that the lady of the mill should dip the freshly caught fish into some of her own flour and brown it quickly in hot butter? The old classical books of cookery, such as Carême's and Urbain Dubois's, do not mention this method at all, and it appears for the first time in Escoffier's writings. Apparently, no writer earlier than Escoffier thought it worthy of mention.

71

Sole à la Meunière à l'Estragon
(Sole with Tarragon)

6 sole
½ cup flour
½ cup clarified butter
juice of ½ lemon
1 tablespoon chopped tarragon
¼ cup sweet butter

HAVE the fish cleaned but not split; leave heads and tails on or not, as preferred. Sprinkle the fish with flour and brown them on both sides in the hot clarified butter. Season with salt during the cooking. Transfer the fish to a hot serving dish and sprinkle with the lemon juice. Blend the chopped tarragon with 2 tablespoons butter and spread the paste on the fish. Brown the remaining butter in a small pan and pour it foaming over the fish. Serve at once.

Flounder is frequently substituted for sole. This method is suitable for almost all small fish and for fish steaks.

THE MAN, who gave his name to the Restaurant Marguery, in Paris, was more than merely the proprietor of that illustrious eating place; he was a chef endowed with great creative genius, and his masterpiece was probably the fillet of sole garnished with oysters and shrimp which is known as *filet de sole Marguery* wherever *haute cuisine* is honored.

Filets de Sole Marguery

6 sole fillets
½ cup dry white wine
juice of 1 lemon
1 tablespoon melted butter
12 small cooked shrimp
12 small poached oysters
1 cup cream sauce
2 egg yolks
4 tablespoons butter

LAY the sole fillets side by side on a buttered baking dish and sprinkle them with salt and the melted butter. Pour the white wine and lemon juice around the fillets and add a little water, if necessary, to cover the bottom of the dish generously. Bake the fish in a moderately hot oven (400°f.) for about 15 minutes, basting occasionally. Transfer the fish to a serving platter. Garnish the platter with the shrimp and

72

oysters and keep all warm while preparing the sauce.

Reduce the cooking liquor over high heat to one third its original quantity. Add the cream sauce, the egg yolks, and the butter. Heat all together without boiling, stirring constantly, and strain over the fillets of sole. Put the platter under the broiler for a moment to glaze the sauce.

Filets de Sole Véronique

FLATTEN the fillets of sole lightly with the flat of a knife and fold them in half. Season with salt and lay the folded fillets side by side on a buttered pan. Pour the fish stock made with the bones and trimmings of the fish and the white wine over the fish. Cook gently for 10 minutes, until the fish is done. Remove the fillets to a platter and garnish the dish with the grapes. Reduce the cooking liquor over high heat to one fourth its original volume. Gradually swirl in the butter, off the fire, and adjust the seasoning. Pour the sauce over the fillets and the grapes and set the platter under the broiler to glaze the sauce.

6 sole fillets
1 cup fish stock
½ cup white wine
2 tablespoons butter
1 cup skinned and seeded
  white grapes

Truites de Rivière, Sauce Verte
(*Brook Trout with Green Mayonnaise*)

CLEAN the trout and lay them side by side in a shallow pan. Add boiling *court-bouillon* to cover the fish. Simmer for 2 or 3 minutes; cover the pan; reduce the heat; and cook for from 10 to 15 minutes longer. Cool the trout in the *court-bouillon,* arrange them on a serving platter, and serve with a sauceboat of green mayonnaise, or *sauce verte*.

6 brook trout
1 quart *court-bouillon*
1 cup *sauce verte*

73

Truites de Mer à la Mirabeau
(*Broiled Sea trout with Anchovy Sauce*)

6 sea trout fillets
2 tablespoons olive oil
½ cup butter
1 tablespoon bottled anchovy
    sauce
6 curled anchovy fillets
6 pitted ripe olives

SEASON the fillets with salt and pepper and brush them with olive oil. Broil on a preheated broiler, basting frequently with the pan drippings. Transfer the fish to a serving dish and pour over it the butter, melted and mixed with the anchovy sauce. Wash and dry the curled anchovy fillets and put an olive in the center of each. Use to garnish the trout.

Truites de Rivière au Bleu
(*Boiled Brook Trout*)

6 live brook trout
2 quarts *court-bouillon*

TAKE the trout from the water and tap them on the head to render them unconscious. Cut off the fins and clean the fish at once. Put the fish on a rack and lower them slowly into a kettle of boiling *court-bouillon*. Reduce the heat to prevent the boiling from agitating the trout so much that they break. Boil for from 8 to 10 minutes, depending upon the size of the fish, and serve with melted butter and boiled potatoes.

Truites de Rivière Rochambeau
(*Brook Trout Rochambeau*)

6 brook trout
4 shallots
2 tomatoes
2 cups white wine
½ pound mushrooms
bouquet made of 1 sprig of
    CONTINUED

CLEAN the trout and lay them side by side in a deep buttered baking dish. Sprinkle with salt, pepper, and paprika, and add the shallots, chopped, the tomatoes, peeled, seeded and coarsely chopped, and the mushrooms, cleaned and sliced. Add the wine and the bouquet, cover the pan with buttered paper, and bake the fish in a moderate oven (350°f.) for about 20 minutes. Transfer the fish to a serving dish and pour the cooking liquid into a small saucepan. Reduce this sauce over high heat to half its original quantity. Remove the pan from the heat, swirl in the butter, and adjust the seasoning. Pour the sauce over the trout and serve hot.

parsley, 1 sprig of thyme, and a bit of bay leaf
2 tablespoons sweet butter

Blanchailles Diablées
(*Deviled Whitebait*)

HAVE the whitebait cleaned. Dip them in milk and in the flour seasoned with the mustard. Put the floured fish in a frying basket and shake off any excess flour. Fry in very hot deep fat to a light brown, drain on absorbent toweling, and season with salt and cayenne pepper. Serve with parsley and lemon wedges. Serves 4.

1 pound whitebait
½ cup milk
1 teaspoon dry mustard
1 cup flour

Merlans Frits
(*Fried Whiting*)

HAVE the whiting cleaned, but not split. Dip them in milk and in flour and shake well in the frying basket before lowering the basket into very hot deep fat. Cook the fish for from 3 to 4 minutes, until they are crisp and golden brown. Drain on absorbent toweling, season with salt, and serve at once with a side dish of *sauce tartare*.

6 whiting
½ cup milk
1 cup flour

Brandade de Morue
(*Salt Codfish Provençal*)

CUT the pound of salt cod into small squares and soak it in cold water for 1 hour or more. Drain well, cover with fresh cold water, and

1 pound salted cod
6 ounces salted cod
CONTINUED

1 cup olive oil
3 garlic cloves
1 cup cream

bring the water to the boiling point. Cook the cod for 12 minutes and drain it thoroughly on a towel. Arrange the 6 ounces of unsoaked cod on a baking dish, sprinkle it with a little olive oil, and bake it in a moderate oven for 15 minutes. This unsoaked cod gives the *brandade* extra flavor. Pound the fish in a mortar until it is very smooth. Add the olive oil slowly, lightly heated with the crushed garlic cloves, stirring constantly to keep the mixture smooth. Add the cream, still stirring, to make a very light, white mixture. Correct the seasoning and serve the *brandade* with croutons of bread browned in butter.

Morue Cardinal
(*Salted Cod Loaf*)

2 cups tomato purée
1 teaspoon chopped parsley
2 garlic cloves
2 eggs
2 egg yolks
1 pound salted cod

BRING the tomato purée to a boil, add the parsley and garlic, both finely chopped, and cook together for 5 minutes. Cool the purée and beat in the eggs beaten with the extra egg yolks and the soaked, boiled, flaked cod. Adjust the seasoning and turn the mixture into a buttered mold. Set the mold in a baking pan in water that comes halfway up the sides. Bake in a moderate oven (350°f.) for about 30 minutes, until the loaf is firm. Unmold the loaf on a serving platter and pour cream sauce over it. Serve hot.

Shellfish

Soft Clams Marinière

4 dozen soft clams
CONTINUED

OPEN the clams and separate the soft portions from the hard. Reserve the hard portions to use for chowder. Put the soft clam meat and the clam juice in a sauce pan, bring the liquid to a boil, and cook for 1 minute. Lift the clams out of the juice with a sieve. Strain the liquid through several thicknesses of cheesecloth and reduce it over moderate heat to one third its original volume. Return the clams to the reduced juice and heat. Blend in the egg yolks mixed with the cream, and heat without allowing the sauce to boil. Finish with the chopped parsley. Neither salt nor pepper is required to season this dish; the fresh clam juice is naturally salty. Serves 2.

2 egg yolks
½ cup cream
1 teaspoon chopped parsley

Crabes Mous Meunière
(*Soft Shell Crabs Meunière*)

WITH a scissors, cut off the segment that folds under the rear of the crab's body. Turn the crab and cut off the "face" behind the eyes. Remove the back shell. Wash the crabs well in cold running water, drain them, and arrange them on a shallow pan. Season with salt and pepper and sprinkle with the cream. Put the crabs in the refrigerator until just before serving time.

Dip the crabs in flour and brown them quickly in the hot clarified butter, shaking the pan constantly to keep the crabs from sticking. Turn and brown the other side. Drain the crabs and serve each on a slice of bread browned in butter. Sprinkle with lemon juice and with freshly chopped parsley, and finally with the sweet butter, cooked to a golden brown color. Serves 3.

6 soft shell crabs
1 tablespoon cream
½ cup clarified butter
1 tablespoon sweet butter
1 teaspoon chopped parsley

77

Hard Shell Crabs

Soak 1 dozen live hard-shell crabs for 5 minutes in cold water containing ½ cup salt. Bring 2 gallons water to a boil with ½ cup salt. Boil the crabs for 10 to 15 minutes, depending upon their size. Put the pot under the cold water faucet and cool the crabs in running water.

Remove the shells carefully, wash them, and dry them thoroughly. Remove and discard the small legs and the lungs. Pick out the meat in the claws and the back, being careful to eliminate the membrane and any bits of shell.

Crabes à la Diable
(*Deviled Crabs*)

meat of 1 dozen hard-shell crabs (about 1½ pounds meat)
1 tablespoon butter
½ tablespoon flour
2 cups hot milk
1 onion
½ cup fresh bread crumbs
2 tablespoons cream
1 teaspoon chopped parsley

Melt the butter, stir in the flour, and cook the *roux* for a minute, stirring constantly with a wooden spoon. Add the hot milk and the onion, chopped, and cook for 10 minutes, stirring from time to time. The sauce should be thin. Add the cream, a little salt and pepper to taste, the bread crumbs, the crabmeat, and the parsley. The mixture should be thick enough to hold its shape. If necessary, add more bread crumbs. Fill prepared crab shells or individual scallop dishes with the crab mixture, mounding it high. Mix some dry mustard to a paste with water and brush the filled shells with it. Sprinkle with bread crumbs and with melted butter and brown quickly in a hot oven. Serve bubbling hot.

If natural crab shells are used, they should not be allowed to rest on the bottom of the baking sheet. Balance each shell on a muffin ring to keep it on a level. A ring of duchesse potatoes may be piped around the edge of the shells before the shells go into the oven to brown.

As FAR as we know, the famous lobster dish called *homard à l'américaine* is Américaine only in that Americans—particularly the Americans who patronized the expensive Parisian restaurants at the turn of the century—enjoyed it very much. The ingredients are typical of those used in the regional cookery of Bordeaux, and history records that the chef of Napoleon III first prepared lobster in this fashion at the Tuileries in about 1860. The first version of the dish to appear on the menu of a restaurant— the Restaurant Bonnefoy in the rue de l'Echelle —was not so spicy as our current preparation, but it achieved instant popularity among gourmets, who called it *homard à la Bonnefoy* until it was ultimately dubbed *à l'américaine*.

Homard à l'Américaine
(*Lobster à l'Américaine*)

CUT up the live lobsters as follows: sever the claws, cut the tails into sections, split the bodies in half lengthwise, and remove and discard the little bag near the head. Reserve the tomalley, or green liver, of the lobster, and the coral, or eggs; these will be used for finishing the sauce. Season the lobster with salt and pepper and toss the pieces in a few tablespoons of hot olive oil over high heat until the meat has stiffened and the shells are red. Pour off and discard the olive oil. Sprinkle the lobster with the shallots and the garlic, finely chopped, and simmer for a few minutes, covered. Add ½ cup

6 lobsters, 1¼ pounds each
4 shallots
3 garlic cloves
1½ cups dry white wine
8 tomatoes or 4 tablespoons tomato purée
1 tablespoon mixed chopped parsley and tarragon
1 cup cognac

cognac, cover the pan, and simmer for 5 minutes. Add the dry white wine, the tomatoes, seeded and chopped, and the chopped herbs. Cover the pan and set it in a moderate oven for 20 minutes. Transfer the lobster to a heatproof serving platter. Reduce the sauce in the pan to one third its original volume and add to it the reserved liver and coral and a little sweet butter. Cook for a minute or two, swirl in 1 tablespoon sweet butter, and adjust the seasoning with salt, pepper, and cayenne. Pour the sauce over the lobster, sprinkle with ½ cup heated cognac, set the spirit ablaze, and serve flaming. Serves 10.

No ONE can state positively whether lobster Newburgh was named for an individual or for the upstate New York city of that name. The recipe first appears in *The Epicurean,* a cookbook by Charles Ranhofer, who was chef at Delmonico's, New York, during the "Gay Nineties." Interestingly enough, the recipe as recorded by Mr. Ranhofer bears some resemblance to the recipe for *homard archiduc* as served at the Maison Paillard, in Paris, at a still earlier date.

Homard à la Newburgh
(*Lobster Newburgh*)

4 lobsters, 1¼ pounds each
1 tablespoon sweet butter
1 cup Madeira or Sherry
1 cup cream
3 egg yolks

PLUNGE the live lobsters into boiling salted water acidulated with ½ cup vinegar and cook them for 20 minutes. Chill in running cold water. Crack the shells and carefully remove the meat in one piece from the tail and claws. Remove and discard the black intestinal vein in the tail and cut the tail into ½-inch-thick slices. Toss the lobster over a hot fire in the melted sweet butter for a few minutes, until the meat acquires a fine red color. Add salt, pepper, and a little cayenne pepper and the hot wine. Simmer for a few minutes longer and add half the cream, also heated. Simmer for 2 minutes longer. Stir in the egg yolks, blended with the remaining cream, and remove the pan from the heat so that the sauce will thicken without danger of curdling. This may be prepared and served in a chafing dish.

Crab meat may be prepared in the same way.

Homard Lafayette

MELT the butter and in it cook the chopped onions until they are soft but not brown. Add the tomatoes, peeled, seeded, and chopped, and cook all together slowly, in a covered pan, for 2 hours.

Sever the tails and claws from the bodies of the lobsters. Boil the bodies in salted water for 10 minutes and clean them well under running water. Set them aside.

Heat the oil in a sauté pan and cook the lobster tails and claws over high heat, stirring constantly, until they turn red. Pour off the cooking oil. Sprinkle the lobster with the shallots and garlic, both chopped, and cook, covered, for 5 to 10 minutes. Add half the cognac, blaze it, and put out the fire by covering the pan. Add the white wine, simmer for a few minutes, and add the previously prepared tomato and onion mixture, the parsley, and the bay leaf. Cover the pan again and cook slowly for 20 to 25 minutes. Turn the contents of the pan into a colander and strain the liquid into a bowl. When the tails and claws are cool

3 tablespoons butter
3 onions
12 ripe tomatoes
6 1-pound lobsters
½ cup olive oil
6 shallots
3 garlic cloves
2 cups dry white wine
½ cup cognac
3 sprigs parsley
1 bay leaf
1 teaspoon chopped tarragon
1 cup *velouté* sauce
2 cups rice
6 slices truffle

enough to handle, remove the meat whole by cutting the shells with a scissors. Put the lobster meat in a sauté pan and sprinkle it with 2 tablespoons of the cooking liquid. Cover the pan and set it in a warm place.

Force the remaining contents of the colander through the sieve and combine this with the cooking liquid. Reduce the mixture over high heat to about 1½ cups.

Make 1 cup chicken *velouté* and make a pilaff with the 2 cups rice.

To serve, arrange the rice along the sides of a long platter. Warm the prepared lobster bodies in hot water and arrange them on the platter across the rice. Put the meat of 1 tail and 2 claws in each body. Combine the lobster sauce with the chicken *velouté,* add the tarragon and the remaining cognac, and pour a little sauce over each body. Garnish with a slice of truffle warmed in butter. Serve very hot.

Homard Thermidor
(*Lobster Thermidor*)

2 lobsters, 1½ pounds each
½ pound mushrooms
1 cup milk
2 tablespoons butter
1½ tablespoons flour
1 teaspoon dry mustard
½ cup cream

Boil the live lobsters, covered, for 20 to 25 minutes in salted water acidulated with 1 tablespoon vinegar for each quart. Put the kettle under the cold water faucet and chill the lobsters thoroughly. Cut each lobster in half lengthwise. Remove the claw meat and the tail meat and cut it in large dice. Wash and rinse the body shells carefully.

Combine the mushrooms, cut in large squares, with 2 teaspoons water, 1 teaspoon lemon juice, and 1 teaspoon butter. Cook, covered, for 6 minutes and drain, reserving the liquid. Combine the mushrooms with the lobster meat.

Melt the butter, stir in the flour, and cook the *roux* for a minute or two, stirring constantly with a wooden spoon. Do not allow the *roux* to brown. Add the mustard, diluted with a little water, and gradually stir in the hot milk and the mushroom liquor. Cook for 2 minutes, stirring constantly, and season with salt, pepper, and cayenne pepper to taste. Add the hot cream and simmer for a minute or so longer. Strain the sauce through a fine sieve over the lobster and mushrooms, and mix well. Fill the lobster shells with the mixture, sprinkle with finely grated Swiss cheese, and set in a very hot oven to brown the topping. Serves 2.

Salade de Homards
(*Lobster Salad*)

SEASON the lobster meat with the French dressing and chill it. Soak the celery in ice water for 1 hour, drain it, and dry it thoroughly. Combine the celery with the lobster, add the mayonnaise, and adjust the seasoning. Serve on lettuce leaves on individual salad plates. Garnish with stuffed olives, capers, slices of pimiento, and quartered hard-cooked eggs. Or mound the salad in a bowl, surround it with quartered hearts of lettuce, and garnish. The salad may be coated lightly with mayonnaise thinned with tarragon vinegar.

1 cup diced, freshly cooked
  lobster meat
1 cup thinly sliced celery
1 tablespoon French dressing
½ cup mayonnaise

MUSSELS HAVE A TENDENCY to secrete sand in the cracks of their purple-black shells, and must be thoroughly scrubbed, preferably under running water. Discard any dead mussels (those with open shells) and any whose unusual heaviness indicates that they are full of sand. Mussels are the least expensive of all shellfish: they are the least appreciated by the uninformed. The most popular of mussel dishes is the simplest to prepare.

Moules Marinière
(*Stewed Mussels*)

1 quart mussels
½ teaspoon chopped shallots
½ teaspoon chopped onion
½ teaspoon chopped parsley
½ cup dry white wine

SCRUB the mussels thoroughly under running water. Put them in a kettle with the wine and ingredients. Add salt and freshly ground black pepper to taste. Cover the kettle tightly and cook over high heat until all the shells are open, for about 5 minutes. Drain the mussels in a colander and put them in a serving dish to keep warm. Pour the cooking liquid off any sediment which may settle to the bottom and reduce it over high heat to one third its original volume. Thicken the sauce, if desired, by stirring in 1 tablespoon butter blended with 1 teaspoon flour. Cook for a minute or two longer and pour the sauce over the mussels. Serves 2.

Moules au Safran
(*Mussels with Saffron*)

2 quarts mussels
3 tablespoons olive oil
1 small onion
white part of 1 leek
1 tomato
2 garlic cloves
1 sprig of thyme
½ bay leaf
1 teaspoon powdered saffron
1 cup white wine

SCRUB 2 quarts mussels thoroughly under running water, tearing off any grass. Heat the oil in a saucepan, add the onion and leek, chopped, and simmer for a few minutes. Add the tomato, peeled, seeded, and chopped, the garlic, thyme, bay leaf, saffron, and wine. Cook slowly until the moisture has all but evaporated. Add the mussels and cover the pan. Cook for about 5 minutes, until all the mussel shells have opened. Remove one shell, or both, if desired, from the mussels, and arrange on a serving dish. Strain the sauce through a fine sieve and pour a little over each mussel. Chill well before serving. Serves 4.

YOUR FISH DEALER will open oysters for you, if you ask him to, but oysters taste so much better when they are freshly opened that I advise to take the trouble of mastering the technique of doing the job yourself. Hold the oysters firmly with the palm of the hand against a towel on the table, deep shell down. Insert the blunt-tipped blade of a knife near the pointed edge and twist the knife to force the shells apart. Slide the knife close to the upper shell and cut the muscle. Then slide the knife close to the lower shell and cut that connection.

Oysters are frequently served as hors d'oeuvre. More oyster recipes will, therefore, be found in the chapter devoted to hors d'oeuvre.

La Soupe aux Huîtres
(*Oyster Stew*)

COOK the milk, parsley, onion, celery, and peppercorns in the top of a double boiler over boiling water for 15 minutes. Strain the milk and return it to the boiler. Beat the egg yolks with the cream, warm the mixture with a little hot milk, and add it to the seasoned milk. Cook, stirring constantly, for from 3 to 4 minutes. Be careful not to let the mixture boil, lest it curdle, and remove it from the heat as soon as it thickens.

Cook the soft part of the oysters in their own juices, discarding the hard part, until the juices boil. Combine oysters and thickened milk, stir, adjust the seasoning, and serve at once. Serves 2.

24 oysters
2 cups milk
1 small stalk of celery
1 small onion
1 small sprig of parsley
6 white peppercorns
2 egg yolks
½ cup cream

85

Huîtres à la Rockefeller
(*Baked Oysters Rockefeller*)

36 freshly opened oysters
¾ cup butter
¾ cup flour
4 cups fish stock
1 tablespoon chili pepper sauce
2 tablespoons tomato ketchup
1 teaspoon Worcestershire
 sauce
4 scallions
6 sprigs of chervil
2 sprigs of parsley
¼ pound washed spinach
 leaves
1 small head of fennel
½ bunch watercress
juice of 2 lemons
¼ cup Absinthe or Pernod

MELT the butter, stir in the flour, and cook, stirring, without allowing the *roux* to take on color. Stir in the fish stock and cook slowly, stirring from time to time, for 30 minutes. Mince all the vegetables finely or put them through the food chopper. Add the vegetables and any juices to the sauce, bring the sauce to a boil, and strain the sauce through a fine sieve. Stir in the ketchup, pepper sauce, and Worcestershire sauce. Add the lemon juice and Absinthe or Pernod, and adjust the seasoning with salt to taste.

Arrange the oysters, in their deep half-shells in a baking pan filled with rock salt. Spoon a little of the sauce over each oyster and bake in a hot oven (400°f.) for about 10 minutes, to glaze the sauce.

Huîtres Casino
(*Oysters Casino*)

12 oysters
1 tablespoon butter
1 tablespoon chopped
 pimientos
1 teaspoon chopped parsley
juice of ½ lemon
2 slices bacon

OPEN large oysters and leave the meat on the deep half-shell. Blend the butter, pimientos, parsley, and lemon juice, and season with salt, pepper, and paprika. Broil the bacon slices slightly and cut them into 1½-inch strips. Cover each oyster with a piece of bacon and some of the seasoned butter. Sprinkle with dry bread crumbs and bake in a hot oven for about 5 minutes. A bed of rock salt makes it easy to balance the oyster shells on the baking pan. Serves 2.

Huîtres Diablées Américaine
(*Deviled Oysters American*)

Mix the mustard to a paste with a little water. Add the oysters, freshly opened and free of beard, and cook, stirring, for 2 minutes. The oysters should be thoroughly coated with the mustard. Remove the pan at once from the heat. Cool the oysters and dip them one by one in beaten egg and fresh bread crumbs. Arrange on a buttered pan, sprinkle with melted butter, and broil quickly to brown both sides. Serve on croutons of bread browned in butter, with *sauce maître d'hôtel*. Serves 2.

12 oysters
1 tablespoon dry mustard
1 egg
1 cup fresh bread crumbs
2 tablespoons *sauce maître d'hôtel*

Huîtres à la Bostonienne
(*Baked Oysters, Boston Style*)

Poach the oysters in their own juices with the butter for about 5 minutes, keeping the liquid below the boiling point. Season to taste with celery salt and a little paprika. Put the toast in individual baking dishes. Cover each piece of toast with a slice of ham and put 6 oysters on the ham. Divide the oyster liquor and butter evenly among the dishes and sprinkle with bread crumbs mixed with grated Swiss or Parmesan cheese. Dot with butter and bake the oysters in a hot oven (400°f.) for about 10 minutes, to brown the topping.

36 freshly opened oysters
½ cup butter
6 slices whole-wheat toast
6 slices ham

Huîtres Florentine
(*Creamed Oysters with Spinach*)

The spinach for this dish should be cooked very quickly in hot butter and highly seasoned. Open the oysters and put a generous teaspoon

36 oysters
1 cup cooked shredded spinach
CONTINUED

87

2 cups Mornay sauce
grated cheese

of the spinach in each deep half-shell. Put the oyster meat on top of the spinach and cover with Mornay sauce. Sprinkle lightly with grated cheese and brown the topping in a hot oven (400°f.). The oyster shells may be set in a pan of rock salt for easier handling.

Huîtres en Coquilles
(*Baked Oysters on the Half-shell*)

36 freshly opened oysters
4 shallots
9 strips bacon
¼ cup butter
juice of 1 lemon
2 tablespoons chopped parsley

ARRANGE the oysters, on their deep half-shells, on a baking pan filled with rock salt. Cook the shallots, chopped, in the butter for a few minutes, add salt and pepper to taste, and pour a little of this mixture on top of each oyster. Cover each oyster with a square of lightly broiled bacon. Bake in a hot oven (400°f.) for 6 minutes. Melt 2 tablespoons of butter, add the lemon juice, and pour over the baked oysters. Garnish with chopped parsley and serve hot.

IN THE UNITED STATES, the scallop is sold ready to cook; the muscle, or edible portion, has been removed from the shell before the scallop comes to the market. If the scallops are to be served whole, the tiny, more delicate bay scallops are preferred; for creamed preparations, the larger, slightly coarser sea scallops may be used.

Pétoncles Meunière
(*Scallops Meunière*)

1 pound bay scallops
½ cup milk
2 tablespoons butter
CONTINUED

COVER the scallops with milk for a few minutes, drain them, and dredge them in seasoned flour. Fry the scallops to a rich brown in hot, deep fat (375°f.). Remove them from the fat and drain them on absorbent toweling. Melt the butter and cook it to a hazelnut brown. Roll the scallops in the browned butter, add the lemon juice and parsley, and season with salt and pepper to taste. Toss well and serve at once. Serves 2–3.

juice of ½ lemon
1 tablespoon chopped parsley

Coquilles Saint-Jacques
(*Scallops in Shells*)

BRING the water and wine to a boil and add the scallops, cut into slices if they are large, and a little salt and pepper. Cook the scallops for 5 minutes and drain them. Reserve the stock.

Melt the butter and cook the onion and shallot, both chopped, for a few minutes. Stir in the flour and cook for a few minutes longer, stirring constantly. The *roux* should not brown.

Cook the mushrooms for 5 minutes in water acidulated with a little lemon juice. Drain the cooking liquid and add it to the *roux* along with the scallop stock. Cook, stirring, until the sauce is very thick. Stir in the hot cream and adjust the seasoning with salt, pepper, and cayenne. The sauce should be highly seasoned. Add the scallops and mushrooms and toss well to combine. Divide the mixture into 6 scallop shells or small individual ramekins. Sprinkle with fresh bread crumbs and a little melted butter, and set in a hot oven (400°f.) for 5 minutes or longer to brown the topping. Serves 2–3.

1 pound scallops
½ cup white wine
½ cup water
1 white onion
1 shallot
2 tablespoon butter
2 tablespoons flour
½ pound mushrooms
½ cup cream

Crevettes au Safran
(*Shrimp with Saffron*)

REMOVE the intestinal vein from the shrimp without removing the entire shell. Use a scissors to facilitate this operation.

24 shrimp
½ cup water
CONTINUED

1 cup white wine
1 carrot
1 onion
1 sprig of parsley
½ teaspoon powdered saffron
juice of 1 lemon

Combine the remaining ingredients, cover the pan, and simmer all together for 10 minutes. Adjust the seasoning with salt, pepper, and cayenne, and add the shrimp. Cover the pan again and cook for 7 minutes, until the shrimp shells are bright pink. Cool before serving. Arrange the shrimp on a serving dish and strain the sauce over them. Each guest removes the shells at the table, either with his hands or with a fish fork and knife, depending upon the formality of the occasion.

Crevettes au Court-Bouillon
(*Shrimp in Court-Bouillon*)

1 pound shrimp
1 cup water
1 cup dry white wine
6 peppercorns
1 bay leaf
2 sprigs of parsley
juice of 1 lemon
1 small onion
2 stalks of celery, including the
  green top

WASH the shrimp and de-vein them, if desired, but do not shell. Combine the remaining ingredients and cook slowly for 15 minutes. Add the shrimp, cover the pan, and cook for from 5 to 7 minutes, until the shrimp are bright pink. Do not overcook them. Remove the pan from the heat and cool the shrimp in the stock. Remove the intestinal vein, if this was not done previously, and the shells, if desired. Serve with mayonnaise or with any cocktail sauce.

Terrapin

IN EARLY COLONIAL DAYS in America, the native terrapin was so plentiful and cheap that slaves rebelled at the frequency with which it was served to them. Unfortunately, that condition no longer holds true; terrapin is neither cheap nor plentiful. Only its status as a delicacy remains unchallenged.

Most of our terrapin comes from the Chesapeake Bay

area, where it lives in tidal waters that are part fresh, part salt, and offer a varied diet of crabs, snails, fish, and grass. Female terrapins have larger heads, smaller tail sections, and deeper bodies than the male, and the shell seems more wedge-shaped. Bull terrapins are not considered choice; the most highly valued terrapin is the female carrying eggs.

Drop the terrapin in tepid water and allow it to swim for 30 minutes. Wash it well and plunge it into boiling water, which will kill it quickly and painlessly. Remove the thin white skin from the feet and tail with a rough cloth. Cut off the claws and draw out the head with a skewer or steel needle. Plunge the head into boiling water to loosen the skin, and rub the skin off.

Put the prepared terrapin in a kettle and cover it with cold water. Add no salt or other seasoning. Bring the water to a boil, cover the kettle, and cook until the terrapin is tender. This takes from 30 minutes to an hour or more: the terrapin is tender when the paws feel soft to the pressure of the finger. Cool the terrapin in the kettle, uncovered, overnight.

To remove the meat, lay the terrapin on its back. Detach the meat from the shells with the tip of a small knife. Break the shell on the flat side and remove the legs, the neck, and the head. Separate the liver and eggs from the entrails. Be careful not to break the gall bladder, which is attached to the liver, as the gall will give a bitter flavor to everything it touches. If the gall bladder should break, wash the meat very carefully in running cold water.

Discard the white meat and the intestines, which are inedible. Use the dark meat, the fat, the liver, and the eggs. Clean and slice the liver and soak it in cold water. Soak the eggs in cold water; the skin should be removed before the eggs are used. Cut the dark meat into pieces the size of a walnut, put it into a bowl, and cover with a wet towel.

Remove the skin from the lower shell and break the shell into pieces. Return the shell and the bones removed from the terrapin to the liquid in which it was cooked. Cook for 10 minutes, strain the broth, and reduce it over low heat, skimming from time to time, until there is just enough clear, light brown stock to cover the terrapin meat in the bowl. This stock is highly gelatinous, and has a strong but pleasant flavor. Store the terrapin in the refrigerator.

Terrapin à la Florham

4 terrapins, 3½ pounds each
2 cups dry sherry
1 tablespoon crushed black
  peppercorns
1 pound sweet butter
3 egg yolks
½ cup heavy cream

PUT the jellied terrapin, prepared as above, in a heavy-bottomed pan and melt it very slowly. Heat 1 cup sherry in a small saucepan with the pepper, stirring constantly, and strain the boiling wine into the terrapin. Add a little salt and cook for 2 minutes. Fit a flannel cloth over a large bowl and put a colander on the cloth. Pour the terrapin and its juices into the colander. Remove the colander and set it, covered, in a warm place. Strain the juices through the cloth and return them to a saucepan. Reduce over high heat, skimming as necessary, until the juices are thick and syrupy. Watch carefully during this process to prevent burning. Add the terrapin to the reduced sauce and swirl in the butter, bit by bit. Heat the remaining cup of sherry and add it to the pan. Adjust the seasoning with salt. If desired, the flavor of the sauce may be modified and the color lightened by the addition of the egg yolks beaten with the cream: this is the Maryland style.

Remove the skin from the terrapin eggs, plunge them into boiling water for a moment, and sprinkle them over the prepared terrapin. The terrapin may be kept hot for serving in a chafing dish. Serves 8.

Frogs' Legs

THE DELICATELY FLAVORED, tender flesh of frogs' legs is as much appreciated by sophisticated diners in the United States as it is in France. The best frogs' legs are of medium size, white, plump, and young; they run from eight to ten to the pound, and three pounds will serve six people. Only frogs from fresh-water ponds are used. They are usually sold skinned and ready to eat. Otherwise the skin must be peeled and the feet cut off and discarded. The flavor of frogs' legs deteriorates very rapidly, so use only very fresh ones.

Frogs' Legs Meunière
(*Frogs' Legs Sauté*)

SOAK the frogs' legs in cold water for 2 hours to plump and bleach the flesh. Dip them in milk, season them with salt and pepper, and dredge them with flour. Brown them on all sides in hot clarified butter and remove them to a serving dish. Pour off any remaining cooking butter, and in the same pan brown lightly the sweet butter. Pour the foaming butter over the frogs' legs and sprinkle with the lemon juice and chopped parsley.

3 pounds frogs' legs
3 tablespoons sweet butter
1 teaspoon lemon juice
1 tablespoon chopped parsley

Frogs' Legs Provençal
(*Frogs' Legs Sauté with Garlic*)

PREPARE the frogs' legs as above, but brown them in olive oil. Pour off the oil and brown the

93

butter in the same skillet, adding 2 cloves of finely chopped garlic. Pour the browned butter over the frogs' legs and sprinkle with lemon juice and parsley.

Frogs' Legs Poulette
(*Creamed Frogs' Legs with Mushrooms*)

3 pounds frogs' legs
2 cups dry white wine
1 teaspoon butter
juice of ½ lemon
1 onion
1 sprig parsley
1 pound mushrooms
2 egg yolks
2 tablespoons cream

SOAK the prepared frogs' legs in cold water for 2 hours to plump and bleach the flesh. Combine the wine, butter, and seasonings and add the frogs' legs. Cover the pan and bring the liquid to the simmering point. Add the mushrooms, which may be peeled if necessary, and cook until the frogs' legs are very tender. Remove the legs and mushrooms to a serving dish. Reduce the cooking liquid over high heat until it measures about 1 cup. Add the eggs, beaten with the cream, and stir for a minute over the heat. Do not allow the sauce to boil. Finish the *sauce Poulette* with a pinch of parsley and a spoonful of sweet butter. Adjust the seasoning, pour the sauce over the frogs' legs and mushrooms, and serve hot.

Bouillabaisse

THE SECRET of the perfect bouillabaisse is fish fresh from the sea; that is why the most famous of bouillabaisses originated in the seaport of Marseilles. Some of the fish used for that classic dish are not obtainable in this country, a condition that does not hold true for other bouillabaisses.

Bouillabaisse à la Parisienne
(Parisian Fish Stew)

CUT the fish in large pieces. Split the lobster and crack its claws. Toss with the remaining ingredients in a large bowl, add a little salt and pepper, and set the bowl in the refrigerator for 1½ hours, until 20 minutes before serving time.

Turn the mixture into a flat pan, add enough hot fish stock or boiling water barely to cover the fish, and bring the liquid to a boil over high heat. Cook, covered, for 12 minutes, or until the fish is opaque and flakes readily at the touch of a fork. Adjust the seasoning of the broth with salt and pepper. Pour the broth over freshly made dry toast in a soup tureen and arrange the fish and lobster on a serving platter. Serve together.

3 pounds bass, redfish, or other rockfish
3 pounds lobsters
1 onion, sliced
1 leek, white only, sliced
3 garlic cloves
1½ teaspoon chopped parsley
1½ teaspoons powdered saffron
¾ teaspoon chopped fennel
1½ tablespoons olive oil
¾ bay leaf
3 cups dry white wine

Bouillabaisse Newportaise
(Newport Fish Stew)

1 small bay leaf
1 quart white wine

CUT the fish in large chunks and the lobsters in halves. Add the remaining ingredients, toss well to blend, and set in the refrigerator for 2 hours. Half an hour before serving time, put fish, seasonings and wine in a large flat pan and bring the liquid quickly to a boil. Reduce the heat, cover the pan, and simmer gently for 15 to 20 minutes. The fish is sufficiently cooked when it is opaque and flakes readily at the touch of a fork. Adjust the seasoning and serve the bouillabaisse in a soup tureen, with toasted French bread. Serves 8.

5 pounds blackfish (tautog)
5 pounds sea robin
3 pounds small lobsters
2 tablespoons chopped onion
2 tablespoons chopped leek, white only
2 cups peeled, seeded, chopped tomatoes
4 garlic cloves
1 tablespoon chopped parsley
2 teaspoons powdered saffron
1 tablespoon olive oil

95

Bouillabaisse de Morue
(Salt Cod Stew)

1 tablespoon olive oil
2 onions
1 leek, white only
6 garlic cloves
2 quarts water
1 tablespoon powdered saffron
A bouquet of 3 sprigs of parsley, 1 stalk of celery, 1 sprig of thyme, and half a bay leaf
3 cups thinly sliced potatoes
3 pounds salt cod

1 tablespoon olive oil
1 tablespoon chopped parsley

SIMMER the onions, leek and garlic, all finely chopped, in the olive oil for a few minutes. Add the water, the saffron, and the bouquet. Add a pinch each of salt and pepper, bring the liquid to a boil, and cook for 10 minutes. Add the potatoes and cook for 12 minutes. Add the cod, which has been cut and soaked in fresh water, and the olive oil. Cover the pan and cook briskly for 15 minutes. Add the chopped parsley, adjust the seasoning with salt and pepper, and serve with a side dish of dry toast moistened with a little of the sauce. Serves 8.

IV

POULTRY *and* GAME

POULTRY

Chicken

UNLESS OTHERWISE SPECIFIED, the chickens used in the recipes which follow are young, tender broilers and fryers, aged from 8 weeks to 4 months and weighing $1\frac{1}{2}$ to $3\frac{1}{2}$ pounds. A roaster is from 4 to 8 months old and weighs from 4 to 6 or more pounds. A pullet is approximately the same age as a roaster, but weighs slightly less. Both roasters and pullets are used for braising and stewing as well as for roasting. The fowl, a bird whose laying days are over, can be identified by its inflexible breastbone and the high proportion of fat under the skin. The flesh of the fowl is not so tender as that of a younger bird, but it has excellent flavor, and makes the best soup.

It is important not to overcook chicken. Test the chicken for done-ness by piercing the second joint with a fork. The juices that follow the fork should be perfectly clear. If there is the slightest trace of pink, the bird needs longer cooking.

The white chicken meat cooks more quickly than the dark. When the chicken is disjointed and the parts are cooked separately, remove the white meat from the pan and continue to cook the dark meat for 10 minutes longer. If the chicken is boned, it cooks even more quickly.

Poulet Sauté à la Maryland
(Maryland Fried Chicken)

1 chicken, 2 pounds
1 egg
1 cup fine bread crumbs
¼ cup clarified butter
juice of ½ lemon
½ cup cream
corn fritters
2 bananas

CUT the chicken in quarters and remove the breast bone and the thigh bone. Make an incision down the leg so that the piece will lie flat in the pan. Season the pieces with salt and pepper, dip them in lightly beaten egg, and roll them in bread crumbs. Brown gently in clarified butter. The white meat will cook first, and may be removed to a heated platter after about 15 minutes. Cook the legs for 10 minutes longer and transfer them to the platter. Add the cream and lemon juice to the pan and stir it to incorporate the brown bits that cling to the bottom and sides. Pour the sauce over the chicken. The customary garnish for Maryland Fried Chicken is broiled bacon: serve with corn fritters and with bananas that have been lightly floured and browned in clarified butter. Serves 2.

Southern Fried Chicken

3 chickens, 2 pounds each
3 cups milk
clarified butter or fat
6 tablespoons butter
3 tablespoons flour mixed with
　1 teaspoon baking powder

HAVE the chickens split in halves. Season the halves with salt and pepper, and cover them with milk. Soak for 1 hour. Fry until golden brown on both sides in about ½ inch hot fat or hot clarified butter in a flame-proof casserole. Cover the pan and finish cooking the chicken in a moderate oven (350°f.) for about 25 minutes. Remove the cover about 10 minutes before the cooking time is over. This restores crispness to the coating. Test the chicken for done-ness by piercing the second joint with a fork; if the juice has any trace of pink, additional cooking is needed.

Remove the chicken to a platter to keep warm. Pour off the fat in the pan and add the

6 tablespoons of butter. Melt the butter, stirring in the brown crustiness that clings to the pan. Stir in the flour and cook, stirring with a fork, for a few minutes. Be careful not to let the *roux* burn. Add the milk in which the chickens were soaked, stirring constantly, and cook the sauce until it is smooth and thickened. The sauce should not be strained, and it should have the color of *café au lait,* a warm beige. Put the sauce on a heated platter and arrange the chicken on top of the sauce.

Poulet en Crapaudine
(Broiled Deviled Chicken)

HAVE the chickens split in half and lightly flattened with the side of a cleaver. Season them with salt and pepper and sprinkle with melted butter. Broil until lightly browned on both sides. Make a paste of dry mustard and water and brush the chicken halves lightly on both sides. Sprinkle both sides with bread crumbs and return the chicken to the broiler to brown the crumbs. Transfer the chicken to a baking pan with a little butter and set the pan in a moderate oven (350°f.) for from 10 to 15 minutes, until the chicken is thoroughly cooked. Remove the chicken to a platter and add to the pan juices the chopped parsley and the lemon juice. Adjust the seasoning of this sauce with salt and pepper and pour it over the chicken on the platter.

3 chickens, 2 pounds each
dry mustard
½ cup fresh bread crumbs
3 tablespoons butter
1 tablespoon chopped parsley
juice of 1 lemon

Poulet Sauté au Thym Frais
(Chicken Sauté with Fresh Thyme)

HAVE the butcher disjoint the chicken and cut it into 8 pieces. Season the pieces with salt and

1 chicken, 2½ pounds
CONTINUED

101

1 tablespoon clarified butter
1 large onion
2 garlic cloves
¼ cup white wine
½ cup foundation stock
2 sprigs thyme

pepper, sprinkle them with flour, and brown them on all sides in the clarified butter. Remove the chicken to a heated dish and keep it in a warm place. In the fat in the pan cook the onion, chopped, for a few minutes. Add the garlic, chopped, the wine, the stock, and the thyme, also chopped. Bring the liquid to a boil, return the chicken to the pan, and simmer the chicken for from 20 to 30 minutes, until it is tender. Adjust the seasoning of the sauce with salt and pepper and serve chicken and sauce together. Serves 2–3.

Poulet Sauté Chasseur
(*Chicken Hunter's Style*)

1 chicken, 3 pounds
1 tablespoon clarified butter
2 tomatoes
1 teaspoon chopped shallots or
   onion
1 pound mushrooms
2 tablespoons brandy
½ cup white wine
½ cup stock or water
1 tablespoon chopped parsley

HAVE the chicken cut into 8 pieces. Season the pieces with salt and pepper, dredge them with flour, and brown them on all sides in the hot clarified butter. Cover the pan, reduce the heat, and simmer the chicken for from 20 to 25 minutes, until it is tender. Remove the chicken to a heated dish and set it aside in a warm place. To the fat remaining in the pan, add the chopped shallots and brown them lightly, stirring constantly with a wooden spoon. Add the mushrooms and the tomatoes, peeled and coarsely chopped, and cook, stirring, until the liquid has almost entirely evaporated. Add the wine, stock, and brandy and bring the liquid to a boil. Adjust the seasoning and return the chicken to the sauce. Heat the chicken and serve chicken and sauce together, sprinkled with chopped parsley. Serves 3–4.

Poulet Sauté à l'Arlésienne
(*Chicken Sauté with Eggplant*)

HAVE the chickens cut into 8 pieces, sprinkle them with salt, pepper, and flour, and brown them on all sides in the hot oil. Remove the chicken to a heated dish and keep it warm. Pour the oil into a skillet and reserve it. To the pan in which the chicken was cooked add the white wine and cook, stirring in the brown bits that cling to the pan, until the wine is reduced by half. Add the tomato juice and the garlic, crushed, and reduce the liquid by half once again. Return the chicken to the pan and simmer it until it is tender.

While the chicken is cooking, peel and slice thinly the onions and the eggplant. Cook the onions in the oil until they are translucent, drain them, and set them aside. Flour the eggplant slices and brown them on both sides in the oil, adding more hot oil if necessary.

Arrange the chicken on a serving platter, pour the sauce over it, and garnish the platter with the fried onions and eggplant slices. Serves 8.

2 chickens, 3 pounds each
¼ cup olive oil
2 cups dry white wine
1 cup tomato juice
2 garlic cloves
2 large onions
1 large eggplant

Poulet Sauté à la Créole
(*Chicken Creole Style*)

HAVE the chicken cut into 4 pieces and season the pieces with salt and pepper. Sprinkle them lightly with flour and brown them on all sides in the clarified butter. Remove the chicken to a heated dish and keep it warm. Slice the onion and brown it in the butter. Add the tomatoes, peeled and sliced, the green peppers, free of

1 chicken, 2½ pounds
2 tablespoons clarified butter
2 tomatoes
1 onion
2 garlic cloves
½ cup stock
CONTINUED

½ cup dry white wine

2 small green peppers

bouquet of 1 sprig of parsley, 1 sprig of thyme, bit of bay leaf

seeds and pith and sliced thinly, the garlic, crushed, and the bouquet. Simmer all together for from 15 to 20 minutes. Add the stock and the wine, bring the liquid to a boil, and season well with salt and pepper. Return the chicken to the pan, cover the pan, and cook for 20 minutes or more, until the chicken is very tender. Serve with boiled rice. Serves 2–3.

Le Coq au Vin Champenois
(*Chicken in Red Wine*)

1 chicken, 2½ pounds

¼ pound lean salt pork

12 small onions

½ pound mushrooms

1 cup red wine

½ cup water

1 garlic clove

bouquet of 1 sprig of parsley, ½ sprig of thyme, and a bit of bay leaf

DICE the salt pork, parboil the dice, and brown them lightly in a heavy-bottomed pan. Have the chicken cut in 8 pieces. Season the pieces, dredge them in flour, and brown them lightly with the pork. Add the onions and cook slowly until they begin to take on color. Add the wine and water and bring the liquid slowly to the boil, stirring with a wooden spoon to incorporate all the brown bits that cling to the pan. Cover the pan and simmer for 10 minutes.

Stew the cleaned mushrooms for a few minutes in a little butter and add them to the chicken. Add also the garlic and the bouquet. Adjust the seasoning and cook the chicken for about 20 minutes, or until it is very tender. Remove and discard the bouquet, skim off any excess fat, and serve hot. Serves 2–3.

Poulet Jambalaya
(*Chicken and Rice*)

1 chicken, 4 pounds

½ cup clarified butter

CONTINUED

HAVE the chicken cut into 12 pieces and brown the pieces on all sides in hot clarified butter. Add the diced ham and pork and cook them for 2 minutes. Add the onion, garlic, peppers, thyme, bay leaf, and red pepper, all finely chopped, and cook for a minute or so longer. Peel the tomatoes, chop them coarsely, and add them to the pan with the chicken stock. Bring the liquid to a boil and simmer for 10 minutes. Adjust the seasoning with salt and pepper. Brown the sausages in a small skillet and add them to the pan with the rice. Cover the pan and put it in a moderate oven (350°f.) for 25 minutes, until the chicken is tender and the rice is cooked. If necessary, add more chicken stock to keep the mixture fairly moist. Taste for seasoning and serve hot. Serves 6.

¼ pound diced raw ham
2 ounces diced lean salt pork
1 onion
2 garlic cloves
2 green peppers
1 sprig thyme
½ bay leaf
1 small red pepper
1 pound tomatoes
4 cups chicken stock
1 cup rice
½ pound link sausages

Poulets Sautés Piémontaise
(Chicken with Saffron Rice)

CUT each chicken in four parts and remove the breast bones and the thigh bones. Make an incision down the legs so that the pieces will lie flat. Season with salt and pepper and moisten with a little cream. Keep the chicken in the refrigerator until about 30 minutes before serving time.

Heat ½ cup of the clarified butter in a saucepan. Sauté the onion, chopped, for about 2 minutes without allowing it to take on color. Add the rice and saffron, and salt and pepper to taste, and cook, stirring, until the grains are well coated with butter. Add the hot chicken stock, cover the pan, and cook over low heat or in a moderate oven (350°f.) for from 15 to 20 minutes, until the rice is tender and the liquid absorbed. If necessary, add a little more hot chicken broth. Add the cheese and toss lightly with a fork. Keep the rice warm.

3 chickens, 2 pounds each
1 cup long grain rice
1 cup clarified butter
1 onion
1 teaspoon powdered saffron
3 cups chicken stock
½ cup grated Swiss cheese
1 cup brown stock

Drain the pieces of chicken, dredge them lightly with flour, and brown them in the remaining clarified butter. Remove the white pieces in about 15 minutes; the dark meat takes about 10 minutes longer to cook.

Spread the saffron rice on a heated platter and lay the chicken on the rice. Decorate each piece of chicken with a slice of truffle warmed in the butter in which the chicken was cooked.

Pour off the excess fat in the pan, add the brown stock, and cook rapidly, scraping in all the brown bits, until the sauce is reduced to ⅓ cup. Strain the sauce over the chicken and rice and serve at once.

Suprême de Volaille Virginienne
(Breast of Chicken with Virginia Ham)

PREPARE and cook 6 chicken breasts as for *poulets sautés piémontaise.*

Trim 6 slices of white bread to fit the chicken breasts and brown them in butter. Trim 6 thin slices of cooked Virginia ham in the same way and warm them in a little Madeira. Cook 1 pound of mushroom caps for 5 minutes in butter with a little lemon juice. Season the mushrooms with salt and pepper and sprinkle them with 1 tablespoon of chopped parsley.

Pile the mushrooms in the center of a round serving dish. Arrange the croutons around the edge of the dish. Top each crouton with a slice of ham, a cooked chicken breast, and a slice of truffle. De-glaze the pan in which the chicken was cooked with ½ cup Madeira and ½ cup brown stock. Reduce the sauce quickly to half its original volume and pour it over the chicken. Serve hot.

How to Carve a Chicken

A FAIRLY SHORT, thick-bladed knife with a sharp point is best for carving chicken. The thin, flexible, long-bladed *trancheur* is intended for slicing meat, not for carving.

Lay the bird on its side, with the legs pointing left. Pierce the upper part of the leg with the carving-fork held in your left hand. Hold the knife against the body and cut off the second joint and leg. A twist of the fork will help to disengage the joint. Lay the piece flat on the board or platter and cut down through the cartilage to separate the thigh from the drumstick. Hold the carcass firmly with the fork and make a vertical cut that takes in part of the breast and the whole wing. Cut the rest of the meat from the breast bone, in one, two, or even three slices, if the bird is unusually large. Use the point of the knife to detach the meat from the bone. The juicy "oysters" under the carcass may be served as tidbits to appreciative connoisseurs.

Poulet Rôti
(*Roast Chicken*)

CHOOSE a plump roaster weighing 5 pounds or more. Tie a sheet of larding pork over the breast and truss the legs and wings close to the body with kitchen string. Sprinkle the bird inside and out with salt and pepper, brush it generously with clarified butter, and roast it in a moderately hot oven (375°f.) for 1 hour, basting frequently and turning it from time to time to insure even browning. Test the bird for doneness; any tinge of red in the juice indicates that further cooking is necessary.

Remove the chicken to a heated platter and let it stand in a warm place for 10 minutes. Pour off the surplus fat in the roasting pan. Add to the juices 1 or 2 tablespoons of water and deglaze the pan by stirring in the brown bits that cling to the bottom and sides. Adjust the seasoning of the sauce and pour it over the chicken.

Farce de Riz pour Volaille
(*Rice Stuffing for Roast Chicken*)

MAKE a rice pilaff *à la française*. Stir into the cooked rice ½ cup diced *foie gras* and 1 tablespoon diced truffles. Or use an equivalent amount of chicken livers browned in butter, or of cooked ham. Use this mixture to stuff the chicken; skewer or sew the opening; and roast in the usual manner.

Poule au Riz
(*Fowl with Rice*)

1 fowl, 4–5 pounds
1 tablespoon salt
1 onion, stuck with a clove
3 stalks celery
2 sprigs parsley
a bit of bay leaf
1 sprig thyme
2 tablespoons butter
1 onion, chopped
1½ tablespoons flour
1½ cups chicken broth
½ cup cream

HAVE the fowl cleaned and truss it with the wings and legs close to the body. Parboil the bird with the neck, feet, and giblets. (To prepare the feet, chop off the nails, scald the feet in boiling water, and peel off the coarse yellow skin.) Drain and cover all with fresh cold water. Add the salt and all the vegetables except the chopped onion. Cook for from 1½ to 2 hours, until the fowl is tender, skimming off the scum as it rises to the surface.

Half an hour before the fowl is tender, cook 1 cup of rice, using half water and half chicken broth for the liquid.

To make the sauce, melt the butter, cook the chopped onion in it for a minute or two, and stir in the flour. Cook the *roux* for a few minutes without allowing it to take on color. Stir in the strained chicken broth and cook, stirring, until the sauce is smooth and thickened. Add the cream and adjust the seasoning to taste.

Make a bed of the hot rice on a serving dish. Carve the fowl and arrange the pieces on the rice. Pour half the sauce over the chicken and rice and pass the rest separately.

Cold Chicken Dishes

THE COLD CHICKEN specialties that follow are intended for display on the cold buffet, but they taste as good as they look, and would be very welcome at any hot-weather meal.

Poulet de Grain en Gelée à l'Estragon
(Tarragon Chicken in Aspic)

TRUSS the chickens as for roasting and parboil them. Put them in a pan with fresh water to cover and add the herbs and vegetables. Season with salt and a few peppercorns. Bring the liquid to the boiling point and simmer the chickens until they are tender, for from 30 to 40 minutes. Cool the birds in the stock.

Remove the chicken to a carving board. Strain the stock. Beat the egg whites slightly and add gradually the strained stock and gelatin, soaked for 5 minutes in ¼ cup cold water. Return the mixture to the stove and heat it, to the boiling point, stirring constantly. Simmer for 10 minutes and strain through a muslin cloth into a shallow bowl. Set the bowl in the refrigerator to cool the aspic.

Carve the chickens and arrange the pieces in a deep silver or glass serving bowl. Blanch

2 chickens, 2½ pounds each
1 onion
1 carrot
1 stalk of celery
1 sprig of parsley
2 sprigs of tarragon
½ bay leaf
2 envelopes gelatin
2 egg whites

leaves of fresh tarragon and use them to decorate the chicken. Pour over the chicken the very cold but still liquid aspic and place the dish in the refrigerator for several hours.

Suprêmes de Volaille Jeannette
(*Jellied Breast of Chicken*)

1 chicken, 5 pounds
6 or 8 slices *foie gras*
2 cups chicken aspic
2 cups *chaud-froid* sauce

COOK the chicken as for tarragon chicken in aspic. Lift off the breast fillets, reserving the rest of the bird for another use. Slice each fillet into 3 or 4 thin ovals, flatten the ovals slightly, and trim them. Cut slices of *foie gras* of the same size and shape as the chicken.

Cover the bottom of a shallow silver or china serving platter with a layer of aspic ½ inch thick. Chill to set the jelly.

Coat the chicken fillets with *chaud-froid* sauce and decorate them with blanched tarragon leaves. Lay the slices of *foie gras* on the bed of aspic, arrange a piece of chicken on each slice, and coat all with more of the clear aspic. Chill well before serving.

Chaud-Froid de Volaille
(*Chicken in Jellied White Sauce*)

1 chicken, 4 to 5 pounds
1 onion, stuck with a clove
12 peppercorns
2 sprigs parsley
1 stalk celery
chaud-froid sauce

PARBOIL the chicken and its giblets and rinse it under running cold water. Add fresh cold water to cover, the onion, the herbs tied together, and the peppercorns wrapped in a square of cheesecloth. Bring the liquid to a boil and simmer the chicken, skimming the broth as necessary, until the bird is just tender. Strain the stock and cool the bird in it. Remove the skin, legs, and breasts left whole or cut, and chill.

Make a *chaud-froid* sauce with the cooking broth. Cool the sauce until it is on the point of setting, and coat the chicken with it. To make a thick coating, return the pieces of chicken to the refrigerator to allow the sauce to set and apply a second coat. Decorate each piece of chicken with truffle cut-outs, leaves of tarragon, and bits of pimiento, as imagination dictates.

Galantine de Volaille
(*Jellied Chicken Roll*)

CLEAN the chicken, cut off the neck, wings, and drumsticks, and split the bird down the back without separating the halves. With a sharp knife, bone the chicken completely and cut out the breast fillets without breaking the skin. Make a stock from the bones and trimmings (reserving the meat of the drumsticks and second joints) and the usual herbs and seasonings.

1 chicken, 6 pounds
1 pound veal
1 pound lean pork
1 small cooked ox tongue
½ cup Madeira
½ cup brandy
3 truffles
1 tablespoon pistachios

Grind the drumstick meat, the veal, and the pork, and season with salt and allspice to taste. Add the Madeira and brandy. Spread a layer of this forcemeat on the chicken skin.

Cut the breast fillets into square strips. Cut the ox tongue into similar strips, and wrap each in a thin sheet of fat larding pork. Cut the truffles into large julienne. Arrange the strips alternately on the forcemeat, to make a mosaic pattern of layers of white, red, and black with the truffles in the center and forcemeat between the layers. Sprinkle with the green pistachio nuts and cover well with the forcemeat. Roll the chicken and wrap the roll in cheesecloth. Tie the roll at the ends and in the middle to hold it securely.

Bring the stock made from the bones to a boil in an oval pan large enough to hold the chicken roll. Cover the pan and cook the chicken roll slowly for about 2 hours. Cool it in the stock, unwrap the roll, rewrap tightly in the cloth, and chill under a weight overnight.

Clarify the galantine stock (see consommé) and use this aspic to garnish the platter. It may be stirred with a fork or cut into decorative shapes.

Leftover Poultry

BECAUSE the French are above all a thrifty people, the classic repertoire includes many recipes for the appetizing use of leftover foods. Of these, those dealing with leftover poultry are perhaps the most popular.

Chicken à la King

3 cups sliced leftover poached
  chicken
1½ cups sliced mushrooms
1 tablespoon shredded green
  pepper
1½ cups chicken broth
4 egg yolks
¾ cup cream

BROWN the mushrooms in a little clarified butter and put them in a saucepan with the chicken and green pepper. Add the hot chicken broth and simmer for 5 minutes. Beat the egg yolks and cream together, warm the mixture with a little hot broth, and stir it into the chicken and mushroom mixture. Heat well without boiling, adjust the seasoning with salt, pepper, and cayenne, and serve on freshly made buttered toast or in puff-paste shells. Because it is less likely to be dry, poached or boiled chicken rather than roasted chicken should be used for chicken à la King.

Salade de Volaille au Cresson
(*Chicken and Water Cress Salad*)

Toss the chicken, celery, and mayonnaise together and season with salt, pepper, and cayenne to taste. Just before serving, strip the leaves
from the water cress, discarding the coarse
stems, and add them to the salad. Garnish with
quarters of peeled tomatoes. Slivered toasted almonds, sliced ripe or green olives, capers, or
hard-cooked eggs may also be added at will,
the proportions adjusted to taste.

3 cups diced cooked chicken
1 cup diced celery
½ cup mayonnaise
1 bunch water cress
tomatoes

Croquettes

HEAT the *sauce velouté* and add to it the egg
yolks beaten with a little cream. Cook the
mushrooms with the butter and lemon juice until the mixture is nearly dry. Combine sauce,
mushrooms, and chicken, and spread on a platter to chill.

Shape the mixture by tablespoons into corks
or other forms, as desired. Roll the croquettes in
flour, in beaten egg, and in bread crumbs. Fry to
a rich brown in deep hot fat (370°f.). Drain on
absorbent toweling and serve at once, with tomato sauce or another suitable sauce. Serves 3.

1 cup diced cooked chicken,
  sweetbreads, meat, fish
  shellfish, or eggs
½ cup *sauce velouté*
2 egg yolks
½ cup mushrooms diced
½ tablespoon butter
½ teaspoon lemon juice

Brochettes de Foies de Volaille
(*Skewered Chicken Livers*)

SELECT large chicken livers and mushrooms for
this dish. Cut livers and mushrooms in half.
Cut the bacon slices in three. Cook the bacon in
a skillet until it is almost done, and remove it to
a paper towel to drain. Cook the livers and

6 chicken livers
9 mushrooms
6 slices bacon

mushrooms in the bacon fat for a few minutes. Fill 6 individual skewers alternately with pieces of liver and mushrooms separated by bacon squares. Roll the skewers in seasoned bread crumbs, sprinkle with melted butter, and broil to a golden brown. Serve with *sauce maître d'hôtel*.

Capon

THE CAPON is a castrated male bird that offers great dividends in flavor and tenderness. Capons reach a weight of 9 or 10 pounds, and have unsurpassed succulence. They are unquestionably the choicest of chickens, and are worth the premium price they command on the market. Carve a roasted capon according to the directions for carving a turkey.

Le Chapon aux Oeufs d'Or
(Capon with Golden Eggs)

1 capon, 7–8 pounds
2 medium truffles
1 pound fresh pork fat
1 can *pâté de foie gras*
duchess potatoes

PREPARE the capon the day before it is to be served. Have it cleaned in the usual way and loosen the skin at the breast and the legs. Reserve 2 thin slices of larding pork and 12 slices of truffles. Put the rest of the pork and the truffle trimmings through the finest blade of the food chopper. Add salt and pepper to season well and spread the mixture smoothly under the loosened skin. Top the layer of stuffing with truffle slices; the truffles will then be directly under the skin. Cover the breast of the bird with the sliced larding pork; truss the legs and wings close to the body. Wrap the bird loosely in waxed paper and let it stand overnight in the refrigerator. The aroma and flavor of the truffles will permeate the flesh.

Next day roast the capon in a slow oven (300°f.) for 2 hours or more, until it is very tender, and the juice that follows the fork when the thigh is pierced is clear and free of any pink tinge. Remove the capon to a heated platter. Skim the excess fat from the roasting pan and reserve the juices.

While the capon is roasting, prepare small egg-shaped croquettes of duchess potatoes. Fry the croquettes in deep hot fat, scoop out a bit of the pulp, and replace it with *pâté de foie gras*.

Pour the pan juices over the capon and garnish the platter with the golden eggs.

Chapon Washington
(*Capon Stuffed with Corn*)

HAVE the capon cleaned through the neck aperture and fill the cavity with the mixture described here. Boil the corn for 5 minutes in salted water and scrape the pulp. Season the pulp with salt and pepper, add the butter and cream, and cook over high heat, stirring, for a few minutes. Cool the corn and stuff the capon. Sew the opening with kitchen string and a large needle. Truss the wings and legs close to the body in the usual fashion. Brown the bird on all sides in clarified butter. Add the vegetables and simmer all together for 10 minutes. Add the wine, stir to incorporate the brown bits, and cover the pan. Roast the capon, covered, in a moderately slow oven (300°f.) for about 2 hours, until the bird is tender and the juices run clear, without any tinge of pink.

Strain the cooking liquor and serve it sepa-

1 capon, 7–8 pounds
12 ears corn
1 tablespoon butter
2 tablespoons cream
1 carrot
1 onion
½ bay leaf
2 sprigs of parsley
2 stalks of celery
1 cup white wine

rately. Carve the capon and garnish the platter with the corn stuffing.

Duckling

A DUCKLING may be stuffed or not, and roasted in the oven or on a spit just as a chicken is roasted, with the exception that the bird should not be trussed, as the legs must cook thoroughly. Duck fat is a great delicacy, and should be poured off as it accumulates in the roasting pan to prevent its scorching. A duckling weighing between 5 and 7 pounds will serve no more than four persons.

How to Carve a Duck

LAY THE DUCK on its side, with its legs pointing left. Hold the bird with the fork in the upper part of the leg and with a firm bladed, sharp-pointed carving knife cut off and detach the leg and second joint. Separate the leg from the second joint and, if desired, cut the second joint in half and remove the bone. Make a vertical incision along the middle of the breast bone and detach the meat from it. Slice the breasts vertically into two or three fillets, cutting the wing at the same time. Turn the bird and carve the other side.

Caneton aux Olives
(*Duckling with Olives*)

1 duckling, 3–4 pounds
1 tablespoon clarified butter
12 small onions
½ pound mushrooms
¼ pound diced lean salt pork
½ cup pitted green olives

HEAT the clarified butter in a flame-proof casserole and brown the duckling on all sides. Season with salt and pepper, cover the casserole, and cook gently for 25 minutes.

In the meantime parboil the pork dice, drain them, and brown them lightly in a skillet. Add the onions and the mushrooms, and cook until the onions are almost tender. Drain well.

Skim off the excess fat in the casserole and add the pork, onions, and mushrooms. Add the olives, cover the casserole, and continue to cook until the duckling is tender, about 1 hour in all. Serves 2–3.

Caneton aux Oranges
(Duckling with Oranges)

BUTTER a heavy pan or Dutch oven, and line the bottom with the vegetables and herbs, all coarsely chopped. Brown the ducklings well on all sides and season them with salt and pepper to taste. Add the wine and the stock, cover the pan, and cook slowly for about 1 hour until the duck is tender. Remove the ducklings to a heated platter. Skim off the excess fat and reserve it for another use. Strain the pan juices and reduce them over high heat to one fourth the original quantity. Thicken the juices, if desired, with the arrowroot stirred to a paste with a little cold water. Shred the outer rind of 2 oranges and add this zest to the sauce. Garnish the platter with slices or wedges of peeled orange.

2 ducklings, 4 pounds each
1 carrot
1 onion
2 sprigs of parsley
1 sprig of thyme
½ bay leaf
2 cups foundation stock
2 cups white wine
1 teaspoon arrowroot or other starch
4 oranges

Caneton aux Navets
(Duckling Braised with Turnips)

USE a flameproof casserole for this preparation.

Brown the duckling on all sides in the clarified butter and remove it to a dish. Pour off the fat and reserve it for another use. Add the wine, brown sauce, stock, and bouquet to the casse-

1 duckling, 5–6 pounds
2 tablespoons clarified butter
1 cup white wine
1 cup brown sauce
CONTINUED

1 cup stock
bouquet made of 1 stalk of
  celery, 1 sprig of parsley,
  1 sprig of thyme, a bit of
  bay leaf
1 pound white turnips
12 small white onions

role, and bring the liquid to a boil, stirring in all the brown bits. Return the duckling to the casserole and cook it, covered, for 30 minutes.

In the meanwhile peel and quarter the turnips and brown them in a little clarified butter, sprinkling them lightly with sugar to glaze them. Peel the small onions and glaze them in the same way.

Remove the duckling to a dish once again. Strain the pan juices and skim the excess fat from the surface. Return the juices to the casserole, add the duckling and the turnips and onions, and cover the casserole. Bake in a moderate oven (350°f.) for about 40 minutes, until the duckling is very tender. Serves 4.

Caneton Montmorency en Gelée
(Duckling in Aspic with Cherries)

1 duckling, 5 pounds
2 cups foundation stock
½ teaspoon chopped shallots
1 sprig of thyme
bit of bay leaf
¼ cup brandy
1 envelope gelatin

CHOOSE a thick-breasted bird and roast it for from 35 to 40 minutes in a moderately hot oven (400°f.). It should be very rare. Cool the bird and remove the breasts and the breast bones so that the rest of the bird forms a container for the stuffing.

Chop the breast bones and the giblets (except for the liver, which will be used for the filling), and brown them quickly in a little butter. Add the shallots, thyme, and bay leaf, and cook for a few minutes longer, stirring constantly. Add the brandy, simmer for 2 minutes, and add the brown stock. Simmer the sauce for 20 minutes and strain it through a cloth. Remove the fat that rises to the surface, and dissolve in the sauce 1 envelope gelatin softened in ¼ cup water. Adjust the seasoning and set the brown jelly sauce in a cool place to thicken.

Cut the breasts into thin slices and coat each slice with cool, but still liquid brown jelly sauce.

Fill the duck cavity with a mousse made of the duck liver and *foie gras* (page 126) and replace the breast fillets with slices of truffle between them. With a pastry bag fitted with a fancy tube, pipe a ring of mousse around the top of the duck. Chill the bird thoroughly and coat it with chicken aspic. Pour a layer of aspic ½ inch thick on a platter and place the platter in the refrigerator until the aspic sets. Arrange the duck on the jellied aspic and garnish the platter with tart shells filled with applesauce and each decorated with a cherry and a little red jelly.

Goose

DESPITE ITS FALL from popularity in recent years, goose deserves its place as the traditional Christmas bird. A fruit stuffing gives pleasant contrast to the very rich and unctuous flesh.

Carve the roast goose as you would a duck or a turkey, depending upon its size. Remove the bones of the legs and second joints and cut this meat into thin slices.

L'Oie du Gourmet
(*Roast Goose*)

HAVE the butcher clean and pluck the goose; if any down or pinfeathers remain, pass the goose quickly through the gas flame to singe it. Use a sharp knife and a tweezers to remove the remaining feathers. Wash the bird well, dry it

1 goose, 12–16 pounds
½ pound prunes
¼ pound almonds
6 large apples

thoroughly, and season with salt and pepper inside and out.

Soak the prunes in water to cover for 1 hour or more, cook them in the same water until they are tender, and pit them. Blanch the almonds in boiling water, slip off the skins, and shred the nuts. Peel, core, and slice the apples and cook them for a minute or two in melted butter. Toss all together gently.

Stuff the goose with the fruit and truss it lightly with kitchen string. Roast on a rack in a moderate oven (350°f.) for about 18 minutes per pound, until the bird tests done. Pour off the fat as it accumulates in the pan, reserving it for another use, and baste the bird every 15 minutes with the pan juices.

Transfer the bird to a serving platter. Skim off the excess fat in the pan and stir into the juices 1 tablespoon of flour. Cook for a few minutes and add 1 cup of stock or water. Cook, stirring, until the sauce is smooth and thickened. Strain the sauce into a sauceboat and serve it separately.

Cassoulet de Castelnaudary
(*Casserole of Goose and Beans*)

1 young goose
1 pound white beans
1 garlic sausage
¼ pound lean salt pork
2 garlic cloves
4 onions
4 cups beef stock
1 sprig of thyme
2 sprigs of parsley
CONTINUED

Soak the beans overnight. Cover them with fresh water, add 2 onions and a little salt and pepper, and cook slowly for about 2 hours. The beans should be about three fourths done.

Have the goose cut into 12 pieces and the garlic sausage into short lengths. Brown both in a little melted butter and transfer them to a *cassoulet,* or shallow earthenware baking dish, which has been rubbed with a cut clove of garlic.

Dice the salt pork, blanch it, and brown it quickly in a skillet. Add the remaining onions, sliced, and the garlic cloves, chopped, and cook until the onions are lightly browned. Sprinkle with 1 teaspoon of flour, and cook, stirring, until the flour is browned. Stir in the beef stock, bring the liquid to a boil, and add the herbs and the tomatoes, peeled and coarsely chopped. Cover the pan and cook the sauce for 20 minutes over low heat.

Drain the beans and spread them over the meat in the *cassoulet*. Pour the sauce over all and bake in a moderate oven (350°f.) for 1 hour. Sprinkle with bread crumbs and return the *cassoulet* to the oven to brown the crumbs.

2 tomatoes
½ bay leaf

Pigeon, or Squab

YOUNG PIGEONS, or squab, have always been a popular favorite for formal dinners, as a whole little bird makes a very attractive serving.

Pigeonneau Rôti
(*Roast Squab*)

ALLOW one squab, weighing about ¾ pound, for each serving. Stuff the birds or not, as desired, and truss the legs and wings close to the body. Brush generously with clarified butter. Roast on a rack in an uncovered pan for about 35 minutes at moderate heat (350°f.), until the squabs are browned, plumped, and tender. Baste frequently with a mixture of butter and stock to keep the birds moist, and season lightly with salt.

Pigeons à l'Anglaise en Casserole
(*Pigeon Pot Pie*)

3 squabs
½ pound rump of beef
3 tablespoons clarified butter
3 hard-cooked eggs
4 shallots
2 cups brown stock
Worcestershire sauce

CUT the squabs in half and slice the beef thin. Brown the squabs and the beef in the clarified butter. Arrange the squabs side by side in a deep pie dish and put the beef slices on top of them. Cut the eggs in half and put them on the beef.

In the butter remaining in the pan in which the meat was browned, cook the shallots, chopped, for a few minutes. Add the stock and bring the liquid to a boil, stirring. Season with Worcestershire sauce to taste and pour the sauce over the meat. Cover the dish with pie dough and bake the pie in a moderate oven (375°f.) for about 1 hour, until the crust is browned and the squabs are tender. Serves 3–4.

Turkey

How to Carve a Turkey

LAY THE TURKEY on its side, with its legs pointing left. Hold the bird by piercing the upper part of the leg with the carving fork, and with a firm-bladed, sharp-pointed carving knife cut the leg and second joint away from the body. Hold the piece flat and detach the second joint from the leg by cutting down through the cartilage. Cut off the end of the wing. Cut the rest of the wing with a slice of the breast. With a *trancheur,* a flexible, thin, long-bladed slicing knife, slice the breast into large, thin, vertical slices. Slice the meat of the second joint parallel to the bone and serve dark and light meat with each portion. The legs may be reserved for other uses. Carve only enough turkey at one time to serve each guest once, as turkey dries quickly when it is off the bone.

Dinde Farcie aux Marrons
(Roast Turkey with Chestnut Stuffing)

CHOP the shallots and cook them for a few minutes in the butter. Add the sausage meat and cook, stirring with a fork, to brown the meat lightly. Add the bread, soaked in milk and well pressed, the cognac, and the parsley. Season with salt and pepper and a pinch of thyme. Peel and cook the chestnuts and cool them. Add them to the stuffing mixture and toss well to blend.

1 turkey, 12–14 pounds
2 shallots
1 tablespoon butter
1 pound sausage meat
½ cup bread crumbs
½ cup cognac
1 teaspoon chopped parsley
2 pounds chestnuts

Fill the turkey loosely with this mixture and sew the opening with kitchen string and a large needle. Truss the legs and wings close to the body and tie a large sheet of larding pork over the breast. Rub well with butter, season with salt and pepper, and roast in a moderate oven (350°f.) for about 15 minutes per pound. Test the bird for done-ness by inserting a fork in the second joint; if the juice shows a tinge of pink, further cooking is needed.

Transfer the turkey to a carving platter and keep it warm. Skim the fat from the pan juices and reserve it for another use. Add about 1 cup of stock or water to the pan and bring it to the boil, stirring in all the brown bits that cling to the pan. Season this pan sauce to taste and strain in into a sauceboat.

Dindonneau Poêlé Farci Gastronome
(Stuffed Baby Turkey)

COOK the onion and garlic, both chopped, in the butter. Add the giblets, finely chopped, and

1 turkey, 8 pounds
CONTINUED

2 tablespoons butter

2 onions

6 garlic cloves

turkey giblets

½ pound sausage meat

1 turkey liver

2 cups day-old bread crumbs

1 cup chopped spinach

1 egg

2 tablespoons mixed chopped parsley and chives

1 cup Chablis

simmer slowly until they are thoroughly cooked. Add the sausage meat and cook, stirring with a fork to break up the particles, until it is browned. Add the turkey liver, finely chopped, and blend for a moment over the fire. Remove the pan from the heat. Blend in the spinach and the bread crumbs, which have been soaked in water and pressed well, and adjust the seasoning with salt, pepper, and a little mace. Add a pinch of sage, if desired. Stir in the egg and the herbs and toss well.

Stuff the turkey loosely with this mixture, sew the opening with kitchen string and a large needle, and truss the wings and legs close to the body. Sprinkle the bird with salt and pepper, rub it with butter, and roast it, breast side down, in a moderately slow oven (325°f.) for about 1½ hours, until it is tender. Do not overcook the turkey; when the juice that follows a fork piercing the second joint is clear of any pink tinge, the bird is done. Turn the turkey during the last 30 minutes of cooking to brown the breast skin.

Add the wine to the pan, stir in the brown bits, and strain the sauce into a sauceboat.

THIS cold, stuffed turkey is an ideal *pièce de résistance* for a New Year's Eve buffet; hence its name. The stuffing is even more important for a turkey to be served cold than for one served hot, for it supplies additional flavor that will not be covered up by the cold.

Dindonneau Froid Nouvel-An
(*Cold Stuffed Turkey*)

1 turkey, 16–18 pounds

CONTINUED

HAVE the butcher prepare the turkey as follows: remove the leg tendons; split the bird down the

back without separating the halves; and remove the breast bones and the thigh bones from
the inside.

Spread the boned turkey, skin side down,
on a tray, and store it in the refrigerator while
you prepare the stuffing. Cut the pork into dice
and brown the dice quickly in a little butter.
Sprinkle with the shallots and garlic, both
chopped, and toss over the heat for a minute.
Turn the mixture out onto a flat platter to cool.
Peel and cook the chestnuts and cool them in
their stock. Put the pork mixture through the
finest blade of the food-chopper and mix it
with the chestnuts and the cognac.

Sprinkle the turkey inside and out with salt
and pepper. Spread the inside thickly with the
stuffing. Lay a cooked ox tongue (these may be
purchased in jars) on one half and fold the
other half over it, thus restoring the natural
shape of the bird. Cover the breast with thin
sheets of larding pork and tie the bird to keep it
in shape. Roast the turkey in the usual fashion
for about 3 hours at 350°f., until it tests done,
basting it frequently with the pan juices.

While the turkey is roasting, make a stock by
cooking the turkey bones and trimmings with
water to cover and a *bouquet garni* of a stalk of
celery and 2 sprigs each of parsley and thyme.

Remove the turkey to a platter to cool.

Skim off the excess fat from the roasting pan
and add the strained stock. Cook, stirring in all
the brown bits, until the gravy is very thick.
Strain the gravy and cool it until it is very cold,
but still liquid. Pour the gravy over the cold
bird and set the bird in the refrigerator until
serving time.

To serve, cut vertical slices down through the
bird so that each portion includes a slice of
tongue.

4 pounds fat loin of pork
6 shallots
3 garlic cloves
1 pound chestnuts
¼ cup cognac
1 ox tongue, cooked

Foie Gras

Foie gras is the liver of a force-fed goose. Force-feeding is not legal in the United States, so we import the fat livers from France. The best *foie gras,* marvelously smooth in texture and a delicate rosy cream in color, comes from Alsace. According to history, the early Romans knew the secret of *foie gras,* but the secret was lost for nearly ten centuries after the decline of their pleasure-loving empire. The marriage of *foie gras* and truffles was consummated after the French Revolution when one François Doyen went to Strasbourg and there revealed the particular wonder of the combination of *foie gras* and the truffles of Périgord. Today, *foie gras* goes around the world wherever gourmets go. It can be purchased in the superbly luxurious form of the whole liver, larded with truffles, cooked and packed in cans, or as a purée. The purée is seasoned, often has truffles added to it, and is called *pâté de foie gras.*

Mousse de Foie Gras et Rouennaise
(*Duck Liver and* Foie Gras *Mousse*)

1 duck liver
shallot, thyme
1 pound additional fresh duck
  livers, or 1 pound *foie gras*
¼ cup cognac
1 cup chicken aspic
2 cups cream

Cook the duck liver (or livers, if no *foie gras* is used) in a little butter with a pinch of chopped shallot and a bit of thyme. Add the cognac and mash the liver to make a smooth paste. Add this *rouennaise* to the purée of *foie gras,* working it with a wooden spoon until the mixture is very light. Slowly add the aspic, which should be cold but still liquid. Fold in the cream, whipped, and adjust the seasoning with salt. pepper, and cayenne pepper.

Poussins à la Souvaroff
(*Squab Chickens with Truffles and* Foie Gras)

HAVE the little chickens cleaned and the breast bone removed from the inside. Season the chickens with salt and pepper, and put in the cavity of each a spoonful of truffled *pâté de foie gras*. This goose liver paste seasoned with truffles is obtainable in cans; lacking it, freshly cooked poultry liver and a bit of truffle may be substituted. Tie a sheet of larding pork over the breasts of the chickens and truss the legs and wings close to the body. Brush with clarified butter and cook in a moderate oven for 10 minutes to a golden color. Drain off the fat in the roasting pan and put the chickens in an earthenware casserole equipped with a tight fitting lid. In the roasting pan, cook the contents of a small can of truffles in Madeira wine for a few minutes. Pour this into the casserole. Cover the casserole and seal the lid with a strip of dough made of flour and water. Set the casserole in a moderate oven (350°f.) for 40 minutes. Remove the dough strip and serve the *poussins* in the casserole.

6 squab chickens, 1 pound each
6 tablespoons truffled *foie gras*
1 small can truffles
½ cup Madeira

Fois Gras Truffé à la Gelée de Porto
(Foie Gras *in Port-Wine Aspic*)

THE flavor of port-wine aspic is especially complimentary to that of *foie gras*. To make a truly memorable dish, spoon a little aspic into an individual serving dish, cool it until it sets, and put a serving of *foie gras* on the aspic. Cover all with more aspic. There are many possible ways to present this dish: the *foie gras* may be sliced, or served with a spoon dipped in hot water, and the dish may be garnished, with water cress or otherwise, for instance, but the way given here is the simplest and most practical.

Escalopes de Foie Gras Cambacérès
(Foie Gras *with* Artichokes)

A VERY elaborate and delicious garnish is made by filling artichoke bottoms with creamed mushrooms and covering them with a slice of *foie gras au naturel,* the whole liver, browned lightly in clarified butter. The *foie gras* is then topped with a slice of truffle and a spoonful of Madeira sauce.

Mousse de Foie Gras Lucullus
(*Goose Liver Mousse*)

1 cup *foie gras*
¼ cup cognac
½ cup *sauce velouté*
1 cup chicken aspic
2 cups heavy cream

PUT 1 cup *foie gras,* in any form, through a fine sieve and work it well with a wooden spoon to make it light and smooth. Season with the cognac and with salt and pepper to taste. Put the bowl in a pan of ice and gently stir in the *sauce velouté* and the cool, but still liquid, chicken aspic. Fold in the cream, whipped, and pour the mixture into a mold. Chill thoroughly and unmold to serve.

GAME

GAME THAT HAS BEEN PROPERLY HANDLED—and I regret
that I cannot here devote the necessary space to this subject—is an inimitable delicacy. In brief, all game should
be cleaned and skinned or plucked as soon as possible after
killing, and it should be stored in a place that offers free
circulation of cool air. Game is naturally more lean than
domestic meat, and requires larding, either in the form of
a sheet of larding pork wrapped around the breast of a bird,
or of strips of larding pork inserted in the flesh of venison
or other meat. Taking these differences into consideration,
wild meat may be cooked in the same ways as its approximate equivalent in domestic meat, except for the difference
in timing, which is noted in the specific recipes, and is most
important.

How to Carve Game Birds

SMALL GAME BIRDS are served whole; larger birds may
be split in half. Wild duck is carved and served like domestic duck, except that the breast may be left whole. The
legs of roast pheasant are not usually served with the rest
of the bird: they are likely to be too rare and too tough
when the breast of the bird is cooked to perfection.

THE legs of a young pheasant are gray, and the
last large feather in the wing is pointed, rather

than round. Only a young pheasant, thus recognized, may be roasted. Older birds should be braised in moist heat, or otherwise treated like domestic fowl.

Faisan Rôti
(*Roast Pheasant*)

CLEAN and truss the pheasant and wrap the breast with a thin slice of larding pork. Roast in a hot oven (400°f.) for from 30 to 35 minutes. Let the birds stand in a warm place for 10 minutes before carving them.

Perdreau Rôti
(*Roast Partridge*)

CLEAN and truss the partridge and wrap the breast with a thin slice of larding pork. Roast in a hot oven (400°f.) for 18 to 20 minutes. The breasts should be slightly pink. Let the birds stand in a warm place for 10 minutes before carving them.

A *chartreuse* is the ideal way to cook a bird that seems to be old and tough.

Faisan en Chartreuse
(*Braised Pheasant with Cabbage*)

1 large pheasant
2 small green cabbages
2 carrots
1 onion stuck with a clove
bouquet of 2 sprigs of parsley,
   CONTINUED

RUB the bird with butter, sprinkle it with salt, and brown it in a hot oven (450°f.) for about 15 minutes.

Cut the cabbages into quarters, cover them with water, and boil for 5 minutes. Drain and cool. Put the cabbage in a flame-proof casserole equipped with a lid. Add the carrots, the onion, and the bouquet, all tied in cheesecloth for easy removal. Lay the pheasant in the center of the bed of cabbage and arrange the sausages around it. Parboil the pork for 5 minutes and add it to the casserole. Season with salt and pepper and add the stock. Cover the casserole with a buttered paper, adjust the lid, and bring the liquid to a boil over direct heat. Finish the cooking in a moderately hot oven (375°f.). After the first 45 minutes, remove the pork and the sausages and reserve them in a warm place. Continue to cook the pheasant until it is very tender, 1½ to 2 hours in all.

To serve, drain the cabbage and pile it in a mound in the center of a serving platter. Carve the pheasant and arrange the pieces on top of the cabbage. Around the cabbage put alternating slices of pork, sausages, and carrots. The remaining contents of the cheesecloth bag may be discarded.

Remove the fat from the liquor left in the casserole and reduce the juices to a few spoonfuls. Pour this sauce over the pheasant. Serve hot.

1 sprig of thyme, ¼ of a bay leaf
½ pound lean salt pork
1 garlic sausage
1 pork sausage
1 quart white stock

To BE at their best, mallards or canvas-back ducks, which feed on celery and other greens rather than on fish, should always be cooked in the ways suggested for domestic ducks, and served rare.

Canard Sauvage Rôti
(Roast Wild Duck)

HAVE the duck thoroughly plucked and cleaned. Singe it by passing it through flame and carefully remove any remaining pinfeath-

3 ducks, about 2½ pounds each
CONTINUED

6 stalks celery, with the leaves

3 tablespoons cognac

ers or down with a sharp knife and a tweezers. Wipe the bird well inside and out with a damp cloth, sprinkle it with salt and pepper, and brush it generously with melted butter. Sprinkle the breast with flour. Stuff the cavity of each duck with 2 stalks of celery and truss the birds lightly with string. Roast the ducks in a very hot oven (450°f.) for from 18 to 20 minutes. Remove the birds from the oven and let them stand for 10 minutes before carving; this period of rest helps them to retain their natural juices. Carve the ducks into quarters and arrange them on a serving platter. Combine the juices that run during the carving with the pan gravy, add the cognac, and heat without boiling. Adjust the seasoning and pour the sauce over the ducks. Serves 6–8.

A FLEXIBLE breast bone indicates a young, tender guinea hen. Allow half a 2-pound hen for each serving.

Pintade au Genièvre
(Guinea Hens with Juniper Berries)

3 guinea hens, 2 pounds each

3 tablespoons crushed juniper berries

3 tablespoons brandy

TRUSS the wings and legs of the hens close to the bodies. Brush generously with clarified butter and roast in a hot oven (400°f.) for 15 minutes, basting frequently with the butter and drippings. Add the juniper berries, crushed, to the pan and roast for 10 minutes more, basting frequently and adding more clarified butter as needed. Remove the hens to a heated dish. Skim off the fat from the roasting pan, return the hens to the pan, and pour the brandy over them. Stir, scraping the pan, for a minute or

two and add ½ cup stock. Cook, stirring, for a
few minutes to blend well. Remove the guinea
hens to the serving platter and cut them in half
lengthwise. Correct the seasoning of the sauce
with salt and pepper and strain it over the birds.

Cailles Rôties
(*Roast Quail*)

QUAIL are so tiny that even the largest makes
only one portion. Brush the little birds well
with butter, season them, and roast them in a
moderately hot oven (400°f.) for about 20 minutes. Baste with the pan drippings three times
during the cooking. Serve on croutons of bread
browned in butter. Pour off the cooking fat and
add to the pan 2 tablespoons brown stock for
each bird. Cook, stirring in the brown bits, for a
few minutes, and pour the sauce over the bird.

Risotto de Cailles
(*Quail with Rice*)

ROAST 6 quail as for *cailles rôties*. Prepare a rice
pilaff. Add to the completed pilaff 1 tablespoon
each of julienne of cooked ham, julienne of truffles, sliced mushrooms, and stewed tomatoes.
Pack the pilaff in a bowl and unmold it by in-
verting the bowl on a large, round platter. Arrange the roasted quail around the rice and
pour the pan sauce over them.

THE marinade serves a double purpose in the
cooking of venison; it at once tenderizes and
flavors the meat.

Marinade à Chaud
(*Cooked Marinade for Venison*)

2 tablespoons olive oil
2 carrots
2 onions
2 stalks of celery
3 sprigs of parsley
2 shallots
2 garlic cloves
1 sprig of rosemary
1 sprig of thyme
1 small bay leaf
12 peppercorns

2 whole cloves
2 cups white wine
½ cup vinegar
2 cups water

HEAT the oil, and in it brown lightly the carrots and onions, both minced. Add the remaining vegetables, all cut fine, the seasonings, and the liquids. Bring the mixture to a boil and simmer it for 10 minutes. Cool the marinade before using it. This recipe makes 1 quart.

THIS recipe may be used for any roasting cut of venison (the cuts correspond to those of the beef animal), but the saddle and legs are considered choice.

Selle de Chevreuil Grand-Veneur
(*Saddle of Venison*)

REMOVE all skin and tendons from the venison and lard it through with strips of fat pork. Use a larding needle for this operation, or cut slits in the meat with a sharp, pointed knife and force strips of pork into the slits. Put the meat in a deep bowl and cover it with *marinade à chaud* (see above). Let the meat stand in the marinade for 2 or 3 days, or even longer if you have reason to suspect that the cut is tough.

Strain the vegetables from the marinade and spread them on the bottom of a roasting pan. Put the venison on the vegetables. Roast the meat in a very hot oven (450°f.) to the rare stage (about 8 minutes per pound). Remove the roast to a platter and pour off the fat in the pan. To the remaining juices, add 2 cups of the marinade and cook for a few minutes, stirring in all the brown bits. Strain this sauce into a bowl. Melt 1 tablespoon of butter, stir in 1 table-spoon of flour, and cook the *roux* for a few minutes. Add the strained pan sauce and cook, stirring, until the mixture is smooth and thick-ened. Add 1 tablespoon of tart currant jelly and stir until the jelly melts. Adjust the seasoning with salt and freshly ground pepper. Serve the sauce separately.

THE recipes for hare apply equally well to wild and domestic rabbit. A *civet* is a game stew.

Lièvre de Garenne en Civet
(*Wild Hare Stew*)

SKIN and clean the hare as soon as possible after killing, reserving the blood. Carefully detach and discard the gall bladder. Reserve the liver. Cut the hare into 8 pieces, sprinkle the pieces with salt and pepper, and marinate them over-night in a mixture of the brandy, olive oil, and red wine with the thyme, garlic, and sliced on-ion. Remove the hare from the marinade, drain well, and dry thoroughly. Dredge with flour and brown lightly in clarified butter. Add the marinade and cook, stirring in all the brown bits, until the sauce thickens. The sauce should be fairly thin; if necessary, add the stock. Cook, covered, for 1½ to 2 hours, until the meat is very tender.

1 young hare or rabbit, 2½ pounds
½ pound lean salt pork
2 tablespoons brandy
2 tablespoons olive oil
1 cup red wine
1 cup foundation stock
1 sprig of parsley
½ sprig of thyme
2 garlic cloves
1 small onion, sliced
2 teaspoons flour
the rabbit liver
20 small onions
20 small mushrooms

135

While the hare is cooking, cut the salt pork into dice and parboil it. Drain and brown the pork dice in a skillet. Add the hare's liver, cut in half, and the whole onions and mushrooms, and cook for a few minutes to glaze the vegetables. About 10 minutes before removing the stew from the heat, add this mixture to the pan. Continue to cook all together, and at the last minute add the reserved hare's blood, warming it with a little of the hot pan juices. Do not allow the sauce to boil after the blood has been added, or it will curdle. Adjust the seasoning with salt and pepper, and serve the stew in a deep platter. Garnish the platter with heart-shaped croutons of bread browned in butter.

Terrine de Lapereau des Gourmets
(*Rabbit in Terrine*)

1 young rabbit, 3–4 pounds
1 cup white wine
¼ pound larding pork
1 pound lean pork
2 truffles
1 pound *foie gras*
3 shallots
2 sprigs of thyme
½ bay leaf
½ cup brandy
1 tablespoon fat
2 cups white wine
2 cups foundation stock

SKIN and clean the rabbit, leaving the head attached. Reserve the blood and mix it with the wine to keep it from coagulating. Remove the bones and tendons without mutilating the meat. Reserve the bones. Cut the fat pork into thin strips and season the strips with a mixture of salt and allspice. Make small slits in the hare and lard it with the strips of fat, using a small, sharp-pointed knife. Put the hare (or rabbit) in a dish, sprinkle it with the shallots and the thyme, both chopped, and add the bay leaf, a few strips of lean pork, and a few truffle dice. Pour a little brandy over all, and set the dish in the refrigerator for several hours.

Grind the remaining pork and mix it with the truffles, cut in small dice, and the *foie gras,* cut in medium cubes. Toss carefully to blend the mixture, and fill the rabbit. Sew the opening and truss the rabbit's head to its back, to give the appearance of the animal at rest. Wrap the rabbit in a sheet of larding pork. Line a deep earthenware terrine, or crock, with thin strips of larding pork and set the rabbit in it. Sprinkle generously with brandy and cook in a hot oven (400°f.) for 30 minutes, uncovered.

While the rabbit is cooking, melt 1 tablespoon of fat. Add the bones and the herbs strained from the marinade. Simmer all together for a few minutes and drain off the fat. Add the white wine and chicken stock, bring the liquid to a boil, and simmer for 30 minutes. Strain this *fumet*. There should be about 2 cups. If neccssary, reduce it further over high heat, or add more wine and stock, in equal parts.

Pour the *fumet* over the rabbit in the terrine, cover the terrine tightly with its lid, and cook for 15 minutes longer. Drain off the liquid and strain it through a cloth. Return it to the terrine. If necessary, add a little more wine and stock to cover the rabbit. Return the terrine to the oven and cook for 15 minutes longer. Cool the rabbit in the terrine and chill it overnight in the refrigerator. If the rabbit is not to be used at once, fill the container to the top with melted lard. To serve, scrape off any fat, loosen the mold by dipping it quickly into very hot water, and unmold it. Invert the mold so that the rabbit is right side up and garnish the platter to taste with water cress. Or put the terrine on a napkin on a serving platter, and bring it to the table. The rabbit is then served in slices cut from the terrine.

V

MEAT

Beef

Côte de Boeuf
(*Rib Roast*)

POSSIBLY the most popular of all roasts is the prime ribs, a standing roast cooked with its bones, which immeasurably enhance its delicious flavor. Buy at least two ribs, and preferably more; the thicker the roast the juicier. Have the short ribs cut off; they may be braised for another meal. Stand the roast on the end of its ribs, fat side up, and season it with salt and pepper. Roast it in a hot oven (400°f.) until it browns lightly, then reduce the heat and finish the cooking in a moderately slow oven (300°f.). Allow about 1¼ hours for an average two-rib roast, 18 to 20 minutes per pound. Beef should be cooked only to the rare stage. Remove the meat from the pan and let it stand in a warm place near the stove for 30 minutes before carving it. The process of cooking will continue for a short time, and the rest period will help the meat to retain its juices when it is carved.

Put the roast on the carving platter with the ribs pointing to the left and cut horizontal slices from right to left across the grain of the meat to the bone. The slices may be thick or thin, according to individual preference. When the first bone has been completely exposed, cut it away and lay it aside.

To make roast beef *au jus,* pour off the excess fat in the roasting pan. Add a little water or brown stock to the pan and cook it for a few minutes, stirring in the flavorful caramelized brown bits that cling to the bottom and sides of the pan. Strain the sauce, reheat it, and adjust the seasoning.

Filet de Boeuf
(Beef Tenderloin)

THE *filet de boeuf,* or beef tenderloin, is cut from the loin of the steer, and is long and comparatively flat. The tenderloin is inevitably tender, but it is dry, and must be larded or wrapped in suet if it is to provide a juicy roast. The ends of the *filet* should be cut off and reserved for another use; the center of the tenderloin makes the most shapely roast. The *filet* should be cooked rare, and because of its shape, never requires more than from 30 to 40 minutes, no matter how heavy it is. The initial cost of the tenderloin may seem high, but as there is no bone, no fat, and therefore no waste, tenderloin is actually a reasonably economical purchase.

Filet de Boeuf Strasbourgeoise
(Beef Tenderloin with Foie Gras*)*

1 tenderloin of beef
1 carrot
2 onions
2 sprigs of parsley
1 sprig of thyme
½ bay leaf
1 cup Madeira
CONTINUED

HAVE the butcher trim the fillet. Reserve the trimmings for another use. As the tenderloin is very lean, it must be larded; that is, thin strips of fat pork must be introduced into the meat with the aid of a larding needle or a very sharp knife. The butcher will perform this operation on request.

Slice the vegetables and put them in the bottom of a buttered roasting pan. Salt the beef and spread it liberally with butter. Lay it on the vegetables and roast it in a very hot oven (450°f.) for 20 minutes, basting it twice and turning it to brown both sides evenly. Add the Madeira and the white wine and cook for from 10 to 15 minutes longer. The tenderloin should be very rare. Transfer the meat to a serving platter. Strain the pan juices and skim off any fat that rises to the surface. Reduce the sauce over high heat to 1 cup in volume and serve it in a sauceboat. Slice the meat and separate the slices with slices of *foie gras* which have been dredged in flour and browned in butter.

1 cup white wine
1 pound *foie gras*

Filet de Boeuf Richelieu
(Beef Tenderloin with Stuffed Tomatoes and Mushrooms)

HAVE the fillet trimmed and larded for roasting. Sprinkle it with salt and pepper. Lay the meat in a roasting pan on some slices of potato and roast it in a hot oven (400°f.) for 30 minutes. Baste it occasionally with the pan drippings, and turn it once to brown both sides. Arrange the meat on a serving platter and garnish the platter with stuffed mushrooms and stuffed tomatoes.

1 tenderloin of beef
6 stuffed tomatoes
6 stuffed mushrooms
potatoes

Filet de Boeuf Wellington
(Beef Tenderloin, Madeira Sauce)

HAVE the butcher trim and lard a beef tenderloin and tie it to keep it in shape. Roast the meat in a buttered pan in a very hot oven (475°f.) for 10 minutes and remove it at once from the oven to cool.

Chop the mushrooms, ham, and onions and

1 beef tenderloin
2 pounds mushrooms
½ pound ham
4 onions
1 tablespoon chopped parsley
CONTINUED

143

6 thin slices back fat pork
puff paste

cook them in a little melted butter. Add salt and pepper and the parsley.

Roll the puff paste into a rectangle ⅜ inch thick and large enough to envelop the fillet. Cover the center of the rectangle with the fat pork and spread it with some of the cooked ham and vegetable mixture. Lay the fillet, which should be quite cold, on the vegetables and coat it with the rest of the mixture. Use the remaining fat pork to hold the vegetables on the meat. Carefully wrap the fillet in the puff paste. Garnish the top of the wrapped meat with cut-outs of puff paste and brush with beaten egg to insure a high gloss. Let the meat stand for an hour. Bake it for 25 minutes in a moderate oven (350°f.) until the paste is nicely browned. Serve with Madeira sauce mixed with finely chopped truffles.

Boeuf Bouilli
(*Boiled Beef*)

BOTTOM round makes an excellent *bouilli,* but plate or brisket may also be boiled. Simmer the meat in boiling salted water—putting the meat to cook in boiling water seals in the juices. Skim the scum as it rises to the surface, and add peppercorns, a bouquet of parsley, thyme, and celery, and a carrot and an onion stuck with a clove. Cover the kettle and cook the meat very gently for several hours, until it is very tender. A 3-pound piece of high-quality bottom round will take about 4 hours. Serve the *bouilli* hot with freshly cooked vegetables and a piquant sauce such as horse-radish or mustard sauce. Or serve the meat cold, sliced, with coarse salt and mustard.

VARIOUS STEAKS are favored in various parts of this country, and the T-bone, porterhouse, rib, and sirloin all have their adherents. The most generally popular of these is the porterhouse, which is cut from the middle of the loin and includes a piece of the tenderloin, a larger piece of sirloin, and a "tail" of flank. These three cuts vary considerably in tenderness, and would benefit from being cooked separately rather than together. All in all, I think the porterhouse a rather curious phenomenon, and prefer the sirloin or rib steaks, or steaks cut from the tenderloin. The flank makes a satisfactory steak by itself, but it must be pounded with the edge of a knife to break down the fibers, and may be marinated for further tenderness. This steak is broiled to the rare stage and sliced in thin diagonal slices to make "London broil."

As a general rule, steaks should be at least 1½ inches thick for broiling. If the meat is any thinner, brown it quickly in a little fat on a skillet, so that it does not dry out.

Most people prefer steak rare, or at least medium rare. The time for broiling depends upon the size and thickness of the steak. When both sides are well browned, you can discover the degree of done-ness by inserting a small, sharp knife at the center of the steak.

Entrecôte Marchand de Vin
(*Rib Steak with Wine Sauce*)

HAVE prime rib steaks cut thick and boned. Allow about ½ pound boned weight for each serving. Spread the steaks with the olive oil and broil them to the rare stage.

While the steaks are broiling, cook the red

2 or 3 rib steaks, 2 inches thick
1 tablespoon olive oil
1 tablespoon chopped shallots
2 cups red wine
CONTINUED

1 tablespoon brown stock
2 tablespoons sweet butter
1 teaspoon chopped parsley
juice of ½ lemon

wine, stock, and shallots over high heat until the liquid is reduced to ½ cup. Stir in the butter, parsley, and lemon juice and add salt and freshly ground pepper to taste.

Season the steaks with salt and remove them to a serving platter. Pour the sauce over the meat and carve the steaks at the table, in diagonal strips.

Steak à l'Estragon
(*Steak with Tarragon*)

2 individual boneless steaks,
  ½ pound each
1 tablespoon chopped tarragon
  leaves
½ cup Beaujolais
½ tablespoon butter
½ tablespoon flour

COOK two teaspoons of the chopped tarragon for a few minutes in the wine (another light-bodied red wine may be substituted for the Beaujolais). Melt the butter, stir in the flour, and cook the *roux* until it is lightly browned. Add the wine and cook the sauce, whisking it constantly, until it is smooth and creamy. Add salt and pepper to taste and whisk in 1 tablespoon of butter, bit by bit. Broil the steaks to the rare stage, pour the sauce over them, and sprinkle with the remaining tarragon leaves. Serves 2.

Steak au Poivre
(*Pepper Steak*)

2 individual boneless steaks,
  ½ pound each
1 tablespoon white
  peppercorns
1 tablespoon olive oil
1 teaspoon chopped shallots
½ cup Burgundy red

PUT the peppercorns in a cloth and pound them well with a hammer. Pat the crushed pepper into both sides of the steaks. Sprinkle the meat with oil and brown it rapidly on both sides under a hot broiler. Or brown the steaks in the oil in a skillet. Simmer the shallots in a little butter, add the wine and a little salt, and cook for 2 minutes. Put the cooked steaks in this sauce for a minute, then remove them to the serving dish. Reduce the sauce over high heat until the moisture is almost entirely evaporated. Remove the pan from the stove and stir in 1 tablespoon of sweet butter, bit by bit. Adjust the seasoning and pour the sauce over the steaks. Serves 2.

Planked Steak

BROIL a sirloin steak, cut 2½ inches thick, to the very rare stage and put it on a seasoned oven plank. (To season the plank, which should be 1 inch thick and made of hickory, oak, or pine, soak it in cold water overnight, dry it, brush it with oil, and put it in a slow oven [250°f.] for 1 hour.) Brush the border of the plank with butter and, with a pastry bag, decorate it with a thick ring of duchess potatoes. Put the plank in a moderately hot oven (400°f.) to brown the potatoes. Be careful not to overcook the steak. Spread the steak with *maître d'hôtel* sauce and garnish it further with bouquets of such vegetables as buttered cauliflower, sautéed mushrooms, broiled tomatoes, and buttered green beans.

Chateaubriand

THE Chateaubriand is the heart of the tenderloin of beef, the luxurious fillet which also yields the *filets mignons* and the *tournedos*. The Chateaubriand should be cut 5 to 6 inches thick, but it is flattened to 3 to 4 inches before broiling. Spread the steak on both sides with clarified butter and broil to the rare stage, about 9 to 10 minutes on each side. Season with salt and pepper and serve with soufflé potatoes and with Béarnaise sauce. Carve at the table in diagonal slices.

Tournedos

THE *tournedos* are cut 1½ inches thick from the fillet or tenderloin of beef. They lie next to the *filet mignon* at the narrow end of the fillet. Sometimes the *tournedos* is spread with butter and broiled, but more often it is quickly browned in butter. Have a strip of fat larding pork tied around the steak to improve its natural leanness.

The most famous of *tournedos* is named for Gioacchino Rossini, composer of operas, who was extremely fond of *foie gras* and truffles.

Tournedos Rossini

Brown in hot butter as many *tournedos* as are required, and season them. Put each steak on a freshly made piece of toast trimmed to fit it. Top with a slice of *foie gras* and a bit of truffle. Serve with Madeira sauce.

Beef Tenderloin Minute Steaks

HAVE the tenderloin cut into very thin slices. Brown the minute steaks quickly in hot butter, season, and serve with a sauce made of the cooking butter, lemon juice, and chopped parsley. The total cooking time should not be longer than 2 or 3 minutes, and the pan and the butter should be very hot.

Sautés de Boeuf Minute
(*Quick Preparations of Beef Tenderloin*)

THE portions of the fillet of beef or tenderloin which cannot be used for steaks—that is, the irregular bits at the ends—are among the most tender and delicious morsals of the entire beef animal. These bits should be cut into slices of uniform size and shape, free of fat and skin, weighing about 1 ounce each. Season them with salt and pepper and brown them quickly in hot butter. Use a pan large enough so that there is no crowding, or, if necessary, cook the meat slices a few at a time, otherwise the meat will not brown quickly enough: it will be stewed in steam, and thus overcooked.

Beef prepared in this way is subject to numerous variations in garnishing which produce what we might call quick beef stews of many kinds.

Boeuf à la Stroganoff
(Beef in Sour Cream)

BROWN the meat quickly in the butter and remove it to a dish to keep warm. Cook the shallots, chopped, in the remaining butter. Add the white wine and bring it to a boil. Add the mushrooms, minced, and the stock, and cook briskly for a few minutes. Add the cup of sour cream. Do not boil the sauce after the cream is added. Adjust the seasoning with salt, pepper, a little freshly grated nutmeg, and a dash of cayenne pepper. Return the beef to the sauce and serve in a ring of buttered rice. Sprinkle with chopped parsley. Serves 2–3.

1 pound sliced tenderloin
4 tablespoons clarified butter
3 shallots
1 cup dry white wine
8 mushrooms
1 tablespoon brown stock
1 cup sour cream

Boeuf à la Deutsch
(Beef à la Deutsch)

BROWN the tenderloin quickly in the clarified butter and remove the meat to a heated platter to keep warm. Chop the onion and brown it

1 pound sliced tenderloin
4 tablespoons clarified butter
CONTINUED

149

1 onion
½ cup dry sherry
8 mushrooms
1 green pepper
1 cup tomato purée
1 tablespoon brown stock

lightly in the same butter. Add the sherry, bring the liquid to a boil, and add the mushrooms and green pepper, both finely minced. Add the tomato purée and the stock and cook all together for a few minutes. Adjust the seasoning, add the beef, and pour all together into a serving dish. Sprinkle with chopped parsley. Garnish the platter with matchstick potatoes browned in clarified butter. Serves 2–3.

Sauté de Boeuf Minute Hongroise
(Paprika Beef)

1 pound sliced tenderloin
4 tablespoons clarified butter
½ cup heavy cream
½ teaspoon paprika
juice of ½ lemon

BROWN the meat in the butter and put it aside. To the butter remaining in the pan add the cream, paprika, and lemon juice. Adjust the seasoning of the sauce with salt, pepper, and cayenne. Combine sauce and meat and serve with buttered noodles. Serves 2–3.

Sauté de Boeuf Minute Provençal
(Beef Provençal)

1 pound sliced tenderloin
4 tablespoons clarified butter
1 green pepper
1 small eggplant
½ cup tomato sauce

BROWN the meat in the butter and reserve it. In the butter remaining in the pan cook until tender the green pepper, sliced and free of pith and seeds, and the eggplant, peeled and cut into small dice. Add ½ cup of tomato sauce and simmer slowly until the vegetables are tender. Return the beef to the sauce and serve all together. Serves 2–3.

BEEF FOR STEWING is cut from the shoulder, hip, bottom round, or chuck. These cuts require long, moist cooking in order to achieve tenderness, but they are rich and flavorful. The most famous of beef stews in classic cuisine is the stew cooked Burgundy style, in red wine.

Boeuf à la Bourguignonne
(*Beef Stew in Red Wine*)

CUT the beef into large, uniform cubes and brown the cubes in the hot butter in a heavy-bottomed pan or a casserole fitted with a cover. Sprinkle with flour, toss over the heat until the flour is browned, and add salt and pepper, the garlic, the wine, and enough water to cover the meat well (about 2 cups). Bring the liquid to a boil, add the bouquet, cover the pan, and braise the stew in a moderate oven (350°f.) for about 2 hours, until the meat is tender. Skim off any excess fat.

Cut the salt pork into dice and brown the dice in a skillet. Peel the onions and brown them lightly. Combine this mixture with the stew and cook all together for 15 minutes longer, until the onions are tender but still firm. Garnish the casserole with mushroom caps cooked in butter with a little lemon juice, and with coarsely chopped parsley.

2½ pounds beef
2 tablespoons butter
1 tablespoon flour
4 cups red wine
2 garlic cloves
bouquet of 1 stalk of celery, 1 sprig each of parsley and thyme, and a bit of bay leaf
½ pound lean salt pork
1 pound small white onions
1 pound mushrooms
chopped parsley

Ragoût de Boeuf Hongrois
(*Hungarian Goulash*)

CUT the beef into uniform cubes and brown the cubes in the hot butter in a skillet. Remove the meat to a casserole and season it with salt and pepper. Chop the onions fine and brown them in the skillet. Add the paprika (you may use as much as 1 tablespoon of paprika for each pound of meat) and flour. Stir over the heat for a minute or two and add the tomato juice and stock. Bring this sauce to the boil, stirring constantly, and pour it over the meat in the casserole. Add the bouquet and the garlic, bring

2½ pounds beef
2 tablespoons clarified butter
2 large onions
1 tablespoon paprika
1 teaspoon flour
1 cup tomato juice
2 cups brown stock
bouquet made of 2 sprigs of parsley, 1 sprig of thyme, 1 bay leaf
3 garlic cloves

the liquid again to the boil, and cover the casserole. Cook the stew in a moderately slow oven (325°f.) for 2 hours or more, until the meat is very tender. Serve with buttered noodles.

Estouffade à l'Espagnole
(*Spanish Beef Stew*)

2½ pounds beef
2 tablespoons olive oil
2 onions
1 tablespoon flour
1 cup purée of tomatoes
3 garlic cloves
3 green peppers

CUT the meat into uniform cubes and brown the cubes in the hot olive oil. Use a Dutch oven or a heavy-bottomed pan. Chop the onions coarse and brown them lightly with the meat. Sprinkle with flour, salt, and pepper, and toss over the heat until the flour browns lightly. Add the purée of tomatoes, made by forcing cooked tomatoes through a sieve, and enough hot water to cover the meat. Bring the liquid to a boil and add the crushed garlic cloves and the peppers, free of pith and seeds and sliced thin. Cover the pan and simmer the stew for 2 hours or more, until the meat is very tender.

Paupiettes de Boeuf au Vin Rouge
(*Beef Rolls in Red Wine*)

round steak, about 2 pounds
1 pound sausage meat
1 onion
1 tablespoon chopped parsley
2 tablespoons clarified butter
½ cup brown stock
1 cup red wine
2 tomatoes
1 pound mushrooms
1 cup pitted green olives

HAVE the steak cut into 6 or 8 uniform-sized thin slices. Put the slices between sheets of waxed paper and pound them well with the flat side of a knife. Season with salt and pepper.

Cook the sausage meat in a heavy skillet, stirring with a fork to break up the meat. Pour off the accumulated fat and add the onion, chopped fine, and a bit of garlic. Cook, still stirring, until the sausage is well done. Add the parsley and salt and pepper to taste.

Spread the sausage mixture evenly on the pounded slices of meat, roll the meat, and fasten the rolls with kitchen string. Dredge the rolls in flour and brown them on all sides in the hot clarified butter. Add the wine, the stock, and the tomatoes, peeled and chopped coarse, cover the pan, and cook slowly for 1 hour, or until the beef is tender.

Arrange the cooked beef rolls in a flame-proof serving casserole. Remove the fat from the pan juices and strain the gravy over the meat. Add the mushrooms, cook for 5 minutes in butter with a little lemon juice, and the olives. Bring the mixture to a boil and serve.

Boeuf à la Mode
(*Braised Beef*)

HAVE the butcher bone the meat, lard it through with fat pork, and tie it. Season the meat with salt and pepper and put it in a bowl with the carrots and onions, sliced, the bouquet, and the wine and brandy. Marinate the meat overnight in the refrigerator, turning it from time to time.

Remove the meat from the marinade, dry it thoroughly, and brown it in hot clarified butter in a heavy-bottomed pan or casserole. Strain the vegetables from the marinade and brown them lightly with the beef. Pour off any excess fat. Add the strained marinade, cover the pan, and simmer for a few minutes. Cut the calf's foot in half crosswise and parboil it for 5 minutes. Add the tomatoes, the garlic, the stock, and the parboiled calf's foot to the meat. Cover the casserole, bring the liquid to a boil, and cook the meat in a moderate oven (350°f.) for 2½ hours, until it is tender.

Remove the meat and the calf's foot from the

beef rump, 3 to 4 pounds
2 carrots
2 onions
bouquet of 1 stalk of celery, 1 sprig each of parsley and thyme, and 1 bay leaf
2 cups dry white or red wine
¼ cup brandy
2 tablespoons clarified butter
1 cup cooked tomatoes
3 cloves garlic
4 cups brown stock
1 calf's foot
1 cup Madeira or sherry

pan. Strain the liquid in the pan through a fine sieve, forcing the vegetables through. Reduce the sauce over high heat to one third its original volume, removing the fat as it rises to the surface. If the sauce seems too thin, thicken it with ½ teaspoon of arrowroot diluted to a paste with cold water. Add the Madeira or sherry.

Remove the string from the beef. Sprinkle the meat lightly with sugar and brown it quickly under the broiler. Garnish the platter with glazed onions, turnips, and new carrots. The calf's foot, cut in large pieces, may also be used as garnish. Slice the meat against the grain, so that the larding fat makes an attractive pattern, and pour some of the sauce over the sliced meat. Serve the rest of the sauce in a sauceboat.

Salisbury Steak

1 pound ground beef
1 tablespoon grated onion
1 tablespoon chopped green pepper
1 chopped garlic clove
1 teaspoon chopped chives
1 teaspoon chopped parsley
thyme
1 tablespoon butter
1 tablespoon ketchup
1 teaspoon lemon juice
Worcestershire sauce
Tabasco sauce
½ teaspoon prepared mustard
1 tablespoon sherry

COMBINE the meat with the vegetables and herbs and season to taste with salt, pepper, and thyme. Blend well. Shape the meat lightly into patties from 1½ to 2 inches thick. Avoid packing the meat solidly. Brush the patties with butter or olive oil and broil them to the desired state of done-ness, about 5 minutes on each side. Do not overcook them.

To make the sauce, melt the butter and add the ketchup, lemon juice, a dash each of Worcestershire and Tabasco, the mustard, and salt and pepper, and a bit of mace, to taste. Add the wine, bring the sauce to the boiling point, and pour the sauce over the Salisbury steaks. Serves 4.

Pain de Boeuf
(*Meat Loaf*)

CHOP the onion and cook it for 2 minutes in hot butter. Combine all the ingredients except the bacon and blend well. Season with salt, pepper, and a pinch of thyme and spoon lightly into a buttered loaf pan. Lay the bacon strips on top of the loaf. Bake in a moderate oven (350°f.) for 1 hour. Serve with tomato sauce. Serves 8.

2 pounds ground beef
1 onion
½ pound ground fresh pork
1 cup soft bread crumbs
½ cup chopped pimientos
2 eggs
½ cup milk
powdered thyme
4 slices bacon

Corned Beef

BRING to a boil all the ingredients except the beef. Test the *saumure,* or brine, by throwing a peeled potato into it. If the potato goes down, add more salt; if it floats too easily, add more water (when the brine has the proper salt content, the potato will float just below the surface). Cool the brine and pour it over the beef brisket in an earthenware crock. The meat should be completely covered with the brine. Weight it down with several plates to keep it under the surface of the liquid. Let the crock stand in a cool place for two weeks. At the end of that time, the meat will be ready to cook.

beef brisket, 3 to 4 pounds
2 gallons water
2 pounds salt
1 ounce saltpeter
¼ pound brown sugar
5 peppercorns
5 juniper berries
1 sprig thyme
1 bay leaf
2 cloves

New England Boiled Dinner

COVER the corned beef with cold water, bring it to a boil, and drain. If the water seems excessively salty, repeat the process. Cover the beef with fresh cold water and cook it for 1½ hours over low heat. Add the cabbages, cut in half,

corned beef, 3 to 4 pounds
3 small green cabbages
4 carrots
2 turnips
CONTINUED

155

2 parsnips
6 onions
6 potatoes

the carrots, turnips, and parsnips, all peeled, and the onions. Continue to cook for 1½ hours longer, until the meat is nearly tender. Add the potatoes, peeled but left whole, and cook for 30 minutes longer. Slice the corned beef and surround the slices with the vegetables, alternating the kinds around the edge of the serving platter.

Oxtail Chez-Soi
(*Oxtail Home Style*)

2 oxtails, 3 pounds each
2 carrots
2 onions
2 white turnips
bouquet of 2 stalks of celery,
  1 sprig each of parsley and
  thyme, 1 bay leaf
cheesecloth bag containing 12
  peppercorns and 4 garlic
  cloves
2 cups dry white wine
18 small white onions
2 cups tomato purée

HAVE the butcher cut the oxtail into 1½-inch lengths. Put the meat in a bowl, cover it with the white wine, and add the carrots, onions, and turnips, peeled and sliced, the bouquet, and the bag of peppercorns and garlic. Season with salt, pepper, and a pinch of allspice. Let the meat marinate overnight in the refrigerator.

Drain and dry the meat and brown it quickly in clarified butter. Transfer it to a casserole fitted with a lid. In the same fat, brown lightly the vegetables from the marinade. Sprinkle with 1 teaspoon of flour and brown the flour, stirring. Stir in the marinade and bring the sauce to the boil, stirring constantly. Add the tomato purée. Pour the sauce over the meat in the casserole and add the bouquet, the bag of peppercorns, and enough stock or water to cover the meat generously. Cover the casserole and cook the stew in a moderate oven (350°f.) for from 3 to 4 hours, until the meat is tender. Fifteen minutes before the stew is done, add the small white onions, peeled and glazed in butter. When the onions are cooked through, but still firm, remove and discard the bouquet and the spice bag. Skim off any excess fat on the surface and adjust the seasoning. Serve the oxtail stew, sprinkled with coarsely chopped parsley, in the casserole.

Suprêmes de Langue au Paprika
(*Jellied Ox Tongue Paprika*)

SOAK the ox tongue in cold water for several hours and drain it well. Cover it with fresh cold water and bring it to a boil. Taste the water; if it is still salty, drain it off and cover the tongue with fresh cold water. Simmer the tongue for about 3 hours, until it is tender and the skin peels easily. Cool the tongue in the stock, peel it, and cut the uniform center portion into about 24 thin diagonal slices. Use the trimmings to make a *salpicon,* as follows:

Cut the trimmings into very small dice and combine them with half their volume in truffles, also cut in small dice. Add 1 cup of paprika sauce and blend well. Adjust the seasoning and cool the mixture.

Pour a layer of aspic jelly ½-inch thick into the bottom of a silver serving dish. Put the dish into the refrigerator to set the jelly.

Lay 12 of the tongue slices on a tray and put a spoonful of the *salpicon* on each. Cover with another slice of tongue, sandwich style. Coat the tongue sandwiches with paprika sauce and set the tray in the refrigerator to set the sauce.

Arrange the tongue sandwiches attractively in the silver dish on the aspic and decorate each with cutouts of hard-cooked egg white and truffles. Pour over the decorations a little very cold but still liquid aspic jelly. Chill thoroughly before serving.

1 ox tongue, smoked or pickled
2 cups paprika sauce
aspic jelly with sherry

157

Tripes à la Mode de Caen
(*Baked Tripe*)

4 pounds fresh beef tripe
2 pounds shank of beef
4 onions, each stuck with a
  clove
4 carrots
3 garlic cloves
4 teaspoons salt
½ teaspoon pepper
1 quart hard cider or white
  wine
½ cup brandy
bouquet garni

WASH the tripe well and cut it into uniform strips. Bone the beef shank and cut the meat into fair-sized pieces. Put the meat in the bottom of a large earthenware casserole fitted with a lid. Add the vegetables and seasonings and spread the tripe over all. Put the *bouquet garni* in the center of the dish and put the beef bones and a few slices of beef suet on the tripe. Add the cider, brandy, and water enough to cover the tripe well. Cover the casserole and seal the cover with a dough made of flour and water. Bake the tripe in a moderately slow oven (325°f.) for 6 hours. (Traditionally, this dish was baked overnight, or for as long as 18 hours, at very low heat.) Discard the beef bones, the suet, the carrots, the onions, and the *bouquet*. Skim off the fat and correct the seasoning. *Tripes à la mode de Caen* keeps very well in the refrigerator, and needs only to be reheated and served piping hot.

LEFTOVER BEEF is frequently eaten cold, thinly sliced, with any of a number of savory sauces. A vegetable salad or a green salad is the usual accompaniment. When the remains of a cold roast are used in a hot dish, it is important not to overcook the meat and thus toughen it.

Côte de Boeuf à la Diable
(*Deviled Ribs*)

DETACH the rib bones from the cold remains of a standing rib roast, leaving as much as possible of the meat on them. Make a paste of dry mustard and water and spread the paste on the bones. Season with salt and pepper and roll in fresh bread crumbs. Sprinkle the crumbs with melted butter and broil the ribs slowly until the crumbs are browned.

Boeuf en Miroton
(Beef with Onions)

SLICE the boiled beef thin and arrange the slices in a shallow baking dish.

Slice the onions thin and brown them slowly in the hot butter. Sprinkle with flour and brown the flour. Stir in the hot beef broth and cook, stirring, until the sauce is thickened and smooth. Add the vinegar, adjust the seasoning, and simmer slowly for 5 minutes. Pour the sauce over the beef, sprinkle with grated cheese, and brown the topping in a moderate oven (350°f.).

2 pounds cold boiled beef
4 onions
1 tablespoon butter
1 tablespoon flour
2 cups beef broth
1 tablespoon wine vinegar

Gratin de Boeuf Parmentier
(Beef Hash)

CHOP the onions and cook them in the butter for 10 minutes, until they are soft and browned. Add the ground beef, the stock, and salt and pepper to taste, and simmer slowly for 30 minutes. Boil, drain, and mash the potatoes and season them to taste with milk, butter, salt, and pepper. Line a buttered baking dish with some of the potatoes and fill the dish with alternating layers of the beef mixture and potatoes, ending with potatoes. The beef mixture should be moist, but not watery. If necessary, cook it a little longer to achieve the de-

2 cups ground leftover cooked beef
2 small onions
1 tablespoon butter
1 cup beef stock
4 potatoes
grated Swiss cheese

159

sired firmness. Sprinkle with grated Swiss cheese and brown the topping in a moderately hot oven (400°f.). Serve very hot. Serves 4.

Veal

VEAL HAS NEVER BEEN so popular in this country as in Europe, principally because the quality of American veal has never equaled the quality of, for instance, American beef. In Europe, meat sold as veal is almost white in color, very fine of texture, and almost entirely free of fat. The veal calf feeds chiefly on milk, and its diet accounts for the delicacy of its flesh. After twelve weeks, the calf begins to vary its diet, and thus begins to acquire some of the characteristics of beef. With the exception of the thin veal scallops, all veal requires long, slow cooking to soften the connective tissues. Being a rather bland meat, it should be well seasoned. The rump and loin of veal may be roasted, as may the leg, but all these cuts are as frequently braised.

Poitrine de Veau Farcie
(Stuffed Breast of Veal)

1 veal breast
1 pound sausage meat
1 egg
1 teaspoon mixed chopped
  tarragon, parsley, and chives
1 cup white stock

HAVE the butcher bone the veal breast and split it open at its thickest part, to form a pocket. Combine the sausage meat and herbs and work in the beaten egg. Fill the pocket with the stuffing and sew the opening with kitchen thread. Season the meat and brown it on all sides in clarified butter. Add 1 cup of stock or water and cover the pan. Braise the veal in a moderate oven (350°f.) for 2 hours or longer, until it is very tender. Baste it frequently with the pan juices. Arrange the stuffed breast of veal on a serving platter and serve the pan gravy separately.

Longe de Veau à la Bonne Femme
(*Roast Loin of Veal with Vegetables*)

HAVE the butcher bone the loin, lard it, and roll it for roasting. Rub the meat generously with the butter, season with salt and pepper, and put it in an open roasting pan in a hot oven (425°f.) to brown on all sides. Add to the pan the sliced vegetables, garlic, herbs, and brown stock. Cover the pan and roast the veal for 1½ to 2 hours in a moderately hot oven (375°f.) until it is very tender. Baste frequently with the liquid in the pan.

Arrange the roast on a heated platter and garnish with the prepared onions, potatoes, and carrots. The salt pork should be cut into narrow strips, parboiled, and browned. Sprinkle these over the vegetables. Remove the excess fat from the liquid in the roasting pan and strain the sauce over the meat. Serves 12.

1 loin of veal, 5 pounds
½ cup butter
2 carrots, sliced
2 onions, sliced
2 crushed garlic cloves
1 sprig of thyme
2 sprigs of parsley
½ bay leaf
1 cup brown stock
24 small white onions, glazed
24 small new potatoes parisienne
24 small new carrots, glazed
½ pound lean salt pork

Noix de Veau Ménagère
(*Veal Cutlet, Home Style*)

SEASON the cutlet with salt and pepper and brown it on both sides in the hot butter. Add the onions and carrots, cover the pan, and simmer for 15 minutes. Add the wine, bring it to the boil, and cook for 4 or 5 minutes longer. Parboil the celery, cut it in large pieces, and add it to the pan along with the stock. Add the bouquet, cover the pan, and simmer gently until the veal is very tender. Skim off the excess fat and adjust the seasoning of the sauce.

1 veal cutlet, 2 pounds
1 tablespoon clarified butter
6 onions
6 carrots
1 cup white wine
1 cup foundation stock
1 head of celery
bouquet of 2 sprigs of parsley, 1 sprig of thyme, a bit of bay leaf, and a garlic clove

Fricandeau à l'Oscille
(*Veal Cutlet with Sorrel*)

HAVE the butcher cut a veal cutlet about 2 inches thick (it will weigh about 4 pounds) and lard the meat with strips of fat pork. Cover the veal with cold marinade (below) and let it stand in a cold place for 2 hours. Turn it from time to time.

Drain and dry the meat thoroughly and brown it quickly on both sides in hot clarified butter. Add the marinade with its vegetables, cover the pan, and cook the veal until it is very tender. Strain the sauce, forcing through as much as possible of the vegetables. Serve with braised sorrel.

Marinade à Froid
(*Cold Marinade*)

1 carrot
1 onion
1 stalk of celery
½ sprig thyme
2 sprigs parsley
2 garlic cloves
1 cup white wine

SLICE the vegetables, add the wine and salt and pepper, and pour the marinade at once over the meat it is to season and tenderize. Cover the bowl and let the meat marinate for about 2 hours.

Oiseaux sans Têtes
(*Veal Birds*)

4 thin slices veal rump
½ pound mushrooms
1 chopped onion
½ pound sausage meat
CONTINUED

POUND the slices of veal flat with the side of a cleaver. Season them with salt and pepper. Mince the mushrooms and cook them with the chopped onion in a little butter until the mixture is pasty and almost dry. Combine this

162

with the sausage meat and divide the filling among the veal slices. Roll the meat around the filling and secure the rolls with string.

Brown the rolls on all sides in the clarified butter. Add the carrot and onion, both sliced, the bouquet, and the garlic. Cover the pan and simmer all together for 15 minutes. Remove the garlic and add the stock. Cover the pan and cook the veal slowly until it is very tender. Remove the strings and put the veal birds in a serving dish. Discard the bouquet, skim off the excess fat, and strain the sauce over the meat. Garnish with mushrooms *sauté* and chopped parsley. Serves 2.

2 tablespoons clarified butter
1 carrot
1 onion
bouquet made of 1 sprig of parsley, ½ sprig of thyme, a bit of bay leaf
3 cloves garlic
2 cups foundation stock or 1 cup each of white wine and water

Sauté de Veau Piémontaise
(*Veal Stew with Rice*)

CUT the meat into uniform pieces, dredge the pieces with flour, and brown them quickly in the hot clarified butter. Season with salt and pepper, add the onions, chopped, and cook for a few minutes. Add the stock, tomato juice, crushed garlic, and the bouquet. Cover the pan and simmer the veal gently until it is almost tender. Adjust the seasoning, add the rice, and cook for about 18 minutes longer, until the rice is tender and has absorbed the liquid.

2 pounds veal for stewing
3 tablespoons clarified butter
2 onions
2 cups foundation stock
1 cup tomato juice
2 garlic cloves
bouquet made of 1 stalk of celery, 1 sprig of thyme, a bit of bay leaf
½ cup rice

Blanquette de Veau à l'Ancienne
(*Old-Fashioned Veal Stew*)

CUT the veal in large pieces and parboil it. Drain it well and wash it. Cover the veal with fresh cold water and add the bag of herbs, the onions, and a little salt. Bring the liquid to a boil, cover the pan, and cook the veal slowly

2 pounds shoulder of veal
a cheesecloth bag containing 1 sprig of parsley, 2 stalks of celery, a bit of bay leaf, half
CONTINUED

a sprig of thyme, 2 garlic cloves, 8 peppercorns, and 1 carrot, sliced
12 small white onions
1 tablespoon butter
2 tablespoons flour
1 pound mushrooms
lemon juice
1 egg yolk
½ cup cream

for 1½ hours, until it is tender. Discard the bag of herbs and strain the stock into another saucepan. Reduce the liquid over high heat to about 2½ cups. In a small saucepan, melt the butter, stir in the flour, and gradually add the reduced stock. Cook, stirring, until the sauce is thickened and smooth.

Wash the mushrooms and simmer them for 5 minutes in very little water with 1 teaspoon of butter and ½ teaspoon of lemon juice. Add the mushrooms to the veal and onion mixture and pour the mushroom liquor into the sauce. Thicken the sauce with the egg yolks beaten with the cream and warmed with a little of the sauce, and heat it without allowing it to boil. Combine sauce, veal, mushrooms, and onions and serve in a heated serving dish, sprinkled with parsley finely chopped.

MADAME DE MAINTENON, who figures largely in the culinary history of a day when the art of cookery was in its glory, has given her name to many famous preparations, among them this one, first prepared under her guidance and that of her brother, the Baron d'Aubigny.

Côtes de Veau en Papillotes, Maintenon
(Veal Chops in Paper Cases)

6 veal chops
½ cup clarified butter
1 small onion
3 shallots
1 pound mushrooms
1 tablespoon brown stock
juice of ½ lemon
12 thin slices cooked ham

HAVE the butcher cut the chops ½ inch thick, trim the bone ends, and lard the meat through with strips of fat pork. Brown the chops on both sides in hot clarified butter, season them with salt and pepper, and simmer them gently, covered, until they are tender, from 15 to 30 minutes. Remove the chops to a heated dish.

Chop the onion and shallots and simmer them for about 10 minutes in the pan in which the chops were cooked. Add the mushrooms, also chopped, and lemon juice, and continue to cook until the mixture is nearly dry. Add the brown stock, or meat extract, and simmer until the mixture is a soft paste. Season with salt and pepper to taste.

Cut six large hearts out of parchment paper or aluminum foil and fold the hearts in half. Brush the paper with olive oil and spread one half nearly to the edge with some of the *duxelles*. Cover the *duxelles* with a slice of ham, cut to fit, more *duxelles,* a chop, *duxelles,* another slice of ham, and finally a thin layer of *duxelles*. Repeat this process for all six chops. Fold the other halves of the hearts over the chops and fold and crimp the edges to seal the packages. Lay the *papillotes* in a baking pan and bake them in a moderate oven (350°f.) for about 8 minutes. Parchment paper will begin to brown; aluminum will merely puff slightly. Serve the chops in the cases. Each guest simply slits a package near the edge and folds back the flap to reveal the contents.

Côtes de Veau Milanaise
(*Breaded Veal Chops with Macaroni*)

SEASON the chops with salt and pepper and dip them in beaten egg and in bread crumbs mixed with grated Parmesan. Press the breading firmly against the chops with the flat of a knife and put the chops in a cool place to dry the coating slightly.

Brown the chops on both sides in a large skillet in hot clarified butter. Cook them slowly,

6 veal chops
1 egg
1 cup bread crumbs
¼ cup grated Parmesan cheese
½ cup clarified butter
½ pound macaroni
1 tablespoon sweet butter
CONTINUED

1 cup tomato purée
1 tablespoon brown stock
1 cup julienne of cooked ham
  and mushrooms

and turn them only once to avoid disturbing the breading, which should form a rich crust.

Cook the macaroni in boiling salted water until it is just tender, and not at all soft, and drain it. Season it with butter, tomato purée, and stock, and toss it with the julienne slivers of ham and mushrooms. Some julienne of truffles may also be added. Put the macaroni in the center of a serving dish and arrange the chops around it. Sprinkle with grated Parmesan and serve at once.

Côtes de Veau de Gourmand
(Veal Chops with Spinach)

6 veal chops
½ cup clarified butter
4 pounds spinach, cooked
1 cup white wine
½ cup light cream
2 tablespoons grated Swiss
  cheese
1 cup Hollandaise sauce

HAVE the butcher lard the chops through with strips of fat pork. Brown the chops on both sides in hot clarified butter and season them with salt and freshly ground black pepper. Cover the pan and simmer the chops until they are very tender.

Season the cooked, well-drained spinach with butter, salt, pepper, and nutmeg. Spread a thick layer of spinach on the bottom of a shallow, buttered baking dish. Lay the tender chops on the spinach.

To the pan in which the chops were browned, add the white wine, stirring to incorporate the brown bits that cling to the pan. Reduce the liquid slightly, add the cream, and cook for a few minutes longer. Strain the sauce into another pan, stir in the grated cheese, and bring it to the boiling point. Cool the sauce to lukewarm and stir in the Hollandaise sauce.

Pour the sauce over the veal chops and spinach and brown the top very quickly under the broiler.

Côtes de Veau en Casserole
(*Veal Chops en Casserole*)

BROWN the chops in a skillet in hot clarified butter, season them with salt and pepper, and transfer them to a heated earthenware or cast-iron casserole. Add the wine and the bouquet and bring the liquid to a boil. Cover the casserole and simmer the meat gently. Brown the mushrooms, adding a little more butter as needed, and put them in the casserole. Brown the onions and add them to the casserole. Cover the pan and simmer for 40 minutes. Add the potatoes and cook all together until the potatoes are cooked through and the meat is tender. Discard the bouquet and serve the chops in the casserole. Serves 2.

2 veal chops
1 tablespoon clarified butter
½ cup white wine
bouquet of 1 sprig each of parsley and thyme and ½ bay leaf
¼ pound mushrooms
6 small onions
6 small potatoes

Escalopes de Veau
(*Veal Scallops*)

THE *escalopes de veau* are thin slices cut across the grain of the loin, rump, or leg of veal. The scallops should be pounded flat with the side of a knife or cleaver. This treatment not only makes the slices thinner, but also tenderizes the meat by breaking down the fibers. Scallops require only brief cooking, at high temperature. Clarified butter, shortening, or oil should be used as a cooking fat, as most other fats burn before they attain the necessary heat. The pan should be large enough to hold all the scallops in a single layer without crowding; if necessary, cook the scallops a few at a time. The meat may be floured or dipped in egg and crumbs, and in this case should be served quickly, while the crust is still crisp. Or it may be carefully dried and browned without embellishment other than salt and pepper. A sauce may be made by adding a little Marsala or other wine to the pan, with additional butter and some herbs, such as fresh tarragon or parsley.

Because this cut of veal is universally popular throughout Europe, it is of some interest to note here that it is called *Schnitzel* in Germany, *Scallopini* in Italy, and *Kalbfilet,* or the local equivalent of that word, in the Scandinavian countries.

Escalopes de Veau Gruyère
(*Veal Scallops with Swiss Cheese*)

2 large, thin scallops of veal
1 egg
1 teaspoon cream
½ cup bread crumbs
2 tablespoons clarified butter
2 slices Swiss cheese

POUND the scallops thin with the side of a cleaver and dip them in seasoned flour, in egg beaten with cream, and in bread crumbs. Cook the scallops slowly in the hot clarified butter until both sides are brown and the meat tender. Lay a slice of Swiss cheese on each scallop and put the meat under the broiler to melt and brown the cheese. Serves 2.

Escalopes de Veau Sautées
(*Veal Scallops Sauté*)

COOK the veal scallops as for *escalopes de veau Gruyère,* above, but omit the cheese. Make a sauce by browning in the pan 2 tablespoons sweet butter. Add the juice of ½ lemon and some chopped parsley, and pour the butter over the scallops. Serves 2.

Escalopes de Veau Viennoise
(*Veal Scallops with Anchovies*)

COOK the veal scallops as for *escalopes de veau Gruyère,* above. Omit the cheese, and garnish each scallop with anchovy fillets washed, sponged dry, and curled in a ring. Top with a pitted green olive. Brown 2 tablespoons butter in the pan in which the veal was cooked, add the juice of ½ lemon and some chopped parsley, and pour the sauce over the veal on the platter. Serves 2.

Escalopes de Veau à la Provençal
(*Veal Scallops Provençal*)

DREDGE the veal scallops with seasoned flour and brown them on both sides in hot olive oil. Add the mushrooms, sliced. (If *cèpes* are available, use them instead of mushrooms.) Simmer the mushrooms and meat together for a few minutes, add the garlic, chopped, and stir in the wine. Peel and cut up the tomatoes and add them to the pan. Cover the pan and simmer all together for 10 minutes. Adjust the seasoning and sprinkle with chopped parsley.

6 large, thin scallops of veal
½ pound mushrooms
2 cloves garlic
scant ½ cup dry white wine
4 tomatoes

Fricadelles de Veau
(*Veal Patties*)

PUT the veal and pork together through the coarse knife of the meat chopper. Soak the bread crumbs in milk and press out the excess moisture. Chop the onions and cook them in a little butter until they are soft, but not browned. Combine all together with the eggs, beaten, and the parsley, and add salt, pepper, and nutmeg to taste. Form flat patties and brown the patties in clarified butter.

1½ pounds boned veal
½ pound lean pork
1 cup soft bread crumbs
2 onions
2 eggs
2 teaspoons chopped parsley
2 tablespoons clarified butter

Sweetbreads

THE SWEETBREADS, the thymus glands of the calf, are highly regarded by gourmets who appreciate their delicate flavor and firm but meltingly tender consistency. The heart sweetbread is round. Slightly less choice is the throat sweetbread, which is elongated and somewhat less fine in texture. Both are treated the same way.

Soak the sweetbreads in ice water for 2 hours or more to make them firm and white. Cover them with fresh cold water, add a little salt, and bring the water slowly to the boiling point. Simmer the sweetbreads for from 3 to 5 minutes and plunge them at once into cold water to cool. Cut away the tubes and connecting tissues before proceeding with any recipe. In most cases, a pair of sweetbreads will serve two.

Ris de Veau Grillé au Jambon
(*Broiled Sweetbreads with Ham*)

PARBOIL and trim the sweetbreads (above), slice them diagonally, sprinkle them with salt and pepper, and brush them with melted butter. Broil them slowly on a rack over a baking pan until they are brown on both sides. Put the broiled sweetbreads in the baking pan and put them in the oven to finish cooking. Test them by touching the edges with a fork; if they seem about to crack or break, the sweetbreads are done.

Arrange the sweetbreads on slices of broiled ham and pour over them a sauce made of 1 tablespoon of melted butter, a little lemon juice, and some chopped parsley. Serves 2.

The ham may be omitted, and the sweetbreads served on freshly buttered hot toast.

Ris de Veau New York
(*Sweetbreads with Apples*)

3 pairs sweetbreads
4 tart, firm-fleshed eating
CONTINUED

SOAK, parboil, and trim the sweetbreads and cut them into thick slices. Sprinkle the slices with salt and pepper, dredge them with flour, and brown them on both sides in ¼ cup of hot clarified butter. Peel and core the apples and cut them into as many round slices as there are sweetbread slices. Brown the apple slices in the remaining butter. Put each slice of sweetbread on a slice of apple and top it with a slice of marrow. To cook the marrow, remove it from the split bone in one piece, slice it, and poach the slices in salted water just under the boiling point, for about 2 minutes.

Pour the sherry into the pan in which the sweetbreads were cooked, add the cream, and bring the liquid to a boil, stirring in all the brown bits. Reduce the sauce over high heat to about half its volume, strain it, and add the chopped parsley. Pour the sauce over the sweetbreads and serve at once.

apples
½ cup clarified butter
cooked marrow, sliced ½ inch thick
½ cup dry sherry
½ cup cream
1 teaspoon chopped parsley

Ris de Veau en Casserole
(Sweetbreads en Casserole)

PARBOIL the sweetbreads and trim them. Heat the clarified butter in a flame-proof casserole fitted with a lid, and brown the sweetbreads on all sides. Add the onion and carrot, both sliced, and the bouquet; salt and pepper to taste. Cover the pan and simmer the vegetables with the sweetbreads for a few minutes. Add the sherry, bring it to the boiling point, and simmer for a few minutes longer. Add the stock, using more if necessary to cover the sweetbreads halfway. Cover the casserole and simmer the sweetbreads for 30 minutes, until they are tender and the edges crack at the touch of a fork. Transfer the sweetbreads to a heated dish to keep them warm. Discard the bouquet. Strain the liquid in the casserole, forcing the vegetables through.

3 pairs sweetbreads
3 tablespoons clarified butter
1 carrot
1 onion
bouquet of 2 sprigs each of parsley and thyme and ½ bay leaf
½ cup sherry
1 cup white stock
1 pound mushrooms

Reduce the sauce a little over high heat and return the sweetbreads to the casserole. Add the mushrooms, browned in butter, and adjust the seasoning of the sauce. Serve very hot, with buttered peas.

Vol-au-Vent de Ris de Veau Toulousaine
(Sweetbreads in Crust)

1 large *vol-au-vent*
2 pairs sweetbreads
1 chicken, 2 pounds
2 egg whites
2 cups light cream
1 pound mushrooms
2 tablespoons butter
4 cups *sauce velouté*
truffle slices

PREPARE the *vol-au-vent*. It should be served warm, and may be reheated at the last moment.

Cook the sweetbreads as for *ris de veau en casserole,* omitting the sherry, and keep them warm.

Cut the meat from the chicken, discarding skin, fat, and tendons. Cut the flesh into small pieces and pound it in a mortar until it is very smooth (or use an electric blender to achieve this end). Work in the egg whites and cream and make the *quenelles* as for *quenelles de brochet.*

Cook the mushrooms for 10 minutes in the butter.

Strain the cooking liquor from the sweetbreads and mushrooms and combine it with the *sauce velouté.* Simmer the sauce to thicken it slightly. Adjust the seasoning and add the sweetbreads, cut in uniform slices, the *quenelles,* and the mushrooms. Fill the *vol-au-vent* and garnish the top with truffle slices. The lid of the *vol-au-vent* should be adjusted so that the contents are visible.

Calf's Brains

CALF's brains are always cooked in a *court-bouillon* (see below) before they are prepared more elaborately. Wash the brains well under running water, removing the membranes and the blood. Soak them in ice water for an hour or more, until they are firm and white. They should be well covered with the water. Cover the brains with cold *court-bouillon,* bring the liquid to a boil, and simmer the brains for about 15 minutes, until they are firm. Cool the brains in the *court-bouillon.*

Court-Bouillon for Calf's Brains

1 sprig of thyme
½ bay leaf
1 stalk of celery

1 quart water
1 tablespoon vinegar
¼ teaspoon salt
6 peppercorns
1 onion, sliced
1 carrot, sliced

COMBINE all the ingredients and boil gently for 30 minutes. Strain before using.

Cervelles de Veau Sautées
(Calf's Brains Sauté)

WASH, soak, and cook the brains in *court-bouillon.* Cool them in the *court-bouillon* and drain and dry them. Cut the brains lengthwise into 3 or 4 slices, dip them in flour, season with salt and pepper, and brown them gently in hot clarified butter on both sides. Serve very hot, with *sauce maître d'hôtel* or with butter cooked to a rich brown and with chopped parsley. A spoonful of capers, washed and dried, may also be sprinkled over the brains.

Amourettes Sautées
(Spinal Marrow Sauté)

THE spinal marrow may be prepared in the same way as the brains. The two are sometimes cooked together.

173

Calf's Tongue

CALF'S tongue may be purchased fresh, smoked, or salted. It is a good idea to put the fresh tongue in a brine, or *saumure,* as for corned beef for 10 days before cooking it. Or, if desired, the tongue may be cooked in a *blanc,* as for *tête de veau vinaigrette,* and garnished and served like ox tongue.

Langue de Veau Bourgeoise
(*Calf's Tongue Country Style*)

1 calf's tongue, fresh or brined
2 carrots
2 onions
1 cup Port
2 cups brown stock
1 cup tomato juice
bouquet made of 1 stalk of celery, 1 sprig each of thyme and parsley, and a bit of bay leaf
3 garlic cloves

COVER the tongue with cold water, bring the water to a boil, and drain and wash the tongue. Brown the tongue gently on all sides in a little fat. Add the carrots and onions, both sliced, and brown them lightly. Add the wine, stock, and tomato juice, and the bouquet and garlic. Bring the liquid to a boil, cover the pan, and simmer the tongue for from 1 to 2 hours, until it is tender. Remove the tongue from the liquid and peel off the skin and trim away the fat and gristle. Slice the tongue and arrange the slices on a serving platter.

Strain the sauce, bring it to the boiling point, and remove the fat from the surface. Adjust the seasoning and pour the sauce over the tongue on the platter. A little sherry may be added to the sauce, if desired, and the sauce may be thickened with ½ teaspoon of arrowroot dissolved in cold water. Serves 2.

Tête de Veau Vinaigrette
(*Calf's Head*)

1 calf's head
a cheesecloth bag containing 2
CONTINUED

HAVE the butcher prepare the calf's head by boning it and cutting it into large, uniform pieces. Have the tongue cut lengthwise into four pieces. Remove the brains and wash under running water, remove the blood and membranes, and cook it for 5 minutes in water acidulated with a little vinegar. It should be diced and added to the *sauce vinaigrette* with which the calf's head is served.

Bring the water to a boil in a large kettle. Mix the flour to a paste with a little cold water and stir it into the kettle, whisking the mixture smooth. Bring this *blanc* to the boil, stirring constantly, and add the meat of the calf's head and the tongue. Add the bag of seasonings and herbs and salt to taste. Simmer the meat for 1½ hours or longer, until it is very tender. Trim the tongue and slice it. Arrange the meat and the tongue on a heated platter and serve the *sauce vinaigrette,* mixed with the diced brain, in a sauceboat.

carrots, 2 onions, 2 sprigs of parsley, 6 stalks of celery, 1 tablespoon peppercorns
4 quarts water
1 tablespoon flour

Foie de Veau à l'Anglaise
(*Calf's Liver and Bacon*)

DREDGE with flour as many slices of calf's liver as are required and shake off the excess flour. Season with salt and pepper and brown quickly on both sides in hot clarified butter. Do not overcook liver. Make a sauce by adding to the pan juices a little sweet butter, lemon juice, and parsley, and pour the sauce over the liver. Serve with crisp bacon.

Foie de Veau à la Bordelaise
(*Calf's Liver with Ham*)

PREPARE and cook the calf's liver as for *foie de veau à l'anglaise.* Omit the bacon and serve the liver with thin slices of Bayonne ham heated in butter. Pour over each serving some *sauce Bordelaise*.

Rognons de Veau Grillés aux Champignons
(Broiled Veal Kidneys with Mushrooms)

2 veal kidneys
½ pound mushrooms
juice of ½ lemon
1 teaspoon chopped parsley

SPLIT the kidneys and cut away the membranes and tubes, using a small curved scissors. Trim off most of the fat, leaving just enough to cover. Brush the kidneys with melted butter and quickly brown them on both sides under the broiler. Remove them to a baking dish, sprinkle with more butter, and bake in a moderate oven (350°f.) for 4 minutes. Do not overcook.

Cook the mushrooms in a little butter until they are tender. Season them with salt, pepper, lemon juice, and parsley. Pour the mushrooms over the kidneys and serve at once. Serves 2.

Lamb

AN EXCELLENT QUALITY of yearling lamb is available in the market all year round, but in May and June, one can purchase spring lamb, the American equivalent of *agneau de lait,* the young animal that has been entirely milk fed. This is an outstanding delicacy. Mutton, the meat of a full-grown sheep, is not as popular in this country as it is, for instance, in England, but if the rather strong flavor of mutton is liked, it can be prepared in many of the ways suggested for lamb, allowing for the possibility that it may not be as tender as lamb, and thus may require longer cooking.

How to Carve Lamb

Hold the leg by the bone with the left hand and cut thin diagonal slices from right to left, turning the leg to cut slices from all sides of the roast, slanting down to the bone each time.

To carve a saddle of lamb, make cuts close to the bone down both sides of the backbone, and remove the fillets from each side in one piece. Turn the saddle over and cut out the fillets on that side. Slice these four fillets lengthwise, making 4 or 5 pieces from each.

Gigot d'Agneau Boulangère
(*Roast Leg of Lamb*)

HAVE the butcher remove the pelvic bone from a thickset leg of lamb. Season the meat with salt and pepper, and make a number of small slits with a small, sharp-pointed knife. Insert in each slit a sliver of garlic. Roast the meat in a moderately hot oven (375°f.) for 30 minutes, until it is well browned. Put the onions and potatoes in the pan around the meat, coating them well with the fat in the pan, and roast for 40 minutes longer, basting from time to time, until the vegetables are cooked through and the lamb is done to the pink stage. For well-done meat, cook the lamb for 18 minutes to the pound instead of 12 minutes, as here stipulated, but pink lamb is much to be preferred.

1 leg of lamb, about 6 pounds
3 garlic cloves
6 onions
6 potatoes

Epaule d'Agneau Farcie
(*Stuffed Shoulder of Lamb*)

HAVE the shoulder of lamb boned but not tied. Mix the remaining ingredients to make a stuffing, and season with salt and pepper. Spread the meat with the stuffing and roll it up. Tie the roll at intervals with kitchen string. Season

1 shoulder of lamb, 3 to 4
  pounds
1 hard-cooked egg
1 cup fresh bread crumbs
CONTINUED

177

1 egg
½ cup chopped parsley

the meat and roast the stuffed shoulder in a moderately hot oven (375°f.) for about 12 minutes per pound for pink meat.

Selle d'Agneau Mireille
(Roast Saddle of Lamb with Artichokes)

1 saddle of lamb, 5 pounds
12 small new potatoes
12 artichoke bottoms, cooked

HAVE the saddle, which includes both loins, trimmed for roasting. Sprinkle it with salt and roast it in a moderately hot oven (375°f.) for from 45 to 50 minutes, the rare stage. Arrange the potatoes and the artichoke bottoms, both sliced, in alternating layers in a buttered baking dish. Sprinkle generously with butter. Bake in a moderate oven (375°f.) until the potatoes are three quarters cooked. Ten minutes before the saddle is done, place it on the potatoes and finish roasting. Carve the meat and serve it in the baking dish with the potatoes. The pan gravy from the roast is served separately.

Selle d'Agneau Farcie Rôtie
(Roast Stuffed Saddle of Lamb)

1 saddle of lamb, 5 pounds
1 onion
½ pound ground lamb
1 cup soft bread crumbs
2 eggs
1 tablespoon cream
1 tablespoon chopped parsley

HAVE the saddle boned from the inside, so that the skin remains intact. Season the meat inside and out with salt and pepper.

Brown the onions lightly in a little butter and mix them well with the remaining ingredients. Season with salt and pepper to taste.

Use the stuffing to fill the saddle. Reconstruct its original shape and tie the saddle securely with kitchen string. Lay the meat in a roasting pan on a mixture of 2 carrots and 2 onions, both sliced, a bay leaf, and a sprig of thyme. Roast the meat in a moderately hot oven (375°f.) for from 45 to 55 minutes, basting it

178

frequently and adding a little stock or water from time to time, as necessary.

Arrange the meat on a serving platter. Strain the pan gravy, forcing through as much of the solid matter as possible. Skim off any excess fat and serve the gravy separately.

Gigot de Mouton Bouilli à l'Anglaise
(Boiled Leg of Mutton)

HAVE the butcher remove the pelvic bone from the leg and shorten the leg in the region of the tibia. Trim away skin and surplus fat and wrap the leg in a large piece of cheesecloth generously buttered and dredged with flour. Put the meat in a large kettle with boiling salted water to cover. Add 2 carrots, the onions, the bouquet, and the garlic, and simmer the meat for about 1 hour. Tie the remaining carrots, the turnips, and the celery, cut in large pieces, in a cheesecloth bag and add them to the pot. Cook the meat for about 1 hour longer, until it is very tender. If necessary, the vegetables may be removed from the pot at this time, and the meat returned to the heat for longer cooking.

To serve, unwrap the leg of mutton and arrange it on a large serving platter. Garnish the platter with the vegetables. Serve separately butter sauce made with mutton broth instead of water and finished with capers and parsley.

1 leg of mutton, 8 pounds
12 carrots
2 onions stuck with 2 cloves
bouquet of 2 sprigs of parsley,
  1 sprig of thyme, ½ bay leaf,
  2 garlic cloves
8 white turnips
1 head of celery
1 tablespoon capers
1 teaspoon chopped parsley

Côtes d'Agneau Grillées
(Broiled Lamb Chops)

CHOOSE loin or rib chops cut as thick as desired and brush them with clarified butter. Broil the chops until one side is richly

179

browned, then turn them and broil the other side until the juices appear on the surface of the cooked side in little globules. Baste the chops with clarified butter to keep them from drying out, and do not salt them until they are cooked. If the salt is applied to the raw meat, it draws off the juices. Lamb chops are not served rare, like beef steaks, but they should not be overcooked, and the inside should be faintly pink and very juicy.

Rib chops may be cut thick and trimmed so that the exposed bone may be covered with a paper frill at serving time. These are the "French" lamb chops. English chops contain the kidney and are cut from the saddle, or double loin. They are also cut thick.

Côtelettes d'Agneau Réforme
(*Breaded Lamb Chops*)

6 rib chops
¼ cup ground cooked ham
¼ cup bread crumbs
white of a hard-cooked egg
½ cup julienne of mushrooms
¼ cup julienne of truffles
¼ cup julienne of cooked ox tongue
1 gherkin
½ cup bottled *sauce Escoffier*

SAUTÉ the rib chops in hot clarified butter to a good brown on both sides. Mix the ham and bread crumbs and pat the mixture firmly against both sides of the chops. Brown the coating on both sides and arrange the chops on a serving platter. Heat the *sauce Escoffier* in a small pan and add the egg white, mushrooms, truffles, ox tongue, and the gherkin, also cut into strips. Bring the sauce to a boil and pour it over the chops. Serve with a dish of currant jelly.

Mixed Grill

4 lamb chops
4 lamb kidneys
CONTINUED

ARRANGE the chops, kidneys, bacon, and sausages on a broiling pan and broil them to the desired degree of done-ness: the bacon should be crisp, the sausages throughly cooked, and the chops and the kidneys cooked through, but not overcooked.

Cut a slice from each end of the tomatoes and dip the cut end of the tomatoes in seasoned flour. Brown them briskly in hot fat. Remove the tomatoes to a serving platter and brown the mushrooms in the same fat. Put the mushrooms on the tomatoes. Arrange the broiled meats on the platter and pour over them a sauce made by mixing the melted butter with the lemon juice and parsley. Serves 4.

4 slices bacon
4 sausages
4 tomatoes
4 mushrooms
juice of ½ lemon
1 teaspoon chopped parsley
1 tablespoon butter, melted

Brochettes d'Agneau à la Turque
(*Turkish Skewered Lamb*)

CUT the lamb into small, uniform squares, and brown them quickly in hot clarified butter. Sprinkle with salt and pepper. Brown the mushrooms in the same butter and reserve them. Cut each strip of bacon into three and brown the squares.

Fill 4 skewers with the ingredients prepared, beginning and ending with a mushroom and putting the mint leaves next to the meat. Roll the skewers in bread crumbs, sprinkle them with melted butter, and brown quickly under the broiler, turning to brown all sides evenly. Serve with rice pilaff. Serves 2.

½ pound tender lamb
8 mushrooms
4 slices bacon
8 mint leaves
1 tablespoon fine bread crumbs
1 tablespoon butter

Ragoût d'Agneau Printanier
(*Spring Lamb Stew*)

HAVE the lamb cut into uniform cubes and brown the cubes over high heat in the clarified butter. Pour off the excess fat and reserve it. Season the meat with salt and pepper to taste

1½ pounds lean lamb
1 tablespoon clarified butter
½ tablespoon flour
CONTINUED

bouquet of 1 sprig of parsley,
   1 stalk of celery, half a sprig
   of thyme, a bit of bay leaf
2 garlic cloves
1 tomato
6 small onions
2 white turnips
2 carrots
½ cup freshly shelled peas
½ cup cut string beans
6 small new potatoes

and sprinkle it with flour. Cook, stirring, for 2 minutes, to brown the flour. Add water or stock to cover all but one third of the meat and bring the liquid to a boil, stirring constantly to prevent scorching. Add the bouquet, the crushed garlic, and the tomato, coarsely chopped. Simmer the stew gently. In the reserved fat, brown the small onions and the turnips, cut lengthwise in 4 pieces. Sprinkle with a pinch of sugar to glaze the vegetables. Add the vegetables to the stew. Add the carrots, also cut lengthwise, the peas, and the string beans, and cook slowly for 40 minutes. Add the potatoes and continue to cook the stew until the meat is tender and the potatoes cooked through. Discard the garlic and the bouquet and skim off any excess fat. Sprinkle with chopped parsley and serve very hot.

Ragoût d'Agneau Irlandais
(*Irish Lamb Stew*)

2 pounds boned shoulder of
   lamb
4 potatoes
4 onions
bouquet of 4 sprigs parsley, 2
   stalks of celery, 1 sprig
   thyme, ½ bay leaf
Worcestershire sauce

HAVE the lamb cut into 1½-inch cubes. Cover the meat with water, bring the water to a boil, and drain it. Fill a saucepan with alternating layers of meat, sliced potatoes, and sliced onions. Season with salt and pepper and lay the bouquet in the center. Add water to cover, and bring the liquid to a boil. Cover the pan and cook the stew in a moderate oven (350°f.) for about 2 hours, until the meat is tender. Discard the bouquet and skim off the excess fat. If a thicker sauce is desired, 1 tablespoon of flour mixed with a little water may be added. Shake and roll the pan over direct heat until the sauce is thick and the vegetables and meat are well coated. Add a dash of Worcestershire, adjust the seasoning with salt and pepper, and dust with chopped parsley. Serve hot.

Haricots de Mouton
(*Lamb Stew with Dried Beans*)

SOAK the dried beans overnight in water to cover; drain them; cover them with fresh water; cook them for 20 minutes; and drain.

Cut the lean salt pork into dice and brown the dice in a skillet. Remove the dice to a flame-proof casserole fitted with a lid. Cut the lamb into large pieces and brown it in the skillet. Season it with salt and pepper and transfer it to the casserole. Pour off all but 1 tablespoon of the fat in the skillet. Add the chopped onion and cook slowly for 10 minutes. Stir in the flour, cook for a minute or two, and add 4 cups of water. Cook, stirring, until the mixture is smooth and boiling. Pour the sauce over the meat, add the garlic and the bouquet, and again bring the liquid to the boil. Add the beans, drained, and cover the casserole. Cook the stew in a moderately slow oven (300°f.) for about 2 hours, until the meat is tender. Remove and discard the bouquet and skim off the excess fat. Sprinkle with chopped parsley and serve hot.

1 cup dry white beans
2 pounds lamb
½ pound lean salt pork
1 onion
1½ teaspoons flour
2 garlic cloves
bouquet of 2 sprigs of parsley, 1 sprig of thyme, a bit of bay leaf.

Sauté d'Agneau au Curry
(*Lamb Curry*)

HAVE the lamb cut into large pieces and brown them in a skillet in clarified butter. Season with salt and pepper, sprinkle with flour, and remove the meat to a flame-proof casserole. Put

3 pounds lean lamb
clarified butter
1½ teaspoons flour
CONTINUED

183

1 large onion
1 tablespoon curry powder
4 cups brown stock
3 garlic cloves
1 cup cooked tomatoes
bouquet of 2 sprigs of parsley,
    2 stalks of celery, ½ sprig of
    thyme and half a bay leaf

the casserole in the oven for 5 minutes. Chop the onion and cook it in the fat remaining in the skillet until it is well browned. Stir in the curry powder and simmer for 1 minute. Add the brown stock and bring the liquid to the boiling point. Pour the sauce over the meat in the casserole and add the garlic, the tomatoes, and the bouquet. Cook slowly for 1½ hours, until the meat is tender. Skim off the excess fat on the surface and remove the meat to a serving dish. Strain the pan juices through a sieve, pressing through as much as possible of the solids, and reduce over high heat to a thick sauce. Return the meat to the sauce, heat it thoroughly, and serve hot, with boiled rice.

Rognons d'Agneau Turbigo
(*Lamb Kidneys Turbigo*)

6 lamb kidneys
6 rounds of bread
6 large mushrooms
12 small sausages
½ cup white wine
½ cup tomato sauce
1 tablespoon brown stock
lemon juice

WASH and split the kidneys, and with a small curved scissors cut out the tubes and membranes. Brown the kidneys quickly in hot clarified butter. Remove them from the pan. Brown the rounds of bread separately in hot clarified butter and arrange the croutons on a heated serving platter. Brown the mushrooms in hot butter and cook the sausages. Put each kidney on a crouton and top it with a mushroom. Put the sausages in the center of the platter. Pour off the excess fat from the pan in which the kidneys were cooked. Add the wine, tomato sauce, and stock, and cook, stirring, for a few minutes, until the sauce is very thick. Add a few drops of lemon juice and a pinch of chopped parsley and pour this sauce over the kidneys. Serves 3.

Rognons Sautés Chasseur
(*Lamb Kidneys with Mushrooms*)

SPLIT the kidneys in half and cut out the fatty core and the tubes, using a small curved scissors. Remove the membrane. Wash the kidneys thoroughly and drain and dry them. Cut them into slices and brown the slices quickly on both sides in hot clarified butter. Sprinkle with the shallots, toss over the heat for a few seconds, and add the flour. Stir for a minute or two, add the Madeira and the white wine, and bring the liquid to a boil, stirring constantly. Add the mushrooms, browned in butter, and salt and pepper to taste. Simmer for 2 or 3 minutes and serve hot, sprinkled with parsley. Serves 3.

6 lamb kidneys
1 tablespoon clarified butter
½ teaspoon chopped shallots
½ tablespoon flour
½ cup Madeira
½ cup white wine
½ teaspoon chopped parsley
¾ pound mushrooms

Pork

Roast Pork

FOR roasting choose the pork shoulder or leg, which may be boned and stuffed, the fresh ham, or the loin. The meat should be well marbled and the fat firm and white. The young animal has grayish pink flesh; the older animal's flesh is deeper in color and less finely grained. Season the meat with salt and pepper, and roast it on a rack in a moderately slow oven (300°f.) for 30 minutes per pound, until the meat is well done and very tender. Pork must always be thoroughly cooked, but it must not be allowed to dry out. Serve with applesauce.

ROAST suckling pig is a classic meat course at Christmas dinner. The pig should be about 1½ months old, and should weigh from 12 to 15 pounds.

To carve the piglet, make a long cut from the shoulders to the legs on each side of the backbone. Remove the loin fillets by running the knife under it, close against the carcass. Slice the meat on a slight diagonal. Cut off the legs and shoulders and slice them as you would the corresponding cuts of lamb.

Cochon de Lait Rôti
(*Roasted Milk-Fed Pig*)

1 piglet, 12–15 pounds
1½ pounds prunes
10 apples
1 pound fresh almonds

SOAK the prunes in water to cover overnight and cook them until they are barely tender. Remove and discard the pits. Shell the almonds and blanch them by dropping them in boiling water for a moment so that the skins may easily be slipped off. Peel, core, and slice the apples and cook them in a little butter in a skillet until they begin to look translucent. Add the prepared prunes and almonds and blend gently. Season this stuffing with salt and pepper and cool it.

Fill the piglet with the cooled stuffing and sew the opening with kitchen thread. Rub the pig with salt, pepper, and powdered thyme. Put a block of wood in the mouth to hold it open. Skewer the hind legs backwards and the forelegs forewards, and tie securely. Slash the skin at intervals on both sides and spread with a little fat. Roast on a rack in a baking pan in a moderate oven (350°f.) If the pig is stuffed, allow 18 minutes per pound; if it is not stuffed, it should cook in 15 minutes per pound. The meat should be very well done and the skin crisp and golden brown. Baste with the pan drippings every 15 minutes.

To give the skin a spicy tang, brush it before

the last 15 minutes of roasting with a paste made of dry mustard and water.

Remove the pig to a serving platter and put a red apple in its mouth. The pig may be further adorned with a necklace of raw cranberries.

Skim the fat from the roasting pan, add a little hot water, and deglaze the pan by stirring in all the brown bits that cling to it. Cook the sauce for a minute or two and strain it into a sauceboat.

Jambon de Porc Frais Braisé
(Braised Fresh Ham)

REMOVE the skin and the excess fat from the ham and rub it well with salt, powdered thyme, and crushed bay leaf. Let the ham stand for about 3 hours to absorb the seasonings.

Put the ham, fat side up, on a rack in a roasting pan. Add white wine, Madeira, or apple cider, to a depth of 1½ inches, and the brown stock. Cover the pan and braise the ham in a moderate oven (350°f.) for about 25 minutes per pound. Baste frequently with the pan drippings. About 30 minutes before the time is up, spread the ham with a paste made of dry mustard and prepared mustard. Continue to cook, basting frequently, until the meat is thoroughly cooked and very tender. Remove the ham to a carving platter. Skim off and discard the fat in the roasting pan and strain the gravy into a sauceboat.

1 fresh ham, 10–12 pounds
white wine, Madeira, or apple cider
1 cup brown stock
dry mustard, prepared mustard

Côtes de Porc
(Pork Chops)

PORK chops are cut from the loin or rib end of the loin. The center loin chops have a greater proportion of meat to bone and fat, and are the most choice and the most expensive. Pork steaks are cut from the leg or shoulder, and are usually braised.

Côtes de Porc à la Flamande
(Braised Pork Chops)

2 pork chops, 1 inch thick
1 onion
½ cup white wine
½ cup stock or water
½ tablespoon butter
½ tablespoon flour
1 teaspoon French mustard

CHOOSE thick, reasonably lean chops. Season them, brown them in hot clarified butter in a skillet, and remove them to a flame-proof casserole fitted with a lid. Pour off most of the fat in the skillet, leaving just enough to cook the onion, sliced. Add the white wine and the stock or water and cook, stirring, for a minute. Pour the sauce over the chops, bring it again to the boil, cover the casserole, and braise the chops in a moderately slow oven (300°f.) for from 1 to 2 hours, until the meat is very tender. Pork must always be thoroughly cooked. Remove the chops to a serving platter. Strain the pan juices and skim off the excess fat.

Melt the butter, stir in the flour, and cook the *roux* for a minute or two. Stir in the strained pan juices and cook, stirring, until the sauce is thick and smooth. Simmer the sauce gently for 10 minutes. Add the prepared mustard and adjust the seasoning. Pour the sauce over the chops and serve hot. Serves 2.

Côtes de Porc Charcutière
(Pork Chops Delicatessen Style)

4 pork chops, ½ inch thick
1 onion
1 tablespoon flour
CONTINUED

BROWN the chops in a little butter and remove them to a warm platter. In the fat remaining in the pan, cook the onion, chopped, until it is soft. Stir in the flour, and cook, stirring, until the mixture begins to brown. Gradually add the wine and the stock, and cook, stirring, until the sauce is smooth and thickened. Add the mustard (or vinegar, if desired) and the sliced gherkins, and adjust the seasoning. Return the chops to the pan and simmer all together for a few minutes. Serves 2.

¾ cup white wine
¾ cup brown stock
2 teaspoons prepared mustard
1 cup sliced gherkins

Basses Côtes de Porc Diablées
(*Deviled Spareribs*)

CHOOSE meaty spareribs, and have the butcher cut them into 2-rib portions. Mix the mustard with enough Worcestershire sauce to make a paste. Add the oil, ketchup, and Tabasco to taste and mix well. Marinate the spareribs in this sauce for 1 hour. Broil the ribs very slowly, basting them frequently with the marinade, until they are crisp, browned, and thoroughly cooked, for 1 hour or longer. Turn the ribs from time to time to ensure even cooking. Serves 2 as a main course.

1½ pounds spareribs
2 teaspoons dry mustard
Worcestershire sauce
1 tablespoon olive oil
1 tablespoon ketchup
Tabasco sauce
bread crumbs

Jambon de Virginie
(*Baked Virginia Ham*)

A VIRGINIA HAM, or aged country-style ham, requires special preparation before it can be cooked. This pre-cooking is sometimes done by the packer, and one should carefully read the information given on the label. If the label indicates that the ham has not been pre-cooked, soak it for 2 days, changing the water twice daily, and scrub it carefully. Cover it with fresh water and simmer it for 30 minutes to the pound. The ham is done when the iliac bone, near the shank, can be readily moved.

Skim the fat from the surface of the stock and let the meat cool in the liquid. Peel off the skin and trim the fat, leaving a generous, uniform layer. Sprinkle with brown sugar spiced with powdered cloves, moisten with a little sherry, and put the ham in a moderate oven (350°f.) to brown the crust. Serve hot or cold, in very thin slices.

Tenderized, or pre-cooked hams, require no boiling, and may be glazed like the Virginia ham.

Jambon en Croûte à l'Ancienne
(*Cold Ham in Crust*)

1 baked ham
pâte à foncer
1 carrot
1 onion
1 stalk of celery
½ pound mushrooms
   duxelles
2 tablespoons chopped truffles
½ cup brown sauce
1½ cups Madeira wine

GLAZE and bake the ham as for *jambon de Virginie*. Use brown sugar, dry mustard, and Madeira to make the glaze.

Prepare the *pâte à foncer,* or pie dough, using 6 cups of flour and increasing the remaining ingredients proportionately. Roll the dough out on a lightly floured board into a large sheet ¼ inch thick and large enough to envelope the ham. Chill it.

Chop the carrot, onion, and celery, and stew them in butter with a pinch of thyme and bay leaf, salt and pepper. To this *mirepoix* add the mushroom *duxelles,* truffles, brown sauce, and Madeira. Cook the mixture until it is reduced to a soft paste. Cool the paste and spread it over the ham.

Lay the ham on the rolled-out dough and envelop it neatly. Trim off the excess dough and roll it out again. This dough may be cut into leaves and other decorative shapes to garnish the ham; or the leaves may be made from *pâté feuilletée.* Brush the leaves with beaten egg so that they will bake to a shining golden brown. Cut a few small decorative slashes in the top to release the steam and keep the crust from buckling. Bake the ham in a very hot oven (450°f.) for about 10 minutes, reduce the heat to moderate (350°f.), and continue to bake until the crust is delicately browned. Serve hot with Madeira sauce or cold with cranberry sauce or fresh pineapple.

La Potée Alsacienne
(*Potted Pork with Beans*)

Soak the beans for 2 hours, in lukewarm water to cover, with the marjoram and rosemary. In a heavy pan melt the butter, and in it brown the onions and garlic, both sliced. Add the meat; the cabbage, sliced and parboiled; the cauliflower, broken into flowerets; the peas; the diced string beans; and the celery, carrots, and potatoes, all sliced. Add the juniper berries, a pinch of ginger, and a little salt and freshly ground black pepper. Add water to cover all generously. Cook the *potée* for 3 hours, very slowly. Cover the pan tightly and shake it from time to time to prevent scorching. Do not stir the mixture and thus mash the vegetables. Serve the vegetable mixture—it will be quite dry—with the sliced pork and with cooked sausages or ham, if desired. Pass horse-radish sauce separately.

2 cups dried white beans
1 sprig marjoram
1 sprig rosemary
2 tablespoons butter
2 onions
1 garlic clove
1 pound lean salt pork, or smoked butt, or ham shoulder
1 small cabbage
1 cauliflower
2 cups green peas
2 cups string beans
1 head of celery
3 carrots
3 potatoes
6 juniper berries

A boiled dinner is the classic mainstay of the sturdy peasants of Burgundy.

Potée Bourguignonne
(*Potted Pork and Vegetables*)

1 smoked butt, 2 pounds
1 pound piece of lean salt pork or bacon
1 fresh pig's knuckle
3 carrots
2 white turnips
3 leeks, white part only
½ pound string beans
1 small head cabbage
4 potatoes

PUT the meat in a stock pot and add the carrots and turnips, peeled and split lengthwise, the leeks, tied together, and the whole string beans. Add water to cover all generously, and simmer for 1 hour. Season the broth with freshly ground black pepper and salt as needed. Add the cabbage, cut in quarters, and the potatoes, peeled but left whole, and cook until the vegetables are tender.

Strain the broth into a soup tureen or individual soup plates over thin slices of French bread. Cover the tureen for 2 minutes and serve the soup as a first course.

Slice the smoked butt and the salt pork and cut the pig's knuckle into pieces. Arrange the meat on a serving platter and garnish the platter with the vegetables.

Choucroute Alsacienne
(*Sauerkraut with Pork*)

2 pounds sauerkraut
3 slices bacon
1 smoked pig's knuckle
1 garlic sausage
1 pound lean salt pork
white stock
white wine
cheesecloth bag containing 1 carrot, 1 onion stuck with a clove, ½ sprig of thyme, 1 sprig of parsley, 1 stalk of
CONTINUED

SOAK the sauerkraut in cold water for 1 hour and drain and rinse it thoroughly. Pull it to pieces with the fingers and season it with salt and pepper to taste. Lay the bacon strips on the bottom of a heavy pan fitted with a lid. Add half the sauerkraut, the cheesecloth bag of herbs and seasonings, and the pig's knuckle. Cover this with the remaining sauerkraut and put the salt pork and the garlic sausage on top. Fill the pan two thirds full with a mixture of equal parts of water or stock and white wine. Cover the pan with a piece of buttered paper cut to fit and bring the liquid to a boil. Adjust the lid and put the pan in a moderately slow oven (300°f.). After 1½ hours, remove the garlic sausage and reserve it. Cover the pan again and continue to cook slowly for 2½ hours longer.

To serve, discard the cheesecloth bag. Put the sauerkraut in the center of the platter and surround it with the pork and sausages, sliced, and the pig's knuckle cut into pieces. Poached frankfurters may also be served, or thin slices of ham.

celery, 1 teaspoon juniper berries, 6 or 8 peppercorns, and a bit of bay leaf

Pieds de Porc Sainte Menehould

WASH the pig's feet thoroughly and put them in a flame-proof, oven-proof pan. Add the vegetables, the seasonings, and the bouquet, and enough water to cover all three times. Bring the water to a boil, cover the pan tightly, and braise the pig's feet in a moderate oven (350°f.) for from 4 to 6 hours, until the meat is very tender and the bones soft enough to be eaten. Cool the meat in its own juices until they are almost all absorbed. Wipe the pig's feet dry and dredge them with fine bread crumbs. Sprinkle with melted butter and bake in a moderate oven (350°f.) until the crumbs are browned. This does not require a sauce.

6 pig's feet
2 carrots
2 onions
12 white peppercorns
3 cloves
bouquet made of 1 stalk of celery, 1 sprig of parsley, 1 sprig of thyme, a bit of bay leaf
2 tablespoons melted butter
bread crumbs

Pieds de Porc Grillés
(*Broiled Pig's Feet*)

CLEAN the pig's feet thoroughly and poach them until tender, about 3 or 4 hours, in salted boiling water or in the seasoned liquid given

6 pig's feet
1 tablespoon dry mustard
CONTINUED

3 tablespoons fine bread
  crumbs

for *pieds de porc Sainte Menehould*. The bones
are not eaten, and the cooking time is therefore
shorter than for the latter dish. Pig's feet may
sometimes be purchased pre-cooked and ready
for broiling.

Wipe the pig's feet dry and brush them with
a paste made of the dry mustard and water.
Dredge them with bread crumbs, sprinkle with
melted butter, and brown the crumbs under the
broiler. Serve with any pungent sauce.

Chou Farci
(*Stuffed Cabbage*)

1 head of cabbage
2 shallots
1 pound sausage meat
2 cups chopped mushrooms
2 teaspoons chopped parsley
2 slices fat pork
1 carrot
1 onion
2 cloves
bouquet of 1 sprig parsley, 1
  sprig thyme, and 1 stalk
  celery

PARBOIL the cabbage in salted water to cover for
10 minutes and cool it in running cold water.
Drain it well. Gently force the top leaves apart
and cut out the center of the head, leaving a
hollow. Simmer the shallots, chopped, in a little butter, add the mushrooms, sausage meat,
and parsley, and season this mixture with salt
and freshly ground black pepper to taste. Stuff
the cabbage, reshape it, and tie it with kitchen
string. Put the fat pork on the bottom of a
heavy pan or casserole. Add the carrot and
onion, both sliced, the cloves, and the bouquet.
Lay the cabbage on this bed and add about 3
cups water. Cover the pan and cook the cabbage in a moderately slow oven (300°f.) for 2
hours. Add a little more water, if necessary,
after the first hour.

Remove the cabbage to a serving dish and
cut away the string. Strain the cooking liquid,
skim off the excess fat, and pour the sauce over
the cabbage.

Andouilles et Andouillettes Grillées
(*Chitterlings*)

CHITTERLINGS are made of the thoroughly cleaned intestines of the pig. Reserve several of the larger intestines and cut the rest into small strips. Fill the larger intestines with the strips, tie these sausages firmly at both ends, and poach them in salt water for 2 hours or until they are very tender. Cool them in the cooking liquid, brush them with butter, and broil them until crisp.

In France, the *andouilles,* or larger intestines, are also smoked. These are broiled and served with mustard, mashed potatoes, and cauliflower. The best known variety of these delicacies is the *andouille de Vire,* which is imported by some fine American stores.

Boudin Grillé
(*Broiled Blood Sausage*)

PRICK the blood sausages well and brush them with melted butter. Broil them slowly until they are very crisp, and serve them hot, with mustard sauce and apple slices browned in butter and sprinkled with sugar and cinnamon.

Fromage de Tête de Porc
(*Headcheese*)

HAVE the butcher bone the pig's head completely and remove the skin in one piece. Only the eyes and the snout should be discarded. Cut the meat into large pieces and roll them in salt.

1 pig's head
2 bay leaves
2 sprigs of thyme

CONTINUED

195

2 sprigs of parsley

12 peppercorns

½ teaspoon allspice

4 stalks of celery, with the
green tops

2 onions, each stuck with 1
clove

Put the salted meat and the skin in an earthen-ware bowl, add the seasonings, and let the mixture stand in a cool place for 24 hours.

Remove the meat from the brine and wipe it dry. Put it in a large saucepan and add cold water barely to cover. Tie the herbs and seasonings in a cheesecloth bag and put the bag in the pan. Bring the mixture to a boil, cover the pan, and simmer gently until the meat is very tender, about 3 hours. Drain off the liquid and reserve it. Discard the bag of spices and herbs.

Line a round or rectangular mold with the pig skin. Cut the meat into small squares and fill the mold. Adjust the seasoning of the cooking stock; it should be very peppery. Pour the stock over the meat and cover the mold with a heavy weight to keep the meat from floating. Chill until firm and serve cold, in slices.

Crépinettes
(*Home Made Sausage*)

½ pound fresh back fat pork

2 pound fresh lean pork

pork intestine cover

2 tablespoons cognac

truffles

chopped parsley

PUT the meat through the finest blade of the meat grinder and season it highly with salt and freshly ground black pepper. Add the cognac and chopped truffles and parsley to taste. Shape the sausage meat into flat portions weighing 3 ounces each. Cover each portion with a piece of pork intestine cover, or *crépine,* and broil or brown in hot, clarified butter. The meat must be thoroughly cooked, but it should not be dry.

VI

VEGETABLES *and* SALADS

VEGETABLES FOR GOURMETS

Modern methods of transportation and preservation make it possible for us to eat any vegetable we prefer at any time, in season and out. But great as this privilege is, to eat vegetables fresh from the garden is a still greater one. Indeed, I am convinced that such vegetables as corn, peas, asparagus, and tomatoes are never fully enjoyed otherwise! Whether the gourmet is fortunate enough to have access to a garden or not, the word "enjoy" is still the keynote to his approach to vegetables. After all, no matter how many valuable minerals and vitamins vegetables may contain, vegetables uneaten on the plate do nobody any good! The cook's duty, therefore, is to prepare vegetables so that they can be enjoyed, so that they can be eaten with pleasure, not because they are good for us, but simply because they taste good.

The first and most important rule of vegetable cookery is this: never overcook any vegetable. Overcooking destroys, or at best alters unfavorably, natural flavor and fresh texture. Vegetables should be cooked until they are just tender, and no longer. Some of them, like string beans, cauliflower, and cabbage, taste best when they are still crisp. Often the only adornment needed to bring out the flavor of vegetables is butter, salt, and pepper, but other spices and chopped fresh herbs may also be used for seasoning, and variety may be achieved by the use of lemon juice, a tart butter sauce, like Hollandaise, or a creamy sauce of the Béchamel family.

Examples are given here of many vegetable preparations; a little imagination will help the cook to adapt to other vegetables the methods described.

The sauces referred to in the recipes that follow will be found in the index.

Artichokes

FRESH young artichokes can be recognized by their bright green color and tightly closed petals. The French variety is globular in shape, the Italian smaller and cone-shaped.

Wash the artichokes thoroughly in a large amount of cold water, swishing them vigorously to remove any dirt lodged in the petals. Cut off the stem and, if necessary, any discolored outer leaves. With kitchen string, tie a thin slice of lemon to the exposed bottom to prevent it from blackening. Cook in salted boiling water generously to cover. Very young artichokes take about 25 minutes; older heads will require from 45 minutes to 1 hour. The artichoke is done when the petals can easily be pulled from the head. Drain the artichokes well and serve hot, with Hollandaise sauce or melted butter, or chilled, with *sauce vinaigrette*.

Allow one French or two Italian artichokes per serving. To eat the artichoke, remove the petals, one by one, and dip them into the sauce. At this point, the fingers are the only possible utensil. Scrape the edible flesh from the petal with the teeth, and discard the hard portion. Remove and discard the hairy choke that hides the bottom, which is the choicest part of the vegetable, and finish the bottom, now using a fork.

Court-Bouillon Blanc pour Légumes
(Court-Bouillon for Vegetables)

Mix 1 tablespoon of flour to a paste with a little cold water and stir it into 2 quarts cold water. Bring the mixture to a boil, stirring. Add the juice of 1 lemon and 2 teaspoons salt. Use this *court-bouillon* instead of plain water for cooking artichoke bottoms, cardoon, and salsify.

Jerusalem Artichokes

The Jerusalem artichoke, or *topinambour,* is not an artichoke at all, but a tuber that somewhat resembles the potato, although it is sweeter and more watery. Cook them in salted water to cover for from 20 to 25 minutes until they are tender. Drain well. Peel the tubers and serve seasoned with butter, salt, and pepper. The cooked *topinambours* may be sliced, browned in butter, and sprinkled with chopped parsley and lemon juice.

Asparagus

Only the tender portion of the asparagus spear is served as a vegetable, although the woody end can contribute some flavor to the soup pot. The stalk breaks readily at the point where the toughness begins. Snap off the ends and peel the stalks below the tips. Wash the tips well to dislodge any dirt that may be hiding there.

Young asparagus will cook in from 15 to 20 minutes; it should be barely tender, not limp. To cook the ends without overcooking the tips, tie the asparagus in convenient bundles of 6 stalks each, and stand the bundles upright in a pan of boiling water. When the pan is covered, the tips cook in steam while the stalks boil. If the bottom of a double boiler is used as a pan, the top of the boiler may be inverted to serve as a cover.

Older asparagus may have a bitter flavor. It should be cooked in a generous amount of boiling salted water, which may be changed toward the end of the cooking time to eliminate any bitterness.

Serve hot asparagus immediately, with melted butter, *sauce Hollandaise,* or bread crumbs browned in melted butter.

If the asparagus is to be served cold, chill it under running water to stop the cooking process, drain well on a napkin, and refrigerate until serving time. Serve cold asparagus with *sauce vinaigrette* or any flavorful French dressing.

Beets

BEETS should be cooked with their skins intact, so that they do not lose their bright red color through "bleeding." Wash the beets thoroughly but carefully. Do not cut off the root, and leave an inch or two of stem intact. Cook beets in boiling salted water in a covered pan for from 30 to 45 minutes, until they are tender. Only very young, small red beets should be served. Drain the beets, cool them under running cold water, and slip off the skins and stems.

Fresh beets may be cut into slices or dice, and reheated with butter, salt, and pepper. Lemon juice, vinegar, and chopped chives or chopped parsley may also be used as seasoning.

Beet Greens

THE leaves and stems of very young, fresh beets may be cooked and served like spinach. Wash the leaves well and cook them for from 10 to 15 minutes in a covered pan. A very little boiling salted water may be added if the moisture that clings to the leaves after washing does not seem to be sufficient to prevent scorching. Drain the beet greens well, and if the liquid seems bitter in taste, rinse them with hot water. Reheat the greens and season them with butter, salt, pepper, and a dash of nutmeg, if desired. Greens may also be mixed with a little *sauce Béchamel*.

Broccoli

BROCCOLI, which the French call *choux-asperges,* or cabbage asparagus, is a plant of the cabbage species. Choose heads with bright green, compact buds, short stems, and small leaves. Soak the broccoli, head down, in salted cold water for 30 minutes to drive out any small insects that may be concealed in the buds. Trim off the tough lower portions of the stalk and strip off the leaves and the skin, peeling it upwards. If the stalks are heavy, split them without cutting into the head. Cook the broccoli in boiling salted water, standing upright in a covered pan so that the heads cook only in steam, for 15 to 20 minutes, until the stalks are barely tender. Drain well and serve hot with melted butter, *sauce Mornay, sauce Hollandaise,* or *sauce Polonaise* prepared as for cauliflower Polonaise.

Brussels Sprouts

DISCARD any browned or withered outer leaves from the tiny cabbage-like heads, trim the stems, and make a small incision in the bottom. Soak the *choux de Bruxelles* in cold salted water for 15 minutes to ensure cleanliness, and cook them in boiling salted water for from 10 to 15 minutes, until they are just tender and not too soft. Drain well and serve with melted butter or with *sauce Hollandaise.* Or toss the cooked sprouts over moderate heat in melted butter for a few minutes, until they are lightly gilded, sprinkle with salt and pepper, and serve hot.

Cabbage

ALL the numerous varieties of cabbage require the same preparation. Discard any wilted leaves and cut out the hard core. Cut the head into wedges or shred or chop the leaves coarsely. Cook the cabbage in boiling salted water, in an open pan, for from 15 to 20 minutes, until the leaves are tender but still crisp. Drain well and serve with butter, salt, and pepper, or with *sauce Mornay* or a similar cream sauce.

Red cabbage takes longer to cook, and a little vinegar or lemon juice added to the water helps to keep it red.

Cardoon

THE cardoon, or *cardon,* is a member of the artichoke family, but it looks more like coarse, prickly celery. Clean and slice the cardoon and parboil it for 5 minutes in salted boiling water. Drain it and cook it until tender in boiling *court-bouillon blanc*. Serve cardoon with *sauce Béchamel,* or one of its variations, or with a brown sauce.

Carrots

FRESH, young carrots have a delicate flavor that is not found in oversized carrots, which are likely to be fibrous and coarse. If the carrots are very young, they need not be peeled or even scraped, but may be simply washed and cooked whole in a covered pan with butter and enough water to prevent scorching. To boil carrots, use boiling salted water barely to cover. Cover the pan, and cook for from 10 to 20 minutes, depending upon the way the carrots are cut.

Carottes Vichy

WASH and scrape or peel the carrots and cut them into very thin slices. Put the slices in a flat pan and add the butter, water, and a little salt and pepper. Cover the vegetables with a buttered white paper, adjust the lid of the pan, and cook very slowly, over low heat or in the oven, for about 30 minutes. The liquid should almost completely evaporate. Sprinkle the carrots with parsley and serve hot. Serves 6.

12 carrots
2 tablespoons butter
1 cup water
2 tablespoons chopped parsley

Carottes Freneuse
(*Carrots with Turnips*)

PEEL and dice 6 carrots and enough white turnips to make 2 cups of each. Cook the vegetables separately in boiling salted water. Drain them well and press them together through a coarse sieve. Season with 2 tablespoons butter, and salt and pepper to taste. Serve hot. Serves 4.

Carottes Glacées
(*Glazed Carrots*)

WASH and scrub 24 very young, small carrots, and put them in a saucepan with enough water to cover them well. Add 1 tablespoon of butter, 1 teaspoon of sugar, and a little salt, and cover the pan tightly. Cook for from 10 to 20 minutes, stirring occasionally, until the carrots are tender and coated with the syrup. Serves 6.

Cauliflower

CAULIFLOWER of good quality is snowy white in color, and has compact, tightly closed flowerets. Soak the cauliflower in cold salted water for 30 minutes. Drain it and trim the stalk and the large leaves. A whole cauliflower will cook in boiling salted water in less than 25 minutes; the flowerets, if they are separated from the stalk, require only about 8 minutes. Cauliflower should not be overcooked; it tastes best when it is *al dente,* resistant to the teeth.

Chou-fleur Polonaise
(*Cauliflower Polonaise*)

1 head cauliflower
¼ cup butter
¼ cup fresh bread crumbs
1 hard-cooked egg

SEPARATE the cauliflower into flowerets, discarding the stalk and the outside leaves. Cook the flowerets in boiling salted water until they are barely tender, about 8 minutes. Drain thoroughly in a colander. Arrange the cauliflower in a heated vegetable dish and sprinkle it with the hard-cooked egg, chopped fine. Melt the butter and brown the bread crumbs in it. Pour the butter and crumbs over the cauliflower, and sprinkle with chopped parsley. Serves 6.

Chou-fleur au Gratin
(Cauliflower with Cheese)

CLEAN, soak, and cook a whole cauliflower (see above). Drain the cauliflower thoroughly in a colander and arrange it on a baking dish. Prepare 1 cup *sauce Béchamel* and pour the sauce over the cauliflower. Sprinkle generously with grated Swiss or Parmesan cheese and set the dish in the oven to melt and brown the cheese. Serves 6.

Celery

BECAUSE of its aromatic properties, celery is widely used as an ingredient of other dishes, but served less frequently than it should be as a vegetable for its own sake. The outer stalks of the head may be used for creamed celery after the hearts have been eaten raw or braised.

Céleri à la Crème
(Creamed Celery)

SCRAPE the celery and cut it into uniform pieces. Simmer the pieces in boiling salted water to cover for from 10 to 15 minutes, until they are tender but not soft. Drain off the cooking stock, reduce it to ½ cup, and add the milk or cream. Melt the butter, stir in the flour, and cook the *roux* for a minute or two. Add the milk and stock, and cook, stirring, until the

4 cups cut celery
1 tablespoon butter
2 tablespoons flour
½ cup milk or cream

sauce is smooth and thickened. Return the drained celery to the sauce, reheat it, and adjust the seasoning with salt, pepper, and cayenne or paprika. Serve hot. Serves 6.

Céleri Braisé
(*Braised Celery*)

6 hearts of celery
beef or chicken stock
3 tablespoons butter
juice of 1 lemon
1 tablespoon chopped parsley

WASH and trim the celery, reserving the leaves for another use. Parboil the bunches in water to cover for 5 minutes, drain them, and lay them side by side in a flat pan. Add rich beef or chicken stock barely to cover, adjust the lid of the pan, and simmer the celery slowly for about 40 minutes, until it is tender. Remove the celery to a serving dish and reduce the pan juices over high heat to a scant ¼ cup in volume. Stir in the butter, lemon juice, and parsley, and pour the sauce over the celery. Serves 6.

Chestnut Purée

A PURÉE of chestnuts is the invariable accompaniment to elegant dishes of game and game birds. Several ways of shelling chestnuts make this tedious job less difficult. My favorite is to cut the nuts in half and shake them for a minute in hot, deep fat. The nuts may then be lifted from the fat with a skimmer and the shells and skins easily removed with a sharp pointed knife. Or you may follow this method: slit the nuts on the convex side with a sharp-pointed knife. Cover them with cold water and bring the water to a boil. Remove the nuts from the water one by one and use the knife to lift off shell and skin.

To cook the shelled nuts, cover them with stock or water and add 2 stalks of celery and a little salt and pepper. Simmer the nuts, covered, for 30 minutes or more, until they are tender. Force the nuts through a fine sieve and season the purée with hot milk or cream, butter, and salt and pepper to taste.

Corn

If corn is young and fresh as it ought to be, with plump, soft kernels that spurt milk when cut, it should cook in no more than 6 minutes. A cup of milk may be added to each gallon of the boiling water used to cook the corn, but neither salt nor sugar should be used at this stage. Butter, salt, and pepper are applied by the diner at the table.

When corn kernels are required for fritters or another dish, they should be scraped from the cob with a corn-scraper, which is designed to take only the pulp and leave the skin. Otherwise, a sharp knife may be used to cut off half the kernels, and the back of the blade used to scrape out the remaining pulp without including the skin. An average ear of corn yields about ½ cup corn pulp.

Corn in Cream

Cook and scrape a dozen ears of young corn. Season the pulp with salt and pepper and stir in 2 tablespoons of heavy cream. Pour the corn into a baking dish, dot it with 2 tablespoons of butter, and bake in a moderate oven until the butter melts and the corn begins to brown. Serves 6–8.

Corn Fritters

1½ cups freshly scraped corn
  pulp
3 egg yolks
1½ tablespoons flour
1 teaspoon baking powder

BEAT the egg yolks and stir in the corn, flour, and baking powder. Season with a scant teaspoon of salt, and pepper to taste. Drop the mixture from a teaspoon into hot olive oil (370°f.), and brown the fritters on both sides. Drain quickly on paper toweling and serve very hot. Serves 2–3.

Cucumbers

COOKED cucumbers are a deliciously delicate vegetable. Peel them, cut them in half lengthwise, and scoop out the seeds. Slice the cucumbers uniformly and parboil them. Drain off the water, barely cover with fresh water, and add salt to taste. Cover the pan and simmer the cucumbers until they are transparent and tender. Drain and add butter and salt and pepper.

Dandelion Greens

YOUNG dandelion greens may be cooked in a generous amount of boiling salted water, well drained, and seasoned like spinach with butter, salt, and pepper.

Eggplant

CHOOSE EGGPLANT that are heavy for their size and have smooth, satiny purple skin.

Aubergine Sautée
(*Fried Eggplant*)

PEEL an eggplant and slice it ¼ inch thick. Dip the slices in milk and in flour, and brown them on both sides in hot clarified butter. Sprinkle with salt and serve hot and crisp.

Aubergine Farcie
(*Stuffed Eggplant*)

CUT the eggplant in half lengthwise and slash the cut surfaces with a sharp knife. Bake the eggplant in a moderate oven for about 10 minutes, until the flesh is soft.

Chop the onion and cook it for a few minutes in the butter. Add the celery and the mushrooms, both chopped, and simmer all together until the mixture is nearly dry.

Scoop the meat from the eggplant, leaving the shell intact. Chop the meat fine and mix it with the onions, mushrooms, and celery. Add the boiled rice, and toss well over moderate heat. Adjust the seasoning and fill the eggplant shells. Sprinkle with bread crumbs and melted butter and bake in a moderate oven (350°f.) until the topping is browned. Sprinkle with parsley and serve hot. Serves 2.

1 small eggplant
1 onion
2 tablespoons butter
1 cup boiled rice
½ pound mushrooms
2 stalks celery

Aubergine Provençale
(*Eggplant with Garlic*)

PEEL the eggplant and slice it ¼ inch thick. Wipe the slices dry and sprinkle them with salt and pepper. Brown the eggplant in the hot oil and arrange the slices on a baking dish. Sprinkle the eggplant with the garlic, finely chopped and mixed with the bread crumbs and a little chopped parsley. Bake in a hot oven (400°f.) for about 5 minutes to brown the topping lightly. Serves 4–6.

1 eggplant
1 cup oil
2 cloves garlic
1 tablespoon bread crumbs

Endive

ALTHOUGH BELGIAN ENDIVE is most commonly used in the United States as a salad green, it is a favorite vegetable in classic cuisine.

Endives au Jus
(*Braised Endive*)

2 pounds Belgian endive
¼ cup butter

WASH the endive and trim the bottom of the heads. Parboil the heads in water to cover for 5 minutes, drain them, and lay them side by side in a flat pan. Add the butter, salt and pepper, and water to cover. Adjust the lid of the pan and simmer the heads of endive slowly for about 40 minutes, until they are tender. Reduce the pan juices over high heat and serve with the endive. Serves 6.

Endives au Gratin
(*Endives with Cheese*)

2 pounds Belgian endive
¼ cup butter
2 tablespoons flour
1 cup hot milk
grated Parmesan or Swiss
   cheese

PREPARE the endive as for braised endive, above. Melt the butter, stir in the flour, and add the hot milk and the reduced pan juices. Cook the sauce, stirring, until it is smooth and thickened. Pour the sauce over the endive on a shallow baking dish, sprinkle generously with grated cheese, and brown the topping in a hot oven (400°f.). Serves 6.

Fennel

FENNEL (*finocchio* in Italian and *fenouil* in French) resembles celery in appearance, but has a distinctive licorice flavor. Fennel may be eaten raw, as a salad vegetable, or it may be prepared in any of the ways suggested for celery.

Leeks

IN FRANCE *les poireaux* are called the asparagus of the poor because they thrive in backyard gardens that could not support the special needs of the asparagus. Leeks may be cooked like asparagus, or braised like celery, and are, of course, widely used for soups.

Chilled cooked leeks, served with a thick French dressing, make an admirable hors d'oeuvre or salad course.

Lima Beans

FRESH LIMA BEANS have full, light green pods, with no trace of the yellow tinge that indicates that the pods were overripe when they were picked. Shell the beans at the last possible moment, as their flavor is elusive.

Haricots de Lima Persillés
(*Lima Beans with Parsley*)

ALLOW about ½ cup of shelled fresh lima beans for each portion. Cook the beans in boiling salted water for from 20 to 30 minutes, depending upon their size. They should be tender, but not soft. Drain well, season with butter, salt, and pepper, and sprinkle generously with chopped parsley.

Lettuce

LIKE CELERY AND ENDIVE, lettuce is far more frequently cooked in France than it is in the United States, where it appears almost exclusively in the salad bowl.

Lettuce may be boiled for about 15 minutes in a generous amount of salted water and seasoned with butter, salt, and pepper. Or it may be parboiled in water, drained, and cooked until tender in beef or chicken stock with a little added fat. Braised lettuce is used to garnish elaborate meat platters.

Laitues Braisés
(Braised Lettuce)

6 hearts of lettuce
1 carrot
1 onion
3 slices beef suet
white stock
1 tablespoon butter
1 teaspoon flour

PARBOIL the lettuce for 5 minutes in boiling salted water and drain well. Slice the carrot and onion and lay them on the beef suet in the bottom of a flat pan. Lay the lettuce hearts side by side on this bed and add white stock barely to cover, and salt and pepper to taste. Adjust the lid of the pan and braise the lettuce over low heat or in a moderate oven (350°f.) for about 30 minutes, until it is tender. Remove the lettuce to a serving dish and reduce the pan juices to ½ cup. Adjust the seasoning. Thicken the sauce with the butter kneaded to a paste with the flour, and pour it over the lettuce. Serves 6.

Mushrooms

Do NOT PEEL the oyster-white skin of fresh mushrooms unless you plan to serve them raw: much of the flavor of the mushroom is in the skin. Simply wipe the mushrooms clean with a damp cloth and cut off the bottom of the stem. Stems and peelings of older, less attractive mushrooms make an excellent addition to the stock pot.

Champignons Sautés
(*Mushrooms Sauté*)

CLEAN and trim 1½ pounds of fresh mushrooms. If the mushrooms are large, slice them vertically. Heat ½ cup of butter in a saucepan and cook the mushrooms quickly for about 2 minutes on each side. Cover the pan and shake it from time to time to prevent sticking. Add salt and pepper to taste, a dash of lemon juice, and some chopped parsley. Serves 6–8.

Champignons à la Provençale
(*Mushrooms with Garlic*)

1 teaspoon chopped parsley
juice of ½ lemon

1½ pounds mushrooms
3 tablespoons olive oil
1 onion
3 cloves of garlic

CLEAN and trim the mushrooms and toss them for a few minutes in the hot oil. Chop the onion and garlic and brown them in the oil. Season with salt and pepper and the lemon juice. Sprinkle with parsley and serve hot. Serves 6–8.

Onions

FOR boiling, choose the tiny white pearl onions. Peel them carefully and boil them gently in a large amount of salted boiling water for about 20 minutes, until they are just tender and can be pierced with a skewer or fork. Serve with melted butter or mask with *sauce Béchamel*.

Oignons Frits
(*French Fried Onions*)

PEEL large, sweet onions and cut them into ¼-inch slices. Separate the rings. Reserve the small center rings for another use. Sprinkle the larger rings with salt, dip them in flour, and fry them to a golden brown in deep, hot fat (370°f.). Drain on paper toweling. A thicker, crisp coating may be achieved by dipping the rings, one by one, in fritter batter and draining them well before frying.

Smothered Onions

PEEL large yellow onions and slice them thin. Sauté the slices very slowly in clarified butter, until they are translucent and tender, but not mushy. Serve with steak and with calf's liver.

Glazed Onions

PEEL small white or yellow onions and cook them slowly in hot butter. When the onions begin to brown, sprinkle them with sugar and continue to cook until the sugar is nearly caramelized. Add sufficient white stock to cover the onions twice, cover the pan, and cook the onions slowly until they are tender and most of the liquid has cooked away.

Peas

COOK freshly shelled peas—the fresher the better—in a small amount of boiling salted water with a few mint leaves, if desired. Tiny, young peas should cook in about 15 minutes; more mature varieties will take 25 minutes or longer. Put the peas in a serving dish, reduce the cooking liquid, if necessary, to a few tablespoons, and pour it over the peas. Season with salt, pepper, and melted butter. Or add a little *sauce Béchamel*. Allow 3 pounds of peas in the pod for 6 servings.

Petits Pois à la Française
(*Green Peas, French Style*)

¼ cup water
1 teaspoon salt
2 teaspoons sugar

4 cups freshly shelled green
  peas
1 tablespoon butter
1 heart of lettuce, shredded
12 small white onions
2 sprigs parsley

COMBINE the ingredients in a saucepan, cover the pan tightly, and simmer all together for 30 minutes or more, until the vegetables are tender. Thicken the liquid by stirring in 1 teaspoon of equal parts of butter and flour, kneaded together. Serve hot. Serves 6–8.

Petits Pois Paysanne
(*Green Peas, Country Style*)

¼ pound lean salt pork, diced
1 tablespoon butter
12 small white onions
½ tablespoon flour
4 cups freshly shelled peas
12 small carrots, sliced

PARBOIL the pork dice and brown them in the butter. Add the onions, and cook for a few minutes, until the onions begin to color. Sprinkle with the flour and add the peas and the carrots. Add sufficient chicken broth or water barely to cover the vegetables, cover the pan, and simmer gently for about 45 minutes, until the vegetables are tender. Serves 6–8.

Potatoes

No ONE has ever determined exactly how many ways there are to cook potatoes, but I am sure that the total would run to several hundred. Obviously, there is no excuse for serving this most versatile of vegetables in the same monotonous fashion day after day.

Of the basic methods of cooking potatoes—boiling, baking, and frying—boiling has the most uses, and comes first in our list.

Tiny new potatoes should be scrubbed, but not peeled, and cooked in boiling salted water until they can be easily pierced with a fork, about 20 minutes. They can be eaten skin and all, or the skins may be slipped off. Older potatoes may also be cooked in their jackets, a method that helps to retain certain nutrients. A circle of the skin should be pared away to keep the potato from bursting as it swells in cooking. If potatoes are peeled before cooking, and this is frequently necessary or convenient, they should be covered at once with cold water to prevent them from darkening on exposure to the air.

Potatoes for boiling and mashing should be waxy in contrast to the floury variety desirable for baking and frying. Long Island potatoes are typical boiling potatoes.

Pommes de Terre Purée
(*Whipped Potatoes*)

6 medium potatoes
½ cup scalded milk
2 tablespoons butter

PEEL the potatoes and cut them into uniform pieces to insure even cooking. Boil gently in salted water until soft, but do not overcook. Drain the potatoes and rub them through a sieve or ricer. Return the purée to the pan and add the butter and salt, nutmeg, and white pepper to taste. With a wooden spoon work in gradually the hot milk, adding it little by little until the purée is light, soft, and fluffy. Serves 6.

Pommes de Terre Duchesse
(*Duchess Potatoes*)

SEASON 4 cups freshly boiled, mashed potatoes with salt, pepper, and grated nutmeg to taste. Beat in ¼ cup of butter and 4 egg yolks, well beaten. This hot potato mixture may be forced through a pastry tube to make a decorative border for serving dishes; the dish is put into the oven or under the broiler to brown. Or the potatoes may be shaped with the tube in mounds on a buttered baking sheet, and baked until brown. Serves 6.

Cold *pommes duchesse* are shaped into rectangles and browned in clarified butter.

Potato Croquettes

SHAPE cold *pommes de terre duchesse* into cones and roll the cones in beaten egg and in bread crumbs. Fry them in hot deep fat (370°f.) to a golden brown.

Pommes de Terre Dauphine
(*Potato Puff Fritters*)

PEEL, boil, and mash the potatoes and combine them with the cream puff paste. There should be approximately equal volume of each. Season the mixture to taste with salt, pepper, and a little freshly grated nutmeg. Scoop up the mixture by the teaspoon and slip it off the spoon with another teaspoon into deep hot fat (390°f.) Fry until the fritters double in size and are a rich golden brown. Drain on absorbent toweling and serve at once. Serves 6.

6 medium potatoes
cream puff paste

Pommes de Terre Parisienne
(*Parisian Potatoes*)

REMOVE the skins from very tiny new potatoes by shaking them in a bag with very coarse salt. Wash the potatoes and cover them with boiling salted water. Bring the water back to the boil and drain the potatoes. Add to the pan 1 tablespoon of clarified butter for every 12 potatoes, and heat well. Return the drained potatoes to the pan and season them with salt. Cover the pan and cook slowly until the potatoes are tender, shaking the pan from time to time to brown them evenly on all sides.

Pommes de Terre Persillées
(Parsley Potatoes)

PEEL 6 medium potatoes and cut them into uniform pieces or balls. Cover with boiling salted water and cook until done. Drain the potatoes well, roll them in melted butter and in chopped parsley, and serve hot. Serves 6.

Pommes de Terre Lyonnaise
(Fried Potatoes and Onions)

3 tablespoons butter
1 onion
6 sliced boiled potatoes
1 garlic clove
2 teaspoons chopped parsley

MELT the butter in a skillet and in it cook the onion, thinly sliced, for a few minutes. Add the sliced potatoes and season them with salt and pepper. Brown the potatoes slowly on both sides. Sprinkle with parsley and with the garlic clove, finely chopped. Serve very hot. Serves 6.

Pommes de Terre Sautées
(Home-Fried Potatoes)

PEEL a strip around the middle of 6 Long Island potatoes and boil them in salted water until they are barely tender. Let the potatoes cool until they can be handled. Peel them, slice them evenly, and sauté in clarified butter until light brown. Sprinkle with chopped parsley, salt, and pepper, and serve at once. Serves 6.

Pommes de Terre au Fromage
(Potatoes au Gratin)

PEEL and slice 6 medium potatoes and cook them in ¼ cup of clarified butter until they are half done. Sprinkle with salt, pepper, and nutmeg to taste. Cover the bottom of a buttered baking dish with a layer of potatoes and sprinkle with grated Swiss or Cheddar cheese. Add another layer of potatoes, more cheese, and a little butter, until all the potatoes and about 1 cup of cheese have been used. Bake in a hot oven (400°f.) until the potatoes are tender and browned. Pour off the cooking butter and serve the potatoes in the baking dish. Serves 6.

Pommes de Terre Provençale
(Potatoes with Garlic)

PEEL and dry the potatoes and brown them in the hot olive oil in a heavy pan, tossing to prevent sticking. Add the onion, sliced, and cook, still tossing, until the onion is lightly browned. Add salt, pepper, and nutmeg to taste and the garlic, finely chopped. Cover the pan and simmer until the potatoes are tender. Arrange on a heated serving dish and serve sprinkled with chopped parsley. Serves 6–8.

18 small new potatoes
2 tablespoons olive oil
1 onion
3 garlic cloves

Pommes de Terre Minute
(Minute Fried Potatoes)

PEEL and cut 6 medium potatoes into matchsticks and cook them in 1 cup clarified butter over a hot fire until they are tender and golden. Drain off the cooking butter and reserve it for another use. Season the potatoes with salt and white pepper and serve at once. Serves 6.

221

Pommes de Terre Frites
(French Fried Potatoes)

PEEL Idaho or Russet potatoes, of the kind also used for baking, and cut them into uniform sticks about 2½ inches long and ⅓ inch thick. Wash them and dry them thoroughly in a towel. Fry the potatoes in hot deep fat (300°f.) until they are cooked through, but not browned. Drain them from the fat and set them aside until just before serving time. Heat the fat to 400°f. and fry the potatoes until they are a rich, golden brown, crisp on the outside and soft inside. Drain well, sprinkle with salt, and serve at once.

Pommes de Terre Soufflées
(Potato Puffs)

WIPE Idaho or Russet potatoes with a damp cloth, peel them, and dry them thoroughly. Cut the potatoes lengthwise into slices ⅟₁₆ inch thick. Have ready two pans of deep fat. Heat the fat in one pan to 350°f. and in the other to 400°f. (a thermometer is essential for the success of soufflé potatoes). Put the potatoes in a frying basket and lower the basket into the fat at 350°f. The temperature will at once go down. Cook the potatoes until they are tender, stirring them to keep them from sticking together, but do not allow the fat to get any hotter than 300°f. Remove the basket from the heat, drain for a minute, and plunge it into the second kettle of fat at 400°f. The slices will puff at once and bob around on the surface of the fat. Turn them to insure even browning, drain on absorbent toweling, and sprinkle with salt.

Pommes de Terre au Four
(*Baked Potatoes*)

SELECT firm, uniform potatoes of the Idaho or Russet varieties, which cook to a mealy, fluffy texture. Scrub the potatoes and dry them. Potatoes may be baked along with other foods, at any temperature from moderate (350°f.) to hot (425°f.); the time of baking depends upon the heat of the oven and the size of the potato. For example, an average Idaho weighing about ½ pound will bake in 50 minutes in a hot oven at 400°f. The potato is done when it is easily pierced with a fork. To serve, cut a cross in the top, press the sides to open the skin and let out the steam, and top with a pat of butter. Season with paprika, salt, and pepper to taste.

Pommes de Terre Macaire
(*Baked Potato Cake*)

BAKE 6 potatoes, as above, until tender. Scoop out the pulp and discard the skins. Season the potatoes with ⅓ cup sweet butter and salt, pepper, and nutmeg to taste. Heat ¼ cup clarified butter in a skillet and spread the seasoned potatoes evenly in the pan. Bake in a hot oven (400°f.) until the top is golden brown. Pour off the cooking butter and invert the skillet to turn the cake out onto a heated platter. Serves 6.

Pommes de Terre au Gruyère
(*Potatoes with Swiss Cheese*)

PEEL and slice thinly 6 medium potatoes and arrange them in a buttered baking dish. Cover each layer of potatoes with thin slices of Swiss cheese, and season with salt and pepper. Sprinkle the whole with 3 tablespoons of melted butter, cover the dish, and bake in a hot oven (400°f.) for about 40 minutes, until the potatoes are cooked through. Invert the baking dish on a heated serving platter and serve hot. Serves 6.

Pommes de Terre Mirette
(Baked Potato Sticks)

CUT 6 medium, peeled potatoes into matchsticks ⅛ inch wide. Melt ½ cup of butter in a skillet and add the potatoes. Season well with salt and pepper and put the skillet in a hot oven (400°f.) until the potato sticks are cooked and golden. Pour off the cooking butter, sprinkle the potatoes with grated Swiss or Parmesan cheese, and return the pan to the oven to brown the topping. Serves 6.

Pommes de Terre Anna
(Molded Potato Cake)

PEEL and trim 6 uniform potatoes to form cylinders of equal size and shape. Slice the cylinders into thin rounds. Butter a small round baking dish or skillet and line it with slices of potato in circles that overlap first in one direction and then in the other, to make an attractive pattern. Spread each layer with clarified butter, using ½ cup in all, and sprinkle each layer with salt and pepper. Bake the mold in a hot oven (400°f.) for about 40 minutes, until the potatoes are cooked through. Drain off the excess butter and invert the dish on a serving platter to unmold it. Serves 6.

Patates au Sucre

(Glazed Sweet Potatoes)

COOK the sweet potatoes in salted water. Don't overcook. Remove from water as soon as done. Peel and cut them in two or three slices lengthwise. Heat the butter in a skillet and brown the potatoes on both sides. Sprinkle with the sugar, turning to coat the potatoes well as the sugar melts. Serves 6.

6 medium sweet potatoes
2 tablespoons powdered sugar
2 tablespoons clarified butter

Soufflé de Patates

(Sweet Potato Soufflé)

BOIL the potatoes in their skins until they are barely tender. Drain, peel, and mash them to make 2 cups purée. Beat in the hot milk, the butter, and the lemon rind, and salt and pepper to taste. Continue to beat the mixture until it is light and fluffy. Fold in the egg whites, beaten stiff but not dry, and pile the mixture in a buttered soufflé dish. The dish should be about three fourths full. Bake in a moderately hot oven (375°f.) for from 30 to 40 minutes, until the soufflé is puffed 1 inch above the rim of the dish and the top is nicely browned. Serves 6.

6 medium sweet potatoes
¾ cup hot milk
⅓ cup butter
1 teaspoon grated lemon rind
3 egg whites

Salsify

THERE are two kinds of salsify, or oyster plant, the white and the black, or viper's grass. Both are cooked in the same way, and have the same flavor, faintly reminiscent of oysters. Scrape the salsify, split them, and cut each into three equal lengthwise pieces. Drop them at once into water acidulated with a little vinegar, which will

225

keep them from darkening. Boil the salsify in a *court-bouillon blanc* for from 1½ to 2 hours, or until they are tender. Let the roots cool in the *court-bouillon* until close to serving time; they will keep well in the refrigerator. Drain and dry the salsify well and serve them in any of a number of ways: they may be sautéed in butter and served sprinkled with parsley, or with *sauce Béchamel,* or covered with cream sauce, grated cheese, and bread crumbs and browned in the oven. Salsify is also dipped into fritter batter and fried in deep hot fat. One bunch (about ½ pound) of salsify will serve 6. There are from 10 to 12 roots to the pound.

String Beans

MOST modern varieties of string beans are actually stringless, and their preparation simply involves snapping off the ends.

Wash the beans well. If there are strings, cut off the thin outer edge of the pod as well. Very small, young beans may be cooked whole. Cut the beans into even lengths, or slice them thin, on the diagonal. The latter method is called "Frenching." Drop the beans into boiling salted water to cover, and cook them, covered, for about 15 minutes, until they are barely tender; they should still be crisp and bright green in color. Serve with butter, salt and pepper. A dash of nutmeg adds interest to beans.

Haricots Verts Persillés
(*String Beans with Parsley*)

1½ pounds string beans, cooked
CONTINUED

COOK the green beans (see above) and drain them. Heat the butter until it is sizzling and lightly browned. Add the drained beans and

226

salt and pepper to taste, and toss together over the heat for a minute or two, until the beans are well coated with the browned butter. Serve sprinkled with parsley. Serves 6.

2 tablespoons butter
1 tablespoon chopped parsley

Haricots Verts Amandine
(String Beans with Almonds)

Cook the green beans as for *haricots verts persillés,* but substitute for the parsley 2 or 3 tablespoons toasted slivered almonds.

Haricots Verts au Gratin
(String Beans au Gratin)

Cook 1½ pounds of string beans (see above.) Combine the beans with 1 cup *sauce Béchamel* and put them in a buttered baking dish. Sprinkle with grated Swiss cheese and bake in a very hot oven (450°f.) for from 10 to 15 minutes, until the topping browns. Serves 6.

Sorrel

Sorrel, which lends its characteristic sour tang to many soups in classic cuisine, is also much liked as a vegetable, especially with veal. To cook the sorrel, wash it, cut it in shreds, and cook it in a covered pan with a little butter, salt and pepper, until it wilts.

Braised Sorrel

Shred the sorrel and wash it in several changes of cold water. Parboil it for a few minutes in water and drain it. Melt the butter, stir in the

2 pounds sorrel
1½ tablespoons butter
CONTINUED

2 tablespoons flour
2 cups white stock
1 tablespoon sugar
½ cup cream

flour, and cook the *roux* for a few minutes without letting it brown. Stir in the white stock, sugar, and a pinch of salt, and cook, stirring, until the sauce is smooth. Add the sorrel and braise in a moderate oven (350°f.) for 1 hour. Force the sorrel through a sieve, adjust the seasoning with salt and pepper, and add the cream. Serve hot, with a little meat gravy, if desired. Serves 6.

Spinach

THE tender, sweet leaves of early spinach can be cooked in the water that clings to the leaves after washing. No more than 10 to 15 minutes, in a covered pan, should be necessary. If the spinach is not young and tender, or if it is of the New Zealand variety, it may be cooked in a generous amount of boiling salted water in an uncovered pan until it is tender. Any strong or bitter taste may then be poured off with the water.

To wash spinach efficiently, swish it in several changes of cold water, lifting the leaves out of the bowl so that the sand can settle to the bottom.

Drain the cooked spinach thoroughly and season it with butter, salt, and pepper. The spinach may be chopped or forced through a sieve, if desired. It may be seasoned with nutmeg or with garlic, or bound with cream sauce or *sauce Béchamel.*

Baked Squash

USE acorn squash, allowing half or a quarter of a squash for each serving, depending upon the size. Or use a large hubbard squash. Cut the squash in half lengthwise, scrape out the seeds, and season the flesh with salt and pepper. Brush generously with butter, and sprinkle with brown sugar mixed with a pinch of ginger. Arrange the shells in a baking dish in an inch of water and bake in a moderately hot oven (400°f.) until the flesh is tender enough to pierce with a fork and the topping is browned. This may take from 30 minutes to 1 hour.

Zucchini Provençale

WASH the zucchini, peel it if necessary, and slice it or cut it into cubes. Slice the onion and brown it lightly in the oil. Add the tomatoes, peeled, seeded, and sliced, the pepper, free of pith and seeds and sliced, the crushed garlic, and the parsley. Add salt and pepper to taste, and cook for 10 minutes. Add the prepared zucchini and cook for from 10 to 15 minutes longer, until the squash is tender but not overcooked. Pour the mixture into a buttered baking dish, sprinkle it with bread crumbs mixed with cheese, and brown the topping lightly in a moderately hot oven (400°f.). Serves 3–4.

1 pound zucchini
1 small onion
1 tablespoon olive oil
4 tomatoes
1 green pepper
1 garlic clove
1 teaspoon chopped parsley
Parmesan cheese
bread crumbs

Tomatoes

TOMATOES are one of our most versatile and useful vegetables, as well as one of the most convenient. With the exception of salads and a few preparations that demand the use of fresh, ripe tomatoes, almost any recipe requiring tomatoes can use the canned product, in one of its several forms, for the fresh. In making this substitution, choose the proper pack: purée, peeled whole tomatoes, stewed tomatoes, tomato paste, tomato sauce. When tomatoes are in season, and at their flavorful best, they may be prepared in any of the following ways.

Tomates Concassées
(*Cooked Fresh Tomatoes*)

16 ripe tomatoes
1 tablespoon butter
2 onions
4 garlic cloves

MELT the butter in a large, flat saucepan, and in it cook the onions, finely chopped, for about 15 minutes, stirring with a wooden spoon. Dip the tomatoes into boiling water and into cold water and slip off the skins. Cut a thin slice from the blossom end and scoop out the seeds. Chop the tomatoes coarsely and put them in the pan with the onions and salt, pepper, and about 1 teaspoon sugar, to taste. Add the garlic, chopped fine, cover the pan, and bake in a moderate oven (350°f.) until most of the moisture has evaporated. This preparation may be served as a vegetable, used for garnishing, or made into soup. Makes about 5 cups, serves 8–10 as a vegetable.

Tomates Grillées
(*Broiled Tomatoes*)

SELECT well-ripened tomatoes of uniform size and shape. Cut them in half, sprinkle them with salt, pepper, and a little cayenne, to taste, and top with fine bread crumbs. Sprinkle the crumbs with olive oil or dot generously with butter. Broil the tomatoes to brown the topping, put the pan in the oven, and cook at moderate heat (350°f.) until the tomatoes are cooked through, but still hold their shape.

Tomates et Champignons Farcis
(*Stuffed Tomatoes and Mushrooms*)

CUT a thin slice from the stem end of each to-mato, and with a small spoon, scoop out the seeds. Turn the tomatoes upside down to drain. Clean the mushroom caps and arrange toma-toes and mushrooms side by side in a buttered baking dish.

Chop the onion and the mushrooms, and cook for a few minutes in the butter. Add the chopped parsley, cook for a minute, and add the beef broth. Simmer the mixture until the liquid is reduced by half. Add salt and pepper to taste, the bread crumbs, and the lightly beaten egg, and blend well. Stuff the toma-toes and the mushrooms with this mixture and sprinkle with more bread crumbs and with melted butter. Bake in a hot oven (400°f.) for about 10 minutes to brown the topping. Serves 6.

6 medium tomatoes
6 large mushroom caps
1 onion
½ pound mushrooms
1 tablespoon chopped parsley
1 tablespoon butter
1 cup foundation stock
1 cup fresh bread crumbs
1 egg

Truffles

IN THE WORDS of the great gourmet, Brillat-Savarin, truf-fles are the *diamants de la cuisine,* the diamonds of cook-ing. Their inimitable flavor and aroma are the distinctive characteristics of many splendid dishes.

Truffles were known even to the early Greeks and Ro-mans, in whose writings there are many references to this mysterious subterranean fungus, but they are still a mys-tery. They cannot be cultivated by any recognized method, and seem to have neither root, stem, nor seed. They grow underground, anywhere from two to twelve inches below the surface, and can be located only by their scent, which is very strong and penetrating. Certain animals, principally dogs and pigs, can be trained to smell out the truffles near the roots of the oak and chestnut trees around which they customarily grow.

Although truffles cannot be cultivated, they can be encouraged to propagate. Soil from known truffle areas is spread around oak and chestnut trees planted in calcareous ground typical of the tuber's native habitat. The ground is lightly plowed and harrowed, and the waiting begins. If the truffles are to appear at all, they do so after about five years. Eight or ten years later, they may be gathered, and in from five to twenty-five years more a maximum yield may be expected. The crop is encouraged by rainy summers and falls, and the harvest begins after the first autumn frosts, in November.

The world's finest truffles come from Périgord, but there are *truffières* in other parts of France, as well as in Germany and other countries, and Italy has long been famous for its white truffles. So far, no one has been able to find truffles in the United States.

The truffle in its natural state is not very handsome; it is roughly globular in shape, and has a leathery-looking skin. But thin slices of this black root, cut into decorative shapes, are used to achieve very elegant effects in garnishing elaborate dishes.

In truffle country, at the height of the harvest, the truffle is served as a vegetable.

Truffes au Champagne
(Truffles in Champagne)

1 tablespoon butter
1 tablespoon diced carrots
CONTINUED

MELT the butter in a saucepan, add the vegetables, a pinch each of thyme and crushed bay leaf, and a little salt, and simmer until the vegetables are soft. Add the Champagne and stock, cover the pan, and simmer the sauce until it is thick enough to coat a spoon. Add the truffles (if canned truffles are used, add their juice also) and simmer all together for a few minutes longer. Cover the pan, reduce the heat or put the pan on an asbestos pad, and let the truffles stand for from 5 to 10 minutes longer. Correct the seasoning with salt and add at the last ¼ cup of cognac. Serves 6.

1 tablespoon diced onion
1 tablespoon diced celery
1 cup Champagne
1 cup white stock
12 fresh truffles (or canned truffles)

Petits Soufflés aux Truffes
(Truffle Soufflé)

MELT the butter, stir in the flour, and cook the roux for a few minutes without allowing it to brown. Stir in the milk and the cream, and cook, stirring, until the sauce is thick and smooth. Season with salt, pepper, and cayenne pepper to taste. Stir in the well-beaten egg yolks and the truffles. If canned truffles are used, add their juice also. Beat the 6 egg whites stiff and fold them into the mixture. Divide the soufflé batter into 6 individual straight-sided soufflé dishes and bake in a moderately hot oven (400°f.) for from 10 to 15 minutes, until the soufflés are puffed and lightly browned. Serve at once. Serves 6.

3 tablespoons butter
3 tablespoons flour
1½ cups hot milk
¾ cup cream
6 egg yolks
¾ cup chopped truffles
6 egg whites

Turnips

YOUNG TURNIPS may be prepared in any of the ways suggested for carrots, which they somewhat resemble. In France navets are a favorite garnish for duck, mutton, and other fatty meats.

Purée de Navets
(*Mashed Yellow Turnips*)

3 large yellow turnips
2 tablespoons butter
3 tablespoons cream

PEEL the turnips and cut them into small uniform pieces. Boil the pieces in salted water until they are tender, for about 10 to 15 minutes, drain thoroughly, and force through a sieve. Beat in the butter and the cream, and adjust the seasoning with salt and pepper. The mashed turnips may be reheated in the top of a double boiler. If desired, the mashed turnips may be combined with an equal volume of mashed potatoes. Serves 6.

Le Gratin de Santé
(*Vegetables au Gratin*)

6 carrots
2 large onions
1 head of celery
2 leeks, white parts only
1 large head lettuce
1 handful chervil
1 tablespoon cream
1 tablespoon butter
1 egg
grated Parmesan cheese

WASH and cut up all the vegetables and cook them separately in very little salted boiling water until each variety is barely tender. Combine the cooked vegetables and chop them together. Add the butter, cream, and beaten egg, blend well, and adjust the seasoning with salt and pepper. Spread the mixture in a well-buttered baking dish and sprinkle it generously with grated Parmesan cheese. Dot with butter and bake in a hot oven (400°f.) until the cheese melts and browns. Serves 6 as a main luncheon dish.

234

SALADS

Green Salad

THE indispensable salad of classic cuisine is the salad of raw mixed greens, tossed with a dressing of oil and vinegar. In addition to the various kinds of lettuces and the endive, chicory, and water cress found in the market the year round, field salad, dandelion greens, young spinach, and fresh beet tops make excellent salads, alone or with other greens.

The greens should be very fresh. Wash them carefully and soak them in ice water in the refrigerator for an hour, until serving time. Leave the leaves whole or tear them into pieces. Endive and small heads of lettuce may be cut into wedges with a silver knife. Drain the leaves well and dry them thoroughly in a towel or in a salad basket so that there is no water on them to dilute the dressing. Toss the salad with the dressing at the last minute. Use just enough dressing to coat every leaf, but not enough to leave a puddle in the bottom of the salad bowl. For more uniform seasoning, add the salt and pepper to the dressing rather than to the greens.

The tossed green salad may be garnished at will with radishes, cucumbers, carrots, hard-cooked egg, and the like. A handful of crisply fried croutons, or of sliced raw mushrooms, water chestnuts, or hearts of palm makes an interesting variation. Chopped herbs are frequently part of the dressing; otherwise chopped chives, chervil, tarragon or parsley, in any combination, may be sprinkled over the salad before it is tossed.

Salade de Légumes Frais
(Vegetable Salad)

COMBINE equal parts of freshly cooked vegetables such as carrots, string beans, peas, lima beans, and celery. The vegetables should be cooked separately until they are barely tender. Toss the vegetables with French dressing, and pile them in the center of a salad bowl. Top the mound with cooked cauliflowerets and garnish the bowl with quartered hearts of lettuce alternating with small mounds of diced cooked beets.

Salade de Chou Vert
(Cole Slaw)

SHRED finely a medium head of green cabbage. There should be 4 cups of cabbage to serve 6 persons. Soak the cabbage in ice water for 1 hour, drain and dry it thoroughly, and mix it with ¼ cup each of finely sliced green pepper and grated raw carrot. Add 1 teaspoon each of chopped chives and chopped parsley, and toss well with French dressing to moisten. Cole slaw may be served crisp or stored in the refrigerator overnight to wilt slightly, as desired.

Salade de Chou Rouge
(Red Cole Slaw)

SUBSTITUTE red cabbage for the green, and omit the green pepper and grated carrot.

236

Chou Rouge Mariné
(*Marinated Red Cabbage*)

REMOVE and discard the tough outer leaves and the stalk of the cabbage. Shred the cabbage and soak the shreds in salt water for 20 minutes. Drain them, spread them on a tray, and sprinkle with salt. Let the tray stand in the refrigerator for 20 hours. Stir the shredded leaves occasionally. Put the cabbage in a bowl, and pour over it the vinegar, which has been boiled and cooled. Add the spices and garlic, tied in a cheesecloth bag, and marinate for several days. To serve, drain off the vinegar and add 2 tablespoons olive oil.

1 medium red cabbage
2 cups vinegar
12 peppercorns
½ bay leaf
3 garlic cloves
2 tablespoons olive oil

Salade de Pissenlits
(*Dandelion Salad*)

WASH the dandelion greens thoroughly and keep them in ice water for 1 hour. Toss with French dressing seasoned with mustard. Add a handful of bread cubes browned in olive oil with a garlic clove. Toss well and serve at once.

Salade de Fenouil et Pommes de Terre
(*Fennel and Potato Salad*)

CLEAN and dice a head of fresh fennel and soak it in ice water for 1 hour. Peel and cook 2 or 3 potatoes and slice them thinly. Chop finely 1 small green pepper, free of pith and seeds. Combine all the ingredients and toss them gently with French dressing or with mayonnaise to moisten.

237

Salade de Tomates
(Tomato Salad)

PEEL the tomatoes by plunging them for a moment into boiling water and then into cold water. The skins will peel readily. Cut them into quarters or thick slices and remove the seeds. Add French dressing to cover, and chill until serving time. Serve on lettuce leaves, with more French dressing, if desired.

Feuilles de Printemps
(Spring Salad)

3 small heads Boston lettuce
2 hard-cooked eggs
1 tablespoon mixed chopped chives and parsley
1 cup well-seasoned mayonnaise

CUT the lettuce in quarters and swish it in cold water until all the sand is washed out. Soak the lettuce in ice water for 1 hour and drain and dry it thoroughly. Arrange 2 wedges side by side on each individual salad plate. Put a little mayonnaise on the lettuce and sprinkle with the egg, chopped, mixed with the herbs.

Salade d'Endives et Betteraves
(Endive and Beet Salad)

3 endives
1 head of lettuce
1 small white onion
½ cup French dressing
6 cooked beets
6 cloves

SPLIT the endives and the lettuce into 6 wedges and soak the greens in ice water for 1 hour. Grate the onion and mix it with the French dressing. Slice the beets, add the cloves, and pour half the dressing over them. Marinate the beets for 30 minutes.

To serve, drain and dry the greens and put them in a ring in a salad bowl. Discard the cloves, and put the beets in the center. Pour the remaining dressing over the greens.

Salade de Lentilles
(*Lentil Salad*)

PICK over the lentils and soak them for about 1 hour. Drain them, cover them with fresh cold water, and bring the water to a boil. Skim carefully. Add the vegetables and a little salt, cover the pan, and simmer gently for about 2 hours, until the lentils are tender. Cool the lentils in the cooking stock and drain them thoroughly. Season with French dressing made in the proportion of 2 parts vinegar to 1 part oil, and sprinkle with onions, chopped fine, and minced parsley to taste. Adjust the seasoning and serve on lettuce leaves.

2 cups dried lentils
1 carrot
1 onion stuck with a clove
2 garlic cloves
bouquet of 2 stalks of celery, 1 sprig of parsley, ½ sprig of thyme

Salade de Poire d'Avocat
(*Avocado Salad*)

ARRANGE on lettuce leaves alternating wedges of grapefruit and oranges, free of pith and membrane, and slices of avocado. Serve with French dressing. Or serve half a pitted avocado for each portion, and fill the hollow left by the pit with sliced oranges.

Corn Salad

Toss 2 cups of corn, scraped from the freshly cooked cob and cooled, with 1 tablespoon mayonnaise. Season well with salt, pepper, and cayenne, and serve on lettuce leaves.

Salad Dressings (Two Servings)

French Dressing

COMBINE thoroughly 3 tablespoons olive oil, 1 tablespoon vinegar, and a pinch each of salt and pepper.

239

Sauce Vinaigrette

To FRENCH DRESSING, above, add ½ teaspoon each of finely chopped onions, mixed herbs, and capers, and 1 teaspoon chopped hard-cooked egg.

Indian Dressing

To FRENCH DRESSING, above, add a pinch of curry powder and 1 teaspoon chopped hard-cooked egg.

Lemon Dressing

SUBSTITUTE lemon juice for the vinegar in the recipe for French dressing, above.

Roquefort Dressing

To FRENCH DRESSING, above, add 2 tablespoons of mashed Roquefort cheese, 1 tablespoon cream, and a pinch of paprika.

Ketchup Dressing

To FRENCH DRESSING, above, add ¼ cup of to-mato ketchup and a pinch each of paprika and dry mustard.

Mayonnaise Salad Dressings

Sauce Rémoulade

To 1 cup mayonnaise add half a hard-cooked egg, chopped, 2 tablespoons of capers, washed, dried, and finely chopped, 1 tablespoon of chopped chives, and 1 tablespoon mixed chopped parsley, tarragon, and chervil.

Russian Dressing

To 1 cup mayonnaise add 3 tablespoons of chili sauce and 1 tablespoon of mixed chopped celery and red and green pepper. A spoonful of caviar may be folded in at the last.

VII

EGGS, CRÊPES, FRITTERS, PASTA,
RICE, CHEESE

EGGS, CRÊPES, FRITTERS, PASTA, RICE, CHEESE

Eggs

THE OMELET PAN is of utmost importance. It should be made of very heavy material that will heat evenly, and it should have a rounded bottom. A French omelet pan or, lacking that, an iron spider or skillet, is my recommendation. If possible, avoid washing the pan with soap or detergents. Simply wipe it out thoroughly with paper toweling or a cloth and, if you can, reserve it exclusively for making omelets.

It is difficult to handle an omelet made with more than 4 eggs. To serve from 4 to 6 persons, make two or three 4-egg omelets.

Omelette

BEAT the eggs with a fork just enough to mingle whites and yolks, add the cream or milk, and salt and pepper to taste.

Heat the pan and melt the butter in it. Tip the pan to make sure that the sizzling hot butter coats the bottom completely. Pour in the eggs and cook over high heat, drawing the cooked portion away from the edges with a fork as you move the pan back and forth over the heat until the entire mass is uniformly soft and creamy.

4 eggs
1 teaspoon cream or milk
2 teaspoons butter

Tip the pan slightly and with the help of a spatula or the fork fold the omelet in half and slip it onto a heated serving dish. The omelet should be slightly golden on the outside, but the inside should be creamy and soft. Serves 2.

Omelette Fines Herbes

ADD to the beaten eggs 1 teaspoon mixed, finely chopped parsley, chervil, and chives.

Omelette Parmentier *
(Potato Omelet)

1 cooked potato
1 tablespoon butter
4 eggs
1 teaspoon chives
1 teaspoon cream or milk

DICE the potato and brown the dice in the hot butter. Beat the eggs lightly, add the browned potatoes, the cream, and the chives, and make the omelet in the usual way. Serves 2.

Omelette au Fromage
(Cheese Omelet)

MAKE a 4-egg omelet in the usual way. Just before folding it, sprinkle it with 2 tablespoons of grated Swiss cheese. Serves 2.

Omelette Truffée
(Omelet with Truffles)

CUT a truffle into large julienne, and cook the strips in a little cognac until the liquid evaporates. Add 1 tablespoon of heavy cream and a

---

* Antoine-Auguste Parmentier (1737–1813) introduced the potato to France, not from Ireland, but from its native South America. His name affixed to any recipe title is certain indication that the dish contains potatoes in some form.

little salt and pepper, and bring the mixture to a boil. Make a 4-egg omelet in the usual way and just before folding it, put the truffles and cream in the center. Serves 2.

Omelette aux Rognons de Veau
(*Veal Kidney Omelet*)

WASH the kidney and cut it into small pieces, discarding the surplus fat and removing the membranes and tubes. Sprinkle with salt and pepper and brown quickly in hot butter. Add the chopped shallots and a pinch of flour, and stir for a minute over the heat. Add the wine and Madeira, and bring the liquid to a boil. Make a 4-egg omelet in the usual way, split the omelet lengthwise in the center, and fill with the stewed kidneys. Sprinkle with parsley. Serves 2.

1 veal kidney
1 tablespoon butter
1 teaspoon chopped shallot
¼ cup dry white wine
¼ cup Madeira

AN OMELET of unsurpassed luxury bears the name of Charles Monselet (1825–1888), poet, literary *gastronome,* and gourmet without peer. The garnish for this omelet is composed of four elements that rank high in the esteem of every gourmet: *foie gras,* truffles, mushrooms, and asparagus tips.

Omelette à la Monselet

RESERVE 2 or 3 slices of truffle and cut the rest into julienne. Combine these with the julienne of mushrooms, and cook for a few minutes in butter. Make a 4-egg omelet. Put the truffles, mushrooms, and *purée de foie gras* in the center of the omelet, fold the omelet, and slip it

1 truffle
1 tablespoon julienne of mushrooms
1 tablespoon *purée de foie gras*

CONTINUED

8 asparagus tips
1 tablespoon Madeira sauce

onto a heated platter. Garnish with the cooked asparagus tips and the truffle slices and pour over all the Madeira sauce.

Omelet for Dessert

An omelet for dessert may be a surprise to unaccustomed palates, but I promise you that it will be a pleasant surprise.

Omelette au Curaçao
(*Curaçao Omelet*)

Make a 3-egg omelet in the usual way, sprinkle it with powdered sugar, and pour over it 1 tablespoon each of warmed Curaçao and cognac. Set the spirits ablaze, and serve the omelet flaming.

Omelette au Rhum
(*Rum Omelet*)

Make a 3-egg omelet in the usual way, sprinkle it with powdered sugar, and pour over it 2 tablespoons of warmed dark rum. Set the spirits ablaze, and serve the omelet flaming.

Omelette Soufflée
(*Puffed Omelet*)

3 egg yolks
½ cup powdered sugar
2 teaspoons potato starch
1 tablespoon dark rum
3 egg whites

Combine the egg yolks, sugar, and starch in a mixing bowl, and beat with a rotary beater until the mixture is very creamy. Beat in the rum and fold in the egg whites, beaten stiff. Spoon the mixture into a buttered baking dish or force it through a pastry bag with a fancy tube, if

248

desired. Bake in a moderate oven (350°f.) for from 15 to 20 minutes, until the omelet is puffed and light gold in color.

Poached Eggs

FILL a shallow, wide saucepan half full of boiling water and add 1 tablespoon vinegar for each quart of water. Break an egg into a small saucer. With a wooden spoon held straight up, stir the water to form a whirlpool. Slip the egg into the center of the whirlpool. The motion of the water helps the egg to keep its shape and prevents it from sticking to the pan. Poach the egg for about 2 minutes, until the white is firm and opaque. If the eggs are to be served hot, remove them with a skimmer to a pan of warm water until all are poached. If they are to be served cold, put them in a pan of cold water.

Oeufs Froids Parisienne
(*Eggs in Aspic*)

COOL the poached eggs and trim them neatly. Arrange them around a shallow dish alternately with slices of ham. In the center of the dish put the vegetable salad, seasoned with mayonnaise. Pour over the eggs very cold, but still liquid aspic jelly. Chill thoroughly and keep in the refrigerator until serving time.

6 poached eggs
6 large slices cooked ham
vegetable salad
aspic jelly

Oeufs Pochés aux Truffes
(*Poached Eggs with Truffles*)

CUT the truffle into large julienne and warm it in a little cognac. Poach the eggs and arrange them on toasted and buttered English muffins.

1 truffle
12 freshly poached eggs
CONTINUED

249

Fold the truffle strips into the Hollandaise and put a spoonful of the sauce on each egg. Serve at once.

6 English muffins
2 cups *sauce Hollandaise*
cognac

Oeuf Mollet

THE *oeuf mollet* is frequently substituted for a poached egg, which it resembles in that the white is firm and the yolk soft. However, this egg is cooked in the shell, for about 5–6 minutes, and peeled like a hard-cooked egg.

Oeufs Mollets Bénédictine
(*Eggs with Codfish*)

6 eggs
6 baked tart shells
½ pound soaked salt codfish
1 large baked potato
½ cup warm cream
½ cup warm olive oil
1 cup *sauce Béchamel*
garlic

SIMMER the codfish in water to cover until it flakes readily at the touch of a fork. Drain it well and combine it with the pulp of the baked potato. Work in the cream and oil, a little at a time, keeping the mixture smooth. Season to taste with salt, pepper, and a little garlic purée. Fill the baked shells with the mixture and top each with an egg, poached or cooked in simmering water in the shell for 6 minutes, until the whites are firm, but the yolks still soft. Pour a little *sauce Béchamel* over each egg and serve hot.

Oeufs à la Bénédict
(*Eggs Benedict*)

12 poached eggs
6 English muffins
12 slices cooked ham
2 cups *sauce Hollandaise*
12 slices truffle

SPLIT the muffins, toast them, butter them, and put a slice of ham, cut to fit, and a poached egg on each half. The ham may be warmed in a little hot butter, if desired. Top the eggs with *sauce Hollandaise,* and garnish with the truffle slices, dipped in *glace de viande* or meat extract, if possible.

250

The origin of the name "Florentine" is uncertain; there is a city in Italy called Florence, of course, and there was an *Abbé* by the name in Arles in the fifth century. But wherever the name Florentine appears on a modern menu, spinach appears also.

Oeufs à la Florentine
(Eggs with Spinach)

For each portion, cover the bottom of a buttered individual baking dish with cooked, seasoned spinach. Cook 2 eggs for 6 minutes, so that the whites are firm and the yolks still soft. Shell the eggs and lay them on the spinach. Coat lightly with Mornay sauce and sprinkle with grated Swiss cheese. Bake in a hot oven (400°f.) just long enough to brown the topping. The eggs should not be overcooked.

Oeufs Mollets Argenteuil
(Eggs with Asparagus)

Clean, pare, and cook the asparagus. Cook the eggs in simmering water for 6 minutes, until the whites are firm and the yolks still soft. Peel the eggs and arrange them on freshly buttered toast in individual baking dishes, two eggs to the portion. Garnish the dish with asparagus tips and pour over all the *sauce Béchamel*. Sprinkle with grated Swiss cheese and bake in a hot oven (400°f.) just long enough to melt and brown the topping. The eggs should not be overcooked.

12 eggs
2 cups *sauce Béchamel*
2 pounds asparagus tips

Oeufs Cuits Durs
(*Hard-Cooked Eggs*)

START the eggs in cold water to cover. (This makes them easier to shell.) Bring the water to the boiling point, lower the heat, and simmer the eggs for 10 minutes. Chill under running cold water to prevent the formation of a greenish ring around the yolk.

If the eggs are to be stuffed, and it is therefore important that the yolks remain exactly in the center of the egg, turn the eggs occasionally during the first 5 minutes of cooking.

Very fresh eggs cannot be smoothly peeled after cooking. It is best to use eggs that have been refrigerated for several days.

Oeufs Anniversaire Escoffier
(*Eggs and Tomatoes au Gratin*)

2 medium onions
6 ripe tomatoes
2 garlic cloves
6 hard-cooked eggs
½ pound mushrooms
1 cup cream sauce
2 tablespoons grated Swiss cheese

SLICE the onions thin and cook them in a little butter until they are transparent. Add the tomatoes, coarsely chopped, and the garlic, crushed. Cover the pan and simmer the vegetables until they are very tender. Adjust the seasoning to taste with salt, pepper, and cayenne, and spread the mixture in a heat-proof baking dish. Slice the hard-cooked eggs, reserving 2 yolks for garnish. Put the eggs over the vegetables. Slice the mushrooms and sauté them for a few minutes in butter. Add the mushrooms to the cream sauce and pour the sauce over the eggs. Sprinkle with grated Swiss cheese and brown the topping in a hot oven (450°f.). Force the reserved yolks through a sieve and garnish the creamed eggs. Serve hot.

252

If desired, this dish may be made with eggs cooked for only 6 minutes, so that the whites are firm but the yolks still soft. Eggs cooked this way may be peeled like hard-cooked eggs.

Oeufs à la Crème au Gratin
(Creamed Eggs au Gratin)

Bring the milk to a boil with the vegetables, cook for a few minutes, and strain.

Melt the butter, stir in the flour, and cook the *roux* for a minute or two without allowing it to take on color. Gradually stir in the hot milk, and cook, stirring with a whisk, until the sauce is smooth and thickened. Season the sauce to taste with salt and pepper. Add the cream and cook for a few minutes longer. Slice the eggs and fold them gently into the sauce. Turn the mixture into a baking dish, sprinkle with grated Swiss cheese, and bake in a hot oven (400°f.) until the topping browns. Serves 2.

2 cups milk
1 slice carrot
1 slice onion
1 sprig parsley
1 tablespoon butter
1½ tablespoons flour
½ cup cream
4 hard-cooked eggs

This dish gets its name from the fact that it looks not unlike a dish of tripe. It is justly famous.

Oeufs à la Tripe
(Creamed Eggs and Onions)

Slice the onion thin and simmer it in butter until it is transparent, but do not allow it to brown. Combine the onions with the *sauce Béchamel*, adjust the seasoning, and fold in the hard-cooked eggs, sliced. Serves 2.

1 large onion
4 hard-cooked eggs
1 cup *sauce Béchamel*

253

Oeufs Frits
(*Fried Eggs*)

THE white of a properly fried egg should be firm, but not tough, and the yolk hot but not hard. Heat about ½ cup oil in a small skillet until it begins to smoke. Break an egg into a cup, season it with salt and pepper, and slide it gently into the hot oil. With a wooden spoon cover the yolk with the curling egg white. As soon as the egg white is set and of a pale golden color, drain it on absorbent paper toweling. Repeat, cooking a single egg at a time.

Oeufs Frits à la Provençale
(*Fried Eggs with Eggplant and Tomato*)

2 fried eggs
2 slices eggplant
2 slices tomato
2 tablespoons butter

SAUTÉ the eggplant and tomato slices, which should be about ½ inch thick, in a little olive oil or butter. Put the tomato on the eggplant and put the freshly fried egg on the tomato. Brown the butter in a small pan and pour it over the egg. Sprinkle with chopped parsley. A bit of garlic, chopped fine, may also be added to the butter. Serves 2.

Oeufs sur le Plat
(*Shirred Eggs*)

BUTTER individual baking dishes generously and carefully break 2 eggs into each dish. Put the dishes in a baking pan in hot water, cover the pan, and bake the eggs in a hot oven (400°f.) until the whites are set. Garnish with grilled sausages, and pour a little hot tomato sauce around the eggs to make *oeufs Bercy*. Bacon, sautéed ham or tomato slices and the like may also be used to garnish these eggs. Salt and pepper should be added to taste at the table.

Oeufs Brouillés
(*Scrambled Eggs*)

BEAT the eggs with a fork until yolks and whites are well mingled. Beat in 1 tablespoon of the cream and salt and pepper to taste. Heat the butter in a heavy-bottomed pan or skillet. Add the eggs and cook over low heat, stirring constantly with a wooden spoon to keep the mixture smooth and free of lumps. Remove the pan from the heat before the eggs are completely set, and stir in the remaining cream. Serves 3.

6 eggs
2 tablespoons cream
2 tablespoons sweet butter

Oeufs Brouillés aux Foies de Volailles
(*Scrambled Eggs with Chicken Livers*)

HEAT the butter in a skillet and cook the chicken livers until they are browned, but not dry. Add the herbs and salt and pepper to taste and pour in the tomato sauce. Heat the mixture and put it in the center of the scrambled eggs on the serving dish. Serves 3.

6 eggs, scrambled
3 chicken livers
1 tablespoon butter
1 teaspoon chopped mixed chervil and tarragon
1 tablespoon tomato sauce

Crêpes

Crêpes for Dessert

BEAT the egg yolks and the whole eggs together and stir them gradually into the flour sifted with the sugar and a pinch of salt. Add the milk slowly, using as much as is needed to make a smooth, light batter about the thickness of

2 egg yolks
2 whole eggs
1 cup flour
1 teaspoon sugar
CONTINUED

2 cups milk
2 tablespoons Kirsch

heavy cream. The batter should just coat the mixing spoon. Add the Kirsch, and let the batter rest in the refrigerator for an hour or more before using it.

Heat a small frying-pan, 5 or 6 inches in diameter, and brush it with melted butter. The pan should be very hot. Pour in about 2 tablespoons of the batter, moving the pan in a circular motion to spread the batter evenly all over the bottom of the pan. Cook the *crêpe* for a minute, until the edges appear brown, and turn it quickly to brown the other side. If the *crêpes* seem too thick, add a little more milk to the batter; if they are so thin that they are difficult to turn, whisk in a little more flour. Turn the *crêpe* out on a towel and continue until all are done. This recipe makes from 18 to 24 *crêpes* for dessert.

Crêpes Cubaines
(*Pineapple Crêpes*)

1 ripe pineapple
¼ cup sugar
½ cup water
2 tablespoons Cuban rum
⅓ cup apricot jam

PEEL and dice a very ripe, sweet pineapple, discarding the spiny eyes and the tough center core. Cook the dice in the sugar and water for a few minutes; the syrup will be absorbed. Add the jam and the rum, and cook for 2 minutes more, watching the mixture carefully to prevent scorching.

Make *crêpes* for dessert, above. Put a spoonful of the pineapple filling on each *crêpe* and roll it. Arrange the filled *crêpes* on a heat-proof serving platter. Sprinkle them generously with powdered sugar and brown the sugar under the broiler. Sprinkle with ¼ cup of heated rum, set the spirit ablaze, and baste the *crêpes* with the syrup until the flame dies out. Serve at once.

THERE have been many stories of the origin of *crêpes Suzette,* but I think that the first *crêpes Suzette* were actually made for and named in honor of an actress who played at the Comédie Française in 1897. Mademoiselle Suzette was playing the role of a serving maid, and the plot required that she serve *crêpes* as part of an intimate supper. The *crêpes* were sent in from a neighboring restaurant, whose proprietor, Joseph, prepared them with his own hands. The actors who had to eat the *crêpes* were gourmets, as artists often are, and informed Joseph that cold *crêpes* were not to be borne. Furthermore, they demanded a variety of hot *crêpes* to relieve the monotony of their on-stage diet. Joseph therefore devised the flaming *crêpes,* which he later perfected and named for the young lady who served them on stage.

Crêpes Suzette, perhaps more often than any other dish, are customarily made at the table, in full view of the appreciative diners. The *crêpes* themselves are prepared in advance, but the cooked *crêpes* and the ingredients for the sauce are brought into the dining-room for the final flourishes.

Crêpes Suzette

MAKE the *crêpes* for dessert and bring them to the table on a heated serving dish.

Rub the lumps of sugar against the orange skin and crush them in the top pan of the chafing dish, over direct heat. Add the lemon juice and butter and stir well. Pour in the orange juice, Curaçao, and Grand Marnier, and bring the sauce to a boil. Put the cooked *crêpes* in the sauce, one by one, turning them to saturate them in the sauce. Fold each *crêpe* and push it

4 lumps sugar
1 orange
1 teaspoon lemon juice
1 tablespoon butter
2 tablespoons Curaçao
2 tablespoons Grand Marnier
2 tablespoons cognac

257

to one side of the pan. When all the *crêpes* are sauced and folded, sprinkle them with the warmed cognac. Set the cognac ablaze and baste the *crêpes* until the flame dies out. Serve at once.

Crêpes Normandie
(*Apple Crêpes*)

PEEL and slice fine 6 tart, firm-fleshed apples, and cook the slices for a few minutes in 2 tablespoons of clarified butter. Sprinkle the fruit with a little sugar.

Make *crêpes* for dessert, as above. Immediately after spreading the batter in the pan, put a spoonful of the apple mixture on the *crêpe*. Pour over the apples a little more batter and turn the *crêpes* to bake the other side. Sprinkle with sugar and serve very hot. The filled *crêpes* will keep warm on a heated platter in a slack oven. Do not stack them, but lay them side by side.

Crêpes Monseigneur
(*Pear Crêpes*)

4 eggs
1 cup flour
1 tablespoon sugar
1 cup milk
1 tablespoon butter
6 ripe pears
Chartreuse liqueur

BEAT the eggs, stir in the flour sifted with the sugar and a pinch of salt, and add the milk slowly, to make a batter about as thick as heavy cream. The batter should just coat the mixing spoon. Brown the butter lightly and stir it into the batter.

Proceed as for *crêpes Normandie,* substituting sliced raw pear for the apples. Pour a spoonful of heated Chartreuse liqueur over each serving, set the liqueur ablaze, and serve flaming.

Blinis
(Buckwheat Pancakes)

SOFTEN the yeast in lukewarm water and dis- solve it in the warm cream. Stir in the buck- wheat flour, cover the bowl with a cloth, and let the dough rise in a warm place for 2 hours. Add the egg yolks, beaten, and the white flour sifted with salt to taste. Fold in the stiffly beaten egg whites and the heavy cream, whipped. To make very small blinis of the kind served with caviar, pour the batter by tablespoons onto a hot grid- dle. Turn the cakes once, when the surface is bubbly and the bottom browned.

½ package yeast
1 cup buckwheat flour
1 cup warm light cream
½ cup white flour
4 eggs, separated
2 tablespoons heavy cream

Fritters

FRITTERS may be made from anything; that is why they can truly be called one of the most useful of preparations. Fritters of leftover meat or fish can provide the main course at another meal; fritters of vegetables make the vegetable course very welcome indeed, and dessert fritters make a substantial sweet for a light meal. All fritters are deep- fried, in fat deep enough to cover them generously. The fat used is usually one of the hydrogenated shortenings or a vegetable oil that can be heated to temperatures upwards of 365°f. without smoking.

There are many fritter batters, some of them all-purpose, some designed for a specific kind of food.

Pâte à Frire pour Légumes
(Fritter Batter for Vegetables)

SIFT the flour with a pinch of salt, and add the butter, the beaten egg yolk, and about 1 cup of

2 cups flour
CONTINUED

259

2 tablespoons melted butter
1 egg, separated

lukewarm water, or enough to make a smooth, light batter. Let the batter stand at room temperature for an hour or two. Just before using it, fold in the egg white, beaten stiff but not dry.

Pâte à Frire
(*Beer Fritter Batter*)

1 cup flour
¼ teaspoon salt
¼ teaspoon sugar
1 tablespoon olive oil
1 tablespoon brandy
2 tablespoons beer

COMBINE all the ingredients and add enough lukewarm water, about ¾ cup, to make a batter the consistency of heavy cream. Cover the bowl with a cloth and let the batter stand in a warm place for an hour or more. Just before using, fold in 1 egg white, beaten stiff but not dry. This is an all-purpose batter.

Beignets d'Oeufs
(*Egg Fritters*)

1 tablespoon butter
3 tablespoons flour
1 cup milk
3 egg yolks
½ pound mushrooms
6 hard-cooked eggs
fritter batter

MELT the butter, stir in the flour, and cook the *roux* for a few minutes without letting it take on color. Gradually stir in the milk, and cook, stirring, until the sauce is smooth and very thick. Beat in the egg yolks, one at a time.

Dice the mushrooms and cook them for 5 minutes in 1 tablespoon of water with a dash of lemon juice and salt and pepper. Stir the mushrooms and their liquid into the sauce, and adjust the seasoning to taste with salt, pepper, and cayenne. Dice the hard-cooked eggs and gently fold them into the sauce. The mixture will be very thick. Spread the mixture on a cold platter to chill. Shape it into croquettes of any desired form, roll the croquettes in fritter batter, and fry them in hot, deep fat (370°f.) to a rich golden brown. Drain on absorbent toweling and serve hot, with any desired sauce.

Fish Fritters

OYSTERS, clams, frogs' legs, mussels, or fillets of flounder or any other fish, cut in uniform, large pieces, may be made into fritters. Season the fish with salt, pepper, chopped parsley, and lemon juice. Drain and dry it well, dust it lightly with flour, and coat it with fritter batter. Fry in the usual way and serve with tartar sauce.

Meat Fritters

MEAT fritters are made of cooked meat. Cut the meat into fairly large, uniform pieces, season the pieces with olive oil, lemon juice, chopped parsley, and salt and pepper, and coat them with fritter batter. Fry in the usual way and serve with tomato sauce.

Vegetable Fritters

FRITTERS may be made of any cooked vegetables, but the most popular are celery, salsify, artichokes, and endive. Dry the vegetables thoroughly and dip them into the batter. Fry in the usual way, and serve with or without sauce.

Fruit Fritters

PEEL and cut fresh fruit into uniform shapes. Sprinkle the fruit to taste with sugar and brandy, rum, Kirsch, or another liqueur, and let it stand for a few minutes. The liquid drained from the fruit may be added to the fritter batter. Dip the fruit in the batter, fry the fritters in the usual way, and serve with a custard sauce or simply sprinkled with powdered sugar.

Beignets aux Mandarines
(*Tangerine Fritters*)

PEEL and separate into sections as many tangerines as are required. Cover them with lukewarm sugar syrup made of equal parts of sugar and water and soak for 1 hour. Dip the sections one by one in fritter batter, and fry the fritters in moderately hot deep fat (370°f.) until they are brown on all sides. Serve hot, with custard sauce.

Beignets Soufflés
(*Soufflé Fritters or French Crullers*)

MAKE cream puff paste, *pâte à chou,* and flavor it to taste with vanilla extract or orange flower water. Scoop up the paste with a dessert spoon and, with the help of a second dessert spoon, slip it off into hot deep fat (370°f.). Fry the fritters for about 5 minutes, until they are well puffed and nicely browned. Remove them from the fat with a skimmer, drain well on absorbent toweling, and sprinkle generously with confectioner's sugar. Serve hot, with a fruit sauce or custard sauce.

To make the fried cake commonly called "French crullers" force the *pâte à chou* through a pastry bag fitted with a star tube. Shape rings of cream puff paste on a piece of buttered paper. Invert the paper over the pan of hot fat, and the rings will drop off into the fat. Fry the crullers for about 5 minutes, until they are browned on both sides, drain them on absorbent toweling, and sprinkle generously with confectioner's sugar. These crullers are sometimes iced with a mixture of confectioner's sugar and milk. Serve at room temperature.

Pasta

PASTA of any shape, whether macaroni, spaghetti, or noodles, should be cooked in a large amount of boiling salted water until it is just tender and not at all soft. The Italians call pasta at this stage *al dente* because it requires chewing. Pasta should be served hot immediately after cooking; it does not bear reheating.

Nouilles au Beurre
(*Buttered Noodles*)

COOK ½ pound of egg noodles and season them with salt, pepper, and a little nutmeg. Add 2 tablespoons or more of butter, to taste, toss well, and serve at once, as an accompaniment to meat or chicken dishes.

Macaroni à l'Italienne
(*Macaroni Italian Style*)

COOK ½ pound of macaroni and toss it quickly but thoroughly over moderate heat with 2 tablespoons of butter and 1 cup of grated Parmesan cheese.

Nouilles Gratinées
(*Noodles with Cheese*)

BOIL the noodles in a large amount of salted boiling water for from 10 to 15 minutes, until

½ pound egg noodles

CONTINUED

1 cup grated Swiss cheese

2 cups *sauce Béchamel*

they are just tender. Drain them well and combine them with the *sauce Béchamel* and ¾ cup of the grated cheese. Adjust the seasoning to taste with salt, pepper, and nutmeg, and pour the mixture into a buttered baking dish. Sprinkle with the remaining cheese and brown the topping under the broiler.

Gnocchi à la Française
(*Gnocchi, French Style*)

1 cup milk

½ cup butter

1 cup flour

4 eggs

1 cup grated Swiss or
Parmesan cheese

2 cups Mornay sauce

BRING the milk and butter to a boil and add salt, pepper, and a pinch of nutmeg to taste. Stir in the flour and work the dough vigorously with a wooden spoon for a minute. Remove the pan from the heat and beat in the eggs, one at a time. Add one half of the cheese and blend well. Force the dough through a pastry bag with a ¼-inch tube into boiling salted water, cutting off small uniform pieces of dough with a knife. Poach the *gnocchi* slowly until they are firm and cooked through, from 5 to 10 minutes. Drain well. Spread some of the Mornay sauce in a baking dish, cover it with *gnocchi,* and add the remaining sauce. Sprinkle with grated cheese and melted butter and brown in a moderate oven (350°f.). Serves 8.

Gnocchi à la Romaine
(*Gnocchi, Roman Style*)

1½ cups semolina or cream of
wheat

4 cups milk

2 egg yolks

1 cup grated Parmesan cheese

BRING the milk to a boil in the top of a double boiler and add salt, pepper, and a dash of grated nutmeg to taste. Stir in the cereal and cook for 10 minutes, stirring occasionally, to make a thick paste. Beat in the egg yolks, and spread the paste on a buttered platter to cool. Cut the cooled mixture into 2-inch squares or circles. PUT the pieces in a shallow, buttered baking dish and sprinkle them generously with grated cheese and lightly with melted butter. Brown the topping in a moderate oven (350°f.). Pour off the excess butter that rises to the top, and serve the *gnocchi* hot.

Rice

PERFECTLY COOKED RICE is dry, fluffy, tender, but not at all mushy; each grain is separate from the others. To achieve this result with any of the processed rices, follow the directions on the package. If you prefer to use long-grain Carolina rice, the Oriental method is best.

Riz à l'Indienne
(Boiled Rice)

PUT the rice in a colander and wash it under running cold water, dipping it into and out of a bowl of cold water beneath the faucet, until the water in the bowl is clear of any trace of white starch. Bring the water to a boil with the salt, and add the rice slowly so that the boiling does not stop. Boil rapidly for 18 minutes, until a grain rubbed between the fingers has no hard center. Drain the rice in the colander and rinse it with boiling water. Sprinkle it with a little melted butter and dry it for a few minutes in a very slow oven or over very low heat.

1 cup rice
3 quarts boiling water
1 tablespoon salt

IN THE Near East, a seasoned dish of rice always accompanies the favorite grilled mutton or lamb. The Turks get credit for bringing rice

265

to the Balkans, and their name for the dish, *pilaff,* is much used. But there are many variations in spelling, *pilau, pilou,* and *pilaw* among them, and many variations in the seasonings used.

Turkish Pilaff

HEAT 1 tablespoon of butter in a heavy-bottomed pan and stir 1 cup well-washed rice in it until the grains are coated with butter. Add 1 teaspoon of salt and 3 cups of boiling water, cover the pan, and simmer the rice for from 15 to 20 minutes, until the water is absorbed and the grains are tender. Stir the rice with a fork to release the steam and return it to the heat until it is very dry.

Part of the water for this pilaff may be replaced by tomato juice. Or a little saffron may be used to color and flavor the rice before the water is added.

Rice Pilaff à la Française

1 tablespoon butter
1 small onion
1 cup rice
3 cups boiling stock

MELT the butter in a heavy-bottomed saucepan, and in it cook the onion, chopped, until it is translucent, but not soft. Add the well-washed rice, and stir over moderate heat until the grains are all coated with the butter. Add the boiling stock—chicken, veal, or beef stock may be used. Cover the pan and simmer the rice for from 15 to 20 minutes, until the liquid is absorbed and a grain of rice rubbed between the fingers is tender.

Cheese

CHEESE, ripened *"à point,"* and removed from the refrigerator an hour or more before serving, is a popular dessert. The flavor of cheese goes as well with fresh fruit as it does with green salads. Serve the cheese with butter, crisp-crusted French bread or richly flavored dark bread, and a selection of unsweetened crackers. At dessert, wine may also be served with cheese and fruit, and beer and cheese make a favorite snack for robust appetites. Because it is such an excellent appetizer, cheese is used for many cocktail tidbits, recipes for which will be found in the chapter on hors d'oeuvre and appetizers.

Soufflé au Fromage
(Cheese Soufflé)

MELT the butter, stir in the flour, and cook the *roux* for a few minutes without letting it brown. Gradually stir in the boiling milk, and cook, stirring, until the sauce is thick and smooth. Add the salt, pepper, and cayenne pepper to taste. Stir in the well-beaten egg yolks, blending thoroughly, and cool the mixture slightly. Stir in the cheese. If desired, this portion of the soufflé may be prepared in advance.

Beat the egg whites stiff and add one fourth of them to the batter, cutting and folding them in very thoroughly. Fold in the remaining egg whites carefully but lightly. Turn the mixture into a generously buttered soufflé dish and bake the soufflé in a hot oven (375°f.) for from 35 to 40 minutes, until the soufflé is well puffed and lightly browned. Serve at once, as the soufflé will fall as it cools.

3 tablespoons butter
4 tablespoons flour
¼ teaspoon salt and pepper
few grains cayenne pepper
little grated nutmeg
2 cups milk
2 cups grated Parmesan or
  Swiss cheese
6 eggs, separated

Cheese Fondue

THIS famous Swiss specialty is usually made in an earthenware pot at the table. In any case, the

½ pound grated Swiss cheese
CONTINUED

267

1 garlic clove
1 cup white wine
½ tablespoon cornstarch
2 tablespoons Kirsch

pot should be kept hot over a table cooking-unit of some kind until the last bit of *fondue* is devoured.

Rub an earthenware casserole with a cut clove of garlic and in it heat the wine to the boiling point. Stir in the cheese and cook, stirring, until the cheese melts and blends with the wine. Mix the cornstarch to a paste with the Kirsch and add it to the wine and cheese. Stir over the heat for a minute or two to cook the starch.

Serve with long French rolls cut into slices. Each guest pierces a slice of roll with his fork and dips it into the common pot. Serve with white wine.

Coeur à la Crème
(*Cheese Heart*)

2 cups cottage cheese
2 cups cream cheese
2 cups heavy cream

FORCE the cheese through a very fine sieve and beat it well with a rotary beater. Whip the cream stiff and stir it into the cheese. Line a heart-shaped basket mold with cheesecloth, and turn the cheese mixture into it. Put the mold on a plate and let it stand overnight in the refrigerator. To serve, unmold the heart on a chilled serving dish and pour some light cream over it. Surround the heart with chilled strawberries sweetened to taste.

VIII

BAKING

BAKING

Pastry, Pies, and Tarts

Feuilletage
(*Puff Paste*)

KNEAD the butter in ice water until it is smooth and waxy, being careful to squeeze out any pockets of water. Shape the butter into a flat rectangular cake and wrap it in wax paper. Keep in the refrigerator.

Sift the flour and salt onto a marble slab or pastry board. Add the ice water gradually, pouring it with the left hand and working it into the flour with the fingertips of the right hand, to make a very firm dough. Dough and butter should be of the same consistency.

Chill the dough for 30 minutes. Roll it into a square and put the cake of butter in the center. Fold all four sides of the dough over the butter to enclose it completely. Chill for 15 minutes. Roll the dough out into a rectangle three times as long as it is wide. Fold the left-hand third over the middle and the right-hand third over the left, thus making three layers. This process of rolling and folding is called a "turn." Make another turn and chill the dough for 20 minutes. Make four more turns, two at a time, chilling between sets and moving the dough a quarter turn to the right before each, so that the

4 cups flour
1 pound sweet butter
1½ cups ice water
½ teaspoon salt

dough will be rolled out in a different direction each time. Chill for 30 minutes after the last turn before using. The puff paste will keep in the refrigerator, wrapped in a dry cloth and a wet towel, for several days. If it is so kept, do the final set of two turns just before using.

Vol au Vent
(*Puff Paste Shell*)

ROLL out puff paste about ⅜ inch thick. Using an overturned plate 7 inches in diameter as a pattern, cut out a 7-inch circle. Moisten a baking sheet with cold water, turn the circle of puff paste over and lay it on the sheet. Cut out another 7-inch circle of puff paste. With a 5-inch plate, or a pattern cut from paper, as a guide, cut the center from this circle, leaving a rim 1 inch wide. Moisten the edge of the first circle and lay this rim on it. Press the rim against the first circle firmly. Lay the cut-out circle lightly inside the rim—this will serve as a cover for the completed shell. With a sharp, small knife, cut decorative criss-cross slashes in the cover. Brush the top with egg beaten with a little milk.

Bake the *vol au vent* in a hot oven (450°f.) for from 10 to 15 minutes, until it is well puffed and lightly browned. Reduce the heat to moderate (350°f.) and continue to bake the shell for from 40 to 45 minutes longer, until the shell is crisp and dry. It is safer not to open the oven door frequently or for any length of time; a sudden draft, shock, or change of temperature has been known to cause a *vol au vent* to collapse.

Remove the center circle with a sharp knife. *Vol au vent* may be filled with any savory mixture, such as sweetbreads and chicken bound with a *sauce velouté*.

Petites Bouchées
(*Patty Shells*)

FOLLOW the procedure given for *vol au vent,* using small cutters or paper patterns cut to the desired size. A 3-inch cutter makes an attractive *bouchée* for luncheon service, and bite-sized *bouchées* are served as cocktail hors d'oeuvre.

Chaussons aux Pommes
(*Apple Turnover*)

PEEL, core, and chop the apples coarsely. Cook them in the melted butter until they are transparent. Season with ½ cup of sugar, more or less, to taste, and the cognac. Grated lemon rind, cinnamon, or a dash of pepper may be added. Cool the fruit thoroughly.

6 firm-fleshed, tart apples
3 tablespoons clarified butter
1 tablespoon cognac
½ cup sugar

Roll out 1 pound puff paste to a thickness of about ⅛ inch. Cut 10 to 12 rounds using a 4- to 5-inch cutter. Spread half the circle with the cooled fruit mixture, leaving the border clear. Brush the edge all around with cold water. Fold the circle and press the edges together firmly to seal, turning the rim up to help hold in the juices. Prick the *chausson* in several places with a fork, and brush it with an egg yolk mixed with a little cold water. Bake in a hot oven (400°f.) for about 30 minutes, until the puff paste is nicely browned. Makes 10 to 12 *chaussons.*

Millefeuilles

(*Thousand Leaves Pastry*)

Puff paste
apricot sauce
crème pâtissière

ROLL out puff paste ¼ inch thick and cut it into rectangles 4 inches wide and as long as desired. Let the rectangles rest on a wet baking sheet for 10 minutes, prick them well with a fork, and bake in a moderate oven (400°f.) until they are crisp and nicely browned. Turn each rectangle at least once during the baking period.

Cool the sheets of pastry and form them into layer cakes, using 3 sheets for each cake. Spread the bottom layer with apricot sauce and a thick layer of *crème pâtissière*. Adjust the second layer and repeat. Cover with the third layer and a final coating of apricot sauce and *crème pâtissière*. Trim the cake evenly and crush the trimmings. Spread the crumbs over the *crème pâtissière* and sprinkle generously with confectioner's sugar. Serve at once, before the cake loses its crispness.

Napoleons

PROCEED as for *millefeuilles* except for the top layer. Spread the top layer lightly with apricot sauce. Coat it with warm white fondant icing. Flavor a little icing with chocolate and, using a paper funnel or *cornet,* quickly draw 3 lines of chocolate icing down the length of the cake. With a sharp pointed knife cut through the lines at 2-inch intervals to give the decorative effect characteristic of Napoleons.

Fondant Icing

1 cup confectioner's sugar
CONTINUED

SIFT the sugar, add the water and a pinch of cream of tartar, and cook in an enamel saucepan, stirring, until the sugar is dissolved. Continue to cook until the mixture forms a thin syrup. With a wooden spoon stir in more confectioner's sugar until the mixture is just thick enough to coat the spoon. This icing should be used lukewarm to achieve maximum brilliance.

Fondant icing may be flavored with chocolate, coffee essence, or any liqueur, and may be colored to taste. It is used for many cakes, for *petits four glacés,* and for cream puffs as well.

THE SECRET of good pie crust is in the handling, more than in the ingredients, though butter gives a flavor that cannot be imitated.

½ cup hot water
cream of tartar

Pâte à Foncer
(*Pie Dough*)

SOFTEN the butter by kneading it to a waxy consistency. Sift the dry ingredients and cut in the butter with a pastry blender. Or rub the ingredients together between the fingers until the fat is evenly distributed and the mixture looks like coarse cornmeal. Add just enough ice water, a little at a time, to hold the mixture together. As each portion of the mixture is moistened, put it aside so that it will not be handled again. Chill the crust for 30 minutes or more before rolling it out on a lightly floured board. Use quick, light movements of the rolling pin, and avoid unnecessary handling. This recipe makes three 9-inch crusts.

1½ cups butter
3¼ cups all-purpose flour
1 teaspoon sugar
½ teaspoon salt

Pâte à Flan
(*Tart Dough*)

SIFT the flour with the sugar and a pinch of salt, and work in the butter with the fingertips or a

2 cups flour
CONTINUED

275

2 tablespoons sugar
½ cup plus 2 tablespoons
  butter
1 egg yolk

pastry-blender until the fat is evenly distributed. Add the egg yolk and, if necessary to make the dough particles adhere, 1 teaspoon of cold water. Chill the dough for an hour or more before rolling it out. This makes two 9-inch tart shells.

Fruit Tarts

ROLL out *pâte à flan,* or tart dough, ⅛ inch thick and cut it into circles. Fit the dough loosely into small tart pans, flute the edges, and prick the dough well. Cover the dough with paper and put a tablespoonful of dried beans into the pan to help the shell hold its shape. Bake the shells in a hot oven (400°f.) for about 15 minutes, until they are browned and thoroughly cooked. Cool the shells and fill them with lightly sweetened fresh fruit or with well-drained cooked fruit. Glaze the fruit with melted tart jelly, with Melba sauce, or with apricot sauce, depending upon its color and flavor. Peach, apricot, and banana tarts are coated with the golden apricot sauce; tarts made with berries, cherries, plums, and the like are coated with the red jelly.

The shells may be half-filled with *crème pâtissière* or with whipped cream before the fruit is added, and the tarts may be further garnished at serving time with whipped cream forced through a pastry bag with a fancy tube.

Pie aux Pommes
(*Apple Pie*)

8 to 10 tart cooking apples
¾ cup sugar
CONTINUED

LINE a pie plate with *pâte à foncer,* or pie dough. Fit the circle of dough lightly into the pie plate without stretching the dough. Peel and core the apples, mix them with the sugar, cinnamon, and lemon rind (taste for sweetness, which varies considerably with the apples used), and pile them high in the pie shell. The fruit shrinks in cooking, and a skimpy pie results if the shell is not generously filled. Dot the fruit with butter. Trim the lower crust even with the rim of the pie plate. Roll out the upper crust, making it somewhat thinner than the lower crust, if desired, and spread it over the apples. Trim the crust about ½ inch beyond the edge of the plate and fold the rim under. After pressing together firmly to seal, flute the edges with the fingers, a fork, or a pastry wheel. Cut a small hole in the middle of the crust to allow for the escape of steam. For a glossy brown crust, brush the top with beaten egg. Bake the pie in a hot oven (450°f.) for 15 minutes, reduce the heat to moderate (350°f.), and bake for 45 minutes longer, until the crust is nicely browned and the apples tender. Serve warm or at room temperature; never serve fruit pies chilled.

¼ teaspoon cinnamon
2 tablespoons butter

One Crust Pies

For most one-crust pies, the shell is baked before the filling is added. To achieve a shapely, well-baked shell, fit the rolled-out dough very loosely into the pie plate, pressing it carefully into the corners of the plate without stretching the dough. Trim the crust ½ inch from the outside edge of the pan. Turn the edge back and flute it between the fingers to make an attractive standing rim. Prick the bottom and sides of the shell thoroughly to prevent air pockets from forming. Line the shell with white paper and fill it with rice or beans kept for this purpose.

Bake the shell in a hot oven (450°f.) for 10 minutes. Remove the rice or beans and the paper, prick any bubbles that may have formed, and bake for 5 minutes longer to a golden brown color.

Tarte aux Cerises
(*Cherry Tart*)

SWEETEN with sugar 4 cups of pitted sour cherries to taste and add a pinch each of salt and nutmeg and a few drops of almond extract. Fill a pie plate lined with *pâte à flan,* or tart dough, and bake in a moderate oven (350°f.) for about 35 minutes, until the crust is browned and the fruit tender. Cool the tart to lukewarm and pour over it ¼ cup of melted, tart currant jelly. Chill long enough to set the glaze.

This recipe may be adapted for use with other fruits.

CATHERINE DE MÉDICIS was responsible for a great many culinary innovations; one of these is the famous tarte *à la frangipane* of Lyons.

Tarte à la Frangipane
(*Almond Cream Tart*)

2½ tablespoons flour
2 eggs
2 cups milk
1 tablespoon butter
6 crushed almonds, 4 sweet,
  2 bitter
  CONTINUED

MELT the butter, add the flour, and stir in the milk and eggs, beating vigorously over moderate heat. Cook for 10 minutes, stirring constantly to prevent scorching. Turn the mixture into a bowl to cool. Add the remaining ingredients, plus powdered sugar to taste, and blend well. Turn the mixture into a baked pie crust

and brown the top lightly under the broiler.
Serve cold.

½ cup macaroon crumbs
½ tablespoon crushed sugar-coated almonds praline
½ teaspoon orange flower water

Tarte de Potiron
(*Pumpkin Pie*)

Mix the sugar and spices together and blend them with the pumpkin. Add the eggs, lightly beaten, and the remaining ingredients. Line a pie plate with pie dough, or *pâte à foncer,* using one third of the recipe. Make a standing, fluted rim, but do not prick the dough. Fill the crust and bake the pie in a moderately hot oven (400°f.) for about 30 minutes, until the crust is well browned and the filling is nearly set, so that a silver knife inserted near, but not at, the center comes out dry. Serve at room temperature.

2 cups purée of cooked pumpkin or squash
¾ cup sugar, half brown, half white
½ teaspoon nutmeg
¾ teaspoon mixed cinnamon and ginger
½ teaspoon salt
3 eggs
1 cup scalded milk
Grated rind of ½ lemon

Pumpkin Chiffon Pie

Put the egg yolks in the top of a double boiler with 1 cup of the sugar and the spices and salt. Stir well to blend, and add the cream and water. Cook, stirring, until the custard is thick and smooth. Soak the gelatin in ½ cup of cold water for 5 minutes and dissolve it in the hot custard. Strain the mixture into a cold bowl set in a pan of ice, and cool it, stirring constantly, until it begins to set. Fold in the pumpkin, the egg whites beaten stiff with ½ cup sugar, and the cream, whipped. Pour into two baked puff-paste pie shells and chill until firm.

1½ cups light brown sugar
6 egg yolks
1 teaspoon salt
1 teaspoon nutmeg
1 teaspoon ginger
2 cups light cream
1 cup water
2 envelopes gelatin
2½ cups cooked pumpkin purée
6 egg whites
½ cup heavy cream

279

Tarte à l'Ananas
(*Pineapple Chiffon Pie*)

1 cup crushed pineapple
4 egg yolks
1 cup sugar
½ teaspoon salt
1 teaspoon grated lemon rind
1 tablespoon lemon juice
1½ envelopes gelatin
4 egg whites
1 cup heavy cream

DRAIN the juice from the crushed pineapple and soak the gelatin in it. Mix ⅔ cup sugar, the egg yolks, the lemon juice and rind, and the salt in the top of a double boiler, and cook, stirring constantly, until the mixture thickens. Add the gelatin, stir to dissolve it, and strain the mixture into a cold bowl set in a pan of ice. Cool, stirring, until the custard begins to thicken. Fold in the crushed pineapple, the egg whites beaten stiff with ⅓ cup of sugar, and the cream, whipped. Pour the mixture into a baked and cooled pie shell made of puff paste. Chill and decorate with whipped cream just before serving.

Tarte au Citron
(*Lemon Chiffon Pie*)

1 tablespoon gelatin
¼ cup cold water
4 egg yolks
1 cup sugar
juice of 4 lemons
juice of 1 orange
½ teaspoon grated lemon rind
4 egg whites
1 cup heavy cream

SOAK the gelatin in the cold water for 5 minutes. Beat the egg yolks in the top of a double boiler with ½ cup of sugar and the citrus juices and rind. Cook over hot water, stirring constantly, until the custard is thick and smooth. Dissolve the gelatin in the hot custard and strain the mixture into a cold bowl set in a pan of ice. Cool, stirring constantly, until the mixture begins to thicken. Fold in the egg whites, beaten stiff with ½ cup sugar and a pinch of salt, and the cream, whipped stiff. Pour into a baked and cooled pie shell and chill until firm.

Pâte à Chou
(*Cream Puff Paste*)

BRING the water to a boil with the butter and salt. Remove the pan from the heat and add the flour all at once. Blend well, return the pan to the heat, and continue to beat with a wooden spoon for about 2 minutes longer, until the dough forms a mass that cleans the sides of the pan. Beat in the eggs, one at a time, beating smooth after each addition. Add a few drops of orange flower water, if desired.

1 cup water
½ cup sweet butter
1 cup flour
4 eggs

Profiterolles

MAKE cream puff paste, above, and shape small puffs on a buttered baking sheet, using a pastry bag or a teaspoon. Bake the puffs in a moderate oven (375°f.) for about 18 minutes, until they are browned and dry, and feel light in the hand. Fill the puffs with *crème pâtissière* and serve them, two or three to a portion, with a little warm chocolate sauce.

Crème Pâtissière
(*Pastry Cream*)

SCALD the milk with a piece of vanilla bean; or use 1 teaspoon of vanilla extract, adding it after the mixture is cooked. Beat the egg yolks with the sugar and flour, and stir in the boiling milk. Cook in the top of a double boiler, stirring constantly, until the cream is thick and smooth, but do not allow it to boil.

Pastry cream, or *crème pâtissière,* may be varied by the addition of melted chocolate, cof-

2 cups milk
vanilla bean
⅓ cup sugar
6 tablespoons flour
6 egg yolks

fee essence, or any desired liqueur, and used to fill puffs of *pâte à chou* or other pastry.

Sauce Chocolat
(*Chocolate Sauce*)

6⅔ ounces German sweet chocolate (5 bars)
1 cup water
1 teaspoon sugar
vanilla extract

MELT the chocolate in the water, add the sugar and a few drops of vanilla extract, and cook all together for a few minutes, stirring constantly.

Meringues Chantilly
(*Whipped Cream Meringues*)

6 egg whites
1½ cups powdered sugar
2 cups heavy cream

BEAT the egg whites with a pinch of salt until they are stiff but not dry. Add the sugar, a little at a time, beating constantly. Put the meringue mixture into a pastry bag fitted with a round tube, and form ovals, an inch apart, on a buttered and floured baking sheet. Bake in a very slow oven (200°f.) for 1½ hours or more. The meringues should be very light gold in color. Take them out of the oven and at once remove them from the baking sheet. The underside will be slightly soft; press this with an egg to form an oval-shaped hollow. Cool and fill the hollow with the cream, whipped and seasoned to taste with sugar and vanilla.

Bread and Cake

Gâteau Vacherin
(*Meringue Layer Cake*)

6 egg whites
1½ cups powdered sugar
½ teaspoon vanilla extract
CONTINUED

BEAT the 6 egg whites until they are stiff but not dry, and gently fold in the 1½ cups of powdered sugar, little by little. Fold in the ½ teaspoon of vanilla.

Cover two well-buttered baking sheets with white paper or dredge them with flour. With a 9-inch plate as a guide, outline 4 circles.

Put the meringue in a pastry bag fitted with a round tube 1 inch in diameter. Cover one of the circles completely with a layer of meringue. Ring each of the remaining three with meringue to form a wreath 1½ inches wide. Sprinkle with confectioner's sugar and bake in a slow oven (250°f.) until the meringue is dry. This may take an hour or more.

Make another meringue with the 2 egg whites, ½ cup of powdered sugar, and vanilla extract. Arrange the wreaths of meringue on top of the solid circle, with uncooked meringue between them to make them set together. Put the remaining meringue in a pastry bag, and with a fancy tube decorate the top and sides of the cake at will. Return the layer cake to the oven at still lower temperature, about 200°f., for an hour or longer, until the meringue is thoroughly dry and very lightly browned. Cool the cake and fill the center with ice cream or with whipped cream flavored with vanilla extract, and garnish with candied violets.

2 egg whites
½ cup powdered sugar
few drops of vanilla extract

SAINT HONORÉ was Bishop of Amiens about A.D. 660; he is the patron saint of pastry chefs and bakers, and the confection that bears his name is composed of several basic preparations known to pastry chefs everywhere.

Gâteau Saint-Honoré
(*Saint-Honoré Cake*)

PREPARE the cream puff paste and the *crème pâtissière* according to the recipes given above. Roll out a 9- or 10-inch circle of tart dough and put it on a baking sheet. Moisten the edge with

cream puff paste
tart dough
crème pâtissière
CONTINUED

½ cup flour

¾ cup sugar

1 tablespoon sweet butter

4 eggs

2 cups scalded milk

1 envelope gelatin

6 egg whites

2 tablespoons confectioner's
  sugar

1 cup sugar

⅓ cup water

¼ teaspoon cream of tartar

a wet pastry brush. Using a pastry bag, force a ¾-inch-thick ring of cream puff paste around the edge of the dough circle. Brush the cream puff paste with egg yolk and bake in a hot oven (425°f.) for 10 minutes. Reduce the heat to moderately slow (300°f.) and continue to bake for from 20 to 30 minutes longer, until the edge is light and brown. Make small cream puffs with the remaining cream puff paste, cool them, and fill them with *crème pâtissière*.

Make the *crème Saint-Honoré* as follows: Combine in a heavy-bottomed saucepan the flour, sugar, butter, a pinch of salt, and the 4 eggs. Work the mixture with a wooden spoon, and gradually stir in the hot milk, scalded with a piece of vanilla bean. Cook, stirring constantly, until the sauce is thick and smooth. Cool slightly, stirring. Soak the gelatin in ¼ cup of cold water and dissolve it over hot water. Add the dissolved gelatin to the first mixture and stir well. Cool the cream, stirring frequently. Beat the egg whites stiff with a pinch of salt and the confectioner's sugar and fold them into the custard. Pile the mixture into the center of the *Saint-Honoré*.

Make an amber syrup by boiling the sugar, water, and cream of tartar together without stirring. Dip the filled cream puffs in the syrup and arrange them around the edge of the cake on the cream puff paste base. Decorate each puff with half a candied cherry. Garnish the cake with swirls of whipped cream forced through a pastry tube.

Croquembouche
(*Cream Puff Tower*)

ROLL out any flaky pastry dough into a circle ¾ inch thick and 9 inches in diameter. Prick the dough well and bake it in a moderately hot oven (400°f.) until it is well browned.

Make 3 dozen small cream puffs with *pâte à chou,* cool them, and fill them with *crème pâtissière.*

Dip the tiny puffs one at a time into the amber caramel syrup prepared as for *gâteau Saint-Honoré* and arrange them in a ring around the edge of the baked pastry crust circle. Continue to pile the cream puffs one on the other in narrowing circles, pyramid fashion. Crown the top of the pyramid with the largest of the puffs.

This *pièce montée* should be attempted only in dry weather. The caramel will harden and crackle in the mouth; hence its name, *croque-en-bouche.*

Each guest detaches puffs from the tower, beginning at the top, with the aid of a serving fork and spoon.

Croissants

(*Crescent Rolls*)

DISSOLVE the yeast in the lukewarm water and add enough of the flour to make a smooth ball of dough. Put the dough in a bowl two thirds full of warm water to rise.

Sift the remaining flour, salt, and sugar onto a pastry board. Work in the risen sponge and the milk, and mix the dough until it is smooth and firm, but not stiff. Let the dough chill for 20 minutes covered with a towel. Roll it out into a rectangle three times as long as it is wide and place in the center the butter, kneaded into a flat cake. Fold the right-hand half of the rectangle over the butter and the left half over the right, thus making three layers of dough. Turn the dough so that the open end faces you and roll it out. Repeat the folding, turning, and roll-

1 cake or envelope yeast
¼ cup lukewarm water
4 cups flour
½ teaspoon salt
1 tablespoon sugar
1½ cups milk
1½ cups butter

285

ing four times more, turning the dough each time so that it is rolled out in a different direction, and chilling between the sets of two "turns" each. Chill the dough thoroughly, overnight if desired, and roll it out ⅛ inch thick. Cut strips 6 inches wide, cut the strips into 6-inch squares, and cut the squares into triangles. Roll the triangles, beginning at the wide end opposite the point. Shape the rolls into crescents and lay them on a lightly buttered baking sheet. Cover the pan and let the crescents rise in a warm place until they are double in bulk, about 1 hour. Brush with beaten egg yolk and bake in a hot oven (400°f.) for from 20 to 25 minutes, until they are nicely browned.

Brioche

½ cake or envelope yeast
½ cup warm water
3 cups flour
1 tablespoon powdered sugar
1 teaspoon salt
1 cup sweet butter
4 eggs

DISSOLVE the yeast in the warm water and mix it with ½ cup of the flour. Knead the dough well and put it in a bowl two thirds full of warm water to rise.

Sift the remaining flour in a mound on a pastry board and make a well in the center. Add the sugar, salt, and the eggs, lightly beaten, and knead thoroughly to make a smooth dough. When the sponge rises to the surface of the warm water, work it into the dough. Soften the butter by kneading it with the hands, and work it into the dough. Put the dough in a bowl, sprinkle it lightly with flour, and set it in a moderately warm place to rise until it is double in bulk, from 2 to 3 hours. Punch the dough down and chill it overnight.

Cut off one fourth of the dough and form it into a ball. Shape the rest into a large ball and put it in a buttered, bowl-shaped *brioche* mold. Cut a cross in the top of the large ball and insert the small ball in it to make the head, or crown of the *brioche*. Let the *brioche* rise in a warm place until it doubles in bulk. Brush with lightly beaten egg yolk and bake in a moderately hot oven (400°f.) for an hour, until the *brioche* is browned and tests done. Individual *brioches* may be made, if preferred, and baked for about 20 minutes.

Kugelhopf

SIFT the flour into a mixing bowl and make a well in the center. Dissolve the yeast in the water and pour it into the well with the eggs, sugar, and Kirsch, and a pinch of salt. Mix the center ingredients and work in the flour, adding as much of the milk or cream as necessary to make a light dough. Beat the dough for a few minutes and work in the butter, which should be kneaded until it is of the same consistency as the dough. Wash the raisins, soak them in warm water, and dry them well. Work in the raisins and continue to knead the dough until it is perfectly blended. Butter and flour a fluted turk's-head mold, and arrange blanched almonds in a decorative pattern on the bottom. Turn the dough into the mold and cover it with a light cloth. Let the cake rise in a warm place for about an hour, until it doubles in bulk. Bake in a moderate oven (350°f.) for about 1 hour, until the cake is well risen and browned, and tests done. Unmold and sprinkle with confectioner's sugar. *Kugelhopf* keeps well in an air-tight cake tin for several days.

2 cups flour
½ cake or envelope yeast
¼ cup lukewarm water
2 eggs
½ tablespoon sugar
1 tablespoon Kirsch
½ cup milk or cream
½ cup sweet butter
½ cup Malaga raisins

Baba au Rhum

SOFTEN the yeast in the lukewarm water, add ½ cup flour, blend well, and set in a warm place, covered with a cloth, to rise for 1 hour,

2 cups flour
1 envelope or cake yeast
CONTINUED

¼ cup lukewarm water
¼ cup milk
½ cup sugar
½ cup butter
3 eggs
2 cups water
1 cup sugar
½ cup rum
apricot sauce

or until the ball of dough doubles in bulk. Cream the butter in a mixing bowl, and work in ½ cup of sugar and a pinch of salt if the butter was not salted. Scald the milk, cool it to lukewarm, and beat it in alternately with the remaining flour. Add the eggs, one at a time, beating well after each addition. Work in the risen dough and continue to beat for about 10 minutes, to make a smooth, light dough. Cover the bowl and let the dough rise in a warm place until it doubles in bulk, for about 1 hour. Stir the dough down and half-fill a buttered *baba* mold or a ring mold. Cover the mold and let the dough rise to the top of the pan. Bake in a moderate oven (350°f.) for 30 minutes or more, until the *baba* is well risen and browned, and tests done when a skewer is inserted in the center. Turn the *baba* out on a rack to cool slightly.

Make a syrup by boiling together the water, 1 cup sugar, and the rum. Soak the warm *baba* in the syrup. Brush with apricot sauce.

THE *génoise,* a butter cake leavened only by eggs, is used to make many fancy pastries. In France, cakes are seldom baked in layer-cake pans. Instead, the cake is baked in a single mold, and split horizontally into as many layers as desired for filling and icing. *Génoise* may also be baked in a flat rectangular pan and cut into small fancy shapes to be decorated as *petits fours.*

Génoise
(*Butter Cake*)

1 cup granulated sugar
8 eggs
CONTINUED

PUT the sugar, eggs, and flavoring into a bowl and set the bowl over hot water. Beat, preferably with the electric mixer, for 5 minutes or more, until the mixture is very light and fluffy and has doubled in bulk. Very gently fold in the flour and the melted and cooled butter. Bake the *génoise* in a buttered pan lined with waxed paper, choosing the size and shape of the pan according to the use planned for the cake. Bake in a moderate oven (325°f.) for 1 hour, or until the cake shrinks from the sides of the pan and springs back from the pressure of a finger, and a tester inserted in the center comes out dry.

few drops vanilla or lemon
  extract
1 cup sweet butter, melted
2 cups cake flour

Gâteau Le Moka
(*Mocha Layer Cake*)

MAKE a *génoise* and split it into 3 horizontal layers. Fill and cover the layers with the following mocha cream:

In the top of a double boiler mix the sugar, egg yolks, and hot milk, and cook, stirring with a wooden spoon, until the mixture coats the spoon. Do not permit it to boil, or it will curdle. Strain the custard into a bowl and cool it. In the meantime, reduce 2 cups of very strong-brewed coffee to 2 tablespoons. Or dissolve 2 tablespoons of instant coffee in 2 tablespoons of water. Soften the butter with a wooden spoon and gradually work in the custard and the coffee essence to make a very smooth, light cream.

Sprinkle the sides of the cake with toasted, chopped almonds, and decorate the top with rosettes of the mocha butter cream pressed through a pastry bag.

1 *génoise*
5 tablespoons sugar
2 egg yolks
1 cup hot milk
2 tablespoons coffee essence
1 cup sweet butter

Butter Cream Icing

SUBSTITUTE for the coffee essence in the recipe for mocha butter cream any desired flavoring, to taste.

Biscuit
(*Sponge Cake*)

4 eggs, separated
½ cup powdered sugar
few drops lemon extract
1 cup less 2 tablespoons cake
  flour

BEAT the egg yolks light, add the sugar and flavoring, and continue to beat until the mixture is pale and fluffy. Beat the egg whites stiff but not dry, and fold them into the first mixture. Fold in the flour, blending it in thoroughly but carefully. Bake in an unbuttered tube pan in a moderately slow oven (300°f.) for about 1 hour, until the cake is lightly browned and springs back from the pressure of a finger. Invert the pan on a cooling rack and let the cake cool thoroughly before removing it from the pan.

Biscuit Roulé au Chocolat
(*Chocolate Roll*)

½ cup flour
¼ cup cocoa
1 teaspoon baking powder
¼ teaspoon salt
4 eggs
¾ cup powdered sugar
1 teaspoon vanilla extract
2 tablespoons water

SIFT the flour, cocoa, baking powder, and salt together. Beat the egg yolks with half the sugar until the mixture is very light and creamy. Add the vanilla and water. Beat the egg whites stiff with the remaining sugar and fold them into the yolk mixture. Gently but thoroughly fold in the sifted dry ingredients. Spread the batter on a shallow baking pan about 8 by 16 inches, buttered and lined with waxed paper. Bake the cake in a moderately hot oven (375°f.) for from 15 to 20 minutes, until it tests done. Invert the cake on a towel sprinkled with powdered sugar, and carefully remove the waxed paper. Roll the cake in the towel and put it on a rack, open side down, to cool. Unroll the cake and spread it thickly with whipped cream, ice cream, *crème pâtissière,* or butter cream icing, to taste. Roll the cake again and finish it with icing, confectioner's sugar, or whipped cream, to taste.

Pain d'Epice à l'Américaine
(*Honey Ginger Bread*)

DISSOLVE the baking soda in the hot water and cool it. Cream the butter, add the spices, the egg, and the honey, and blend well. Stir in the cool soda and water and beat in the flour. Beat until the mixture is very smooth. Turn the batter into a large loaf pan lined with heavy paper and bake in a moderate oven (350°f.) for 1 hour or longer, until the cake tests done. Honey cake scorches easily, so remove it from the oven the moment the tester comes out dry and the cake springs back from the pressure of a finger.

The cake may be iced with chocolate fondant icing, or it may be decorated before baking with blanched almond halves and angelica arranged to resemble flowers.

5 teaspoons baking soda
1 cup hot water
3 tablespoons butter
1 egg
2 teaspoons cinnamon
2 teaspoons ginger
1 pound honey
4 cups flour

Gâteau aux Raisins
(*Raisin Cake*)

AN ELECTRIC MIXER is almost essential for the success of this cake. Beat the butter and sugar until the mixture is very light and fluffy, and beat in the eggs, one at a time, beating for 5 minutes after each addition. Add the lemon extract. In the meantime, soak the raisins for 10 minutes in warm water. Dry them well on a towel and mix them with the flour, baking powder, and salt, sifted together. Stir the flour mixture slowly into the batter. Pour the batter into a buttered pan lined with waxed paper and bake the cake in a moderately slow oven (300°f.) for 1½ hours, until a tester inserted in the cake comes out dry, the cake shrinks from the sides of the pan, and the top springs back from the pressure of a finger.

1 cup sweet butter
1¼ cups powdered sugar
5 small eggs
¼ teaspoon lemon extract
½ pound seedless raisins
2 cups cake flour
1 teaspoon baking powder
1 teaspoon salt

Petits Fours Secs

Madeleines

½ cup sugar
4 egg yolks
2 whole eggs
1 teaspoon vanilla extract
1 cup cake flour
¼ cup melted butter

BEAT the sugar, egg yolks, and eggs for 10 minutes; use an electric mixer if possible. Stir in the flour and the melted butter. Butter Madeleine pans (small, fluted, oval-shaped molds) with clarified butter and dust them with flour. Divide the batter evenly into the molds—this makes about 24 small cakes—and bake in a moderate oven (350°f.) for from 15 to 20 minutes, until the cakes are lightly golden in color.

Sablés Fondant
(*Sand Cookies*)

1½ cups butter
¾ cup sugar
3 egg whites
4 cups flour
1 teaspoon vanilla extract

CREAM the butter and sugar together and work in the egg whites. Add the flour gradually. Flavor with the extract and a pinch of salt. Chill the dough for an hour or more, and roll it out on a lightly floured board. Cut into any desired shapes and bake in a moderately hot oven (375°f.) for about 10 minutes, until the cookies begin to brown slightly.

Langues de Chat
(*Cats' Tongues*)

5 tablespoons sweet butter
½ cup granulated sugar
½ teaspoon vanilla extract
4 egg whites
1 cup cake flour

CREAM the butter and sugar together and add the vanilla extract. Work in the unbeaten egg whites, one at a time, and then add the flour. Press the batter through a pastry tube in strips 3 inches long on an unbuttered baking sheet. Bake in a hot oven (400°f.) for from 8 to 10 minutes, until the tongues are lightly browned.

292

Macarons
(*Macaroons*)

SOFTEN the almond paste with a wooden spoon and work in the egg whites, the sugar, and the flavoring. Blend thoroughly, and force the mixture through a pastry bag fitted with a plain tube onto a baking sheet covered with white paper. Bake the macaroons in a moderately slow oven (300°f.) for about 20 minutes, until they are delicately browned. Cover the cake rack with a wet towel and lay the paper on it. In a few minutes, the macaroons may be easily removed from the wet paper.

½ pound almond paste
½ cup granulated sugar
½ cup powdered sugar
3 egg whites, unbeaten
½ teaspoon vanilla extract

Petits Fours Secs
(*Almond Paste Cookies*)

BLEND the butter and almond paste together, and work in the sugar, the flavoring, and the egg yolk. Slowly add the flour, working the mixture with a wooden spoon to ensure even blending. Chill the dough for 30 minutes to facilitate handling. Force the dough through a cookie press onto an unbuttered baking sheet, or roll the dough out on a lightly floured board and cut it into any desired shapes. Bake in a moderately hot oven (375°f.) for from 8 to 10 minutes, until the cookies just begin to color and are firm. Cool on a cake rack.

¼ pound almond paste
½ cup sweet butter
½ cup sugar
1 egg yolk
½ teaspoon vanilla or lemon extract
1 cup cake flour

Biscuits à la Cuiller
(*Lady Fingers*)

BEAT the egg yolks, using an electric mixer if possible, until they are very light and fluffy. Beat in two thirds of the sugar and the extract,

7 eggs, separated
½ cup sugar
CONTINUED

293

1 teaspoon flavoring extract
⅞ cup cake flour

which may be vanilla, lemon, or orange flower. Beat the egg whites stiff with the remaining sugar and carefully fold them into the yolks. Fold in the flour, lightly but thoroughly.

Line a baking sheet with white paper and press the batter through a pastry bag fitted with a flat tube to make strips 4 inches long. Sprinkle the strips lightly with confectioner's sugar and bake in a moderately slow oven (300°f.) for about 30 minutes, until the cakes are firm and lightly golden in color.

Tartines Russes
(*Russian Jelly Slices*)

½ cup butter
½ cup brown sugar
¼ pound filberts
¼ cup Kümmel
1 egg
currant jelly

CREAM the butter and sugar, and work in the filberts, roasted and ground, the Kümmel—a caraway-flavored liqueur—and the egg. Blend the dough thoroughly and, with a spatula, spread it thinly on a buttered baking sheet. Bake in a moderate oven (350°f.) for about 15 or 20 minutes, until the dough is firm and lightly colored. Cut the cake in half and spread one half with a thin coat of currant jelly. Cover with the other half, sandwich fashion, and sprinkle with confectioner's sugar. Cut into 1½-inch squares.

IX

SWEETS

SWEETS

Fruit Desserts

Pommes à la Canelle
(*Cinnamon Apples*)

PEEL and quarter the apples—use a crisp, slightly acid eating apple such as the Winesap or Jonathan. Boil the remaining ingredients for 5 minutes. Add the apples to the syrup, cover the pan, and cook until the wedges are transparent. Cool in the syrup and serve chilled.

6 firm-fleshed red apples
3 tablespoons sugar
2 cups water
1 cinnamon stick
3 cloves

Melon Rafraîchi au Kirsch
(*Kirsch-flavored Honeydew*)

CHOOSE a ripe, sweet melon and, with a small knife, cut a circular plug from the stem end just large enough to permit the removal of the seeds and fibers. Clean the melon and pour into the cavity ½ cup Kirsch. Replace the plug and chill the melon in the refrigerator until serving time. To serve, remove the plug and pour off the liqueur. Strain the liqueur and combine it with grenadine syrup, to taste. Cut the melon into wedges and pour a little of the Kirsch and grenadine syrup over each portion.

IN 1892 MME NELLIE MELBA, the Australian prima donna, gave a party at the Savoy Hotel in

London. In her honor the great Escoffier created a new dessert. A swan carved of ice (to commemorate the swan in *Lohengrin*) was in the center of this masterpiece, and around it were arranged poached peaches on a bed of vanilla ice cream. Later M. Escoffier improved upon perfection by adding a purée of fresh raspberries and a sprinkling of shredded green almonds. This *pêches Melba* first appeared on the menu of the Carlton Hotel at its opening in London on July 15, 1899.

Pêches Melba
(*Peaches with Ice Cream and Raspberry Sauce*)

CHOOSE ripe, perfect peaches, plunge them for a minute into boiling water, and slip off the skins. Cut the peaches in half and pit them; if this is done at the last minute, the peaches can be served raw, but as they darken quickly, it is safer to poach them in advance. Prepare a sugar syrup of 1 cup each of sugar and water by boiling the mixture for 5 minutes. A piece of vanilla bean or a cracked peach pit may be added to the syrup for flavor. Poach the peaches in this mixture for a few minutes, until the fruit is barely tender, and not at all mushy. Chill the fruit. Put a portion of vanilla ice cream in each serving dish, lay the peach half, rounded side up, on the ice cream, and pour over all a spoonful of *sauce Melba* (see below).

Sauce Melba

1 pound raspberries
1 8-ounce jar currant jelly

WASH the raspberries and force them through a fine sieve. Squeeze the jelly through a cheesecloth. Combine the two thoroughly and serve very cold.

298

Compote de Pêches
(*Stewed Peaches*)

PREPARE the peaches for stewing as in the recipe for *pêches Melba,* above. Flavor the syrup with the juice of ½ lemon, and simmer the peaches, covered, until they are just tender. Serve chilled.

Poires au Vin Rouge
(*Spiced Pears in Red Wine*)

BOIL the wine, sugar, and spices together for 5 minutes. Peel, halve, and core the pears, and simmer them in the syrup until they are just tender. Cool the fruit in the syrup. Remove the spices and serve cold.

6 firm-fleshed winter pears
1 cup red wine
1 cup sugar
1 stick cinnamon
3 cloves

Poires Hélène
(*Pears with Chocolate Sauce*)

PEEL, halve, and core 1 ripe pear for each serving. Or use poached pears, prepared like the peaches for *pêches Melba,* adding a little lemon juice to the syrup. Cool the pears well. Put a scoop of vanilla ice cream in each dessert dish, cover it with the pear halves, and spoon a little chocolate sauce over the fruit.

Compote de Fraises
(*Stewed Strawberries*)

BRING the sugar and water to the boiling point and simmer for a minute or two. Add the vanilla extract and the berries, carefully hulled and washed. Cover the pan, bring the syrup

2 quarts strawberries
¼ cup sugar
1 cup water
1 teaspoon vanilla extract

299

again to the boil, and remove the pan from the heat. Let the berries stand in a warm place, covered, for 15 minutes. They will cook without losing their shape. Serve chilled.

Fraises Melba
(*Strawberries with Ice Cream and Raspberry Sauce*)

SURROUND each serving of vanilla ice cream with 2 tablespoons sliced strawberries that have been chilled for an hour or longer with powdered sugar and Kirsch to taste. Pour a spoonful of *sauce Melba* over the ice cream and serve at once.

Ananas et Framboises au Sucre
(*Pineapple and Raspberries*)

PEEL a ripe, sweet pineapple deeply to remove all the spines. Cut the fruit into thin slices and cut out the hard core of each slice. Arrange the fruit in a glass serving bowl. Sprinkle with sugar to taste and a little Sauternes, if desired. Just before serving, cover the pineapple with fresh raspberries, washed and lightly sugared to taste.

Macédoine de Fruits au Kirsch
(*Fruit in Kirsch*)

COMBINE in a glass serving bowl equal parts of any fruits in season, cut up. Make a syrup of 1 cup of sugar and 1 cup of water, boil the syrup for 5 minutes, and let it cool to lukewarm. Add 2 tablespoons of Kirsch and pour the syrup over the fruit. Chill for at least 2 hours before serving.

Fraises et Ananas Créole
(Strawberries and Pineapple in Kirsch)

COMBINE equal parts of strawberries and fresh, ripe pineapple, cut in thin slices, and sprinkle with powdered sugar and a little Kirsch, to taste. Chill for at least 2 hours before serving.

Mandarines au Kirsch
(Tangerines in Kirsch)

PEEL and separate the tangerines into sections. Sprinkle with powdered sugar and Kirsch to taste, and chill for at least 2 hours before serving.

Compote de Rhubarbe
(Stewed Rhubarb)

TRIM off the leaves of the rhubarb, but do not peel the stalks unless they are very large and tough. Wash well, split the stalks lengthwise, and cut them into 2-inch lengths. Cook the sugar and water together for 5 minutes, add the rhubarb, cover the pan, and cook slowly for about 5 minutes, until the rhubarb is tender, but not mushy. Serve chilled, with *sauce Anglaise*.

2 pounds rhubarb
1 cup sugar
2 tablespoons water

Hot Desserts

FOR all rice puddings, use long-grain Carolina rice rather than processed rice. Processed rice resists cooking down to a smooth paste, and will not make a creamy rice pudding.

Pouding de Riz
(*Rice Pudding*)

1 quart milk
½ cup rice
½ cup light cream
2 tablespoons sugar
vanilla bean

Scald the milk in the top of a double boiler with a piece of vanilla bean. Wash the rice in several waters and add it to the milk with the sugar and a pinch of salt. Cook over hot water for 1½ hours, stirring from time to time. Add the cream. Turn the pudding into a buttered baking dish and bake it in a moderate oven (350°f.) until the top forms a brown crust. Grated lemon rind, nutmeg, cinnamon, or any of these and ½ cup of raisins may be added to the pudding, if desired.

Gâteau de Riz à l'Ananas
(*Pineapple Rice Pudding*)

Make a rice pudding as described above. Add with the cream 2 lightly beaten eggs. Fill the buttered baking dish with alternate layers of the rice pudding mixture and ½ cup of diced canned pineapple, well drained. Begin and end with rice. Bake the pudding in a moderate oven (350°f.) until the top begins to brown.

Peel, core, and dice 3 large sour apples, and cook them until soft in a little water. Add the pineapple juice and simmer for a few minutes. Strain the sauce and serve it hot or cold with the pineapple rice pudding, which may be served warm or chilled.

Pouding au Pain
(*Bread and Butter Pudding*)

5 slices day-old bread
½ cup raisins
2 cups milk
CONTINUED

Trim the crusts from the bread, butter the slices, and cut them into uniform cubes. Put the bread in a buttered pudding dish. Soak the raisins in warm water until they are plump. Drain them and sprinkle them over the bread. Scald the milk with a piece of vanilla bean and the sugar, and stir it slowly into the beaten eggs. Pour this custard mixture over the bread and bake the pudding in a moderate oven (350°f.) for about 25 minutes, until the top is brown and a knife inserted near the center comes out clean. Serve warm, with apricot sauce. Serves 3–4.

½ cup sugar
2 eggs

A *tourtière* is a pie plate, and, by extension, one of certain pies baked in a *tourtière*. One of the most famous of these comes from the Morvan, in central France.

La Tourtière
(*Apple Custard*)

PEEL and core the apples and cut them into very thin slices. Cook in a little clarified butter until the fruit is tender. Beat the eggs well and add the scalded milk gradually. Add a pinch of salt and a few drops of flavoring, to taste. Mix the flour and sugar, add a little of the milk mixture, stir well to make a smooth paste, and add the rest of the milk, stirring. Combine this mixture with the fruit and pour into a well-buttered *tourtière,* or pie plate. Bake in a moderately hot oven (400°f.) for about 30 minutes, until the custard is set and a knife inserted near the center comes out clean. Sprinkle with confectioner's sugar and serve hot.

2 tart, firm-fleshed apples
2 cups milk
2 eggs
1 tablespoon flour
1 tablespoon sugar
lemon extract or orange flower
  water

Pouding de Figues
(*Fig Pudding*)

PUT the figs and the suet through the finest blade of the food-chopper twice and work the mixture with a wooden spoon until it is soft

½ pound dried figs
3 ounces beef suet
CONTINUED

303

1 cup fresh bread crumbs
1 cup milk
2 eggs
⅓ cup sugar
zest of 1 lemon and 1 orange
⅓ cup flour
1½ teaspoons baking powder
2 tablespoons rum

and well blended. Soak the bread crumbs in the milk and add the eggs, sugar, grated citrus rinds, and a pinch of salt. Combine this mixture with the figs and suet and blend well. Add the flour, sifted with the baking powder, and beat in the rum. Turn the mixture into a buttered pudding dish, cover it with brown paper, and set the dish in a pan of hot water. Bake the pudding in a moderate oven (350°f.) for 2 hours. Unmold on a heated serving platter and serve with whipped cream or custard sauce flavored with rum.

Crème Anglaise
(*Custard Sauce*)

2 cups milk
½ cup sugar
4 egg yolks

SCALD the milk with a piece of vanilla bean. Beat the egg yolks with the sugar, and briskly stir in the hot milk. Return the mixture to the pan, and cook over hot water, stirring constantly, until the sauce is thick enough to coat the spoon. Do not allow the sauce to boil. Strain the sauce into a cold bowl and cool it, stirring from time to time. Remove the vanilla bean before serving.

Savetier aux Pêches
(*Peach Cobbler*)

1 whole egg
2 cups peaches, sliced fine
2 eggs, separated
1 tablespoon powdered sugar
1 tablespoon potato starch
lemon extract

SWEETEN the peaches to taste with sugar, and toss them with the beaten whole egg. Crack the peach stones, blanch the nuts and add them to the mixture. Pour the fruit mixture into a well-buttered pudding dish.

Beat the egg yolks well and beat in the sugar and starch. Continue to beat until the mixture falls from the mixing spoon in a ribbon, and is very light and fluffy. Add a few drops of lemon extract and fold in the egg whites, beaten stiff with a pinch of salt.

Pour this batter over the fruit and bake the pudding in a moderately hot oven (400°f.) for about 30 minutes, until the cake is nicely browned and tests done. Serve warm, with custard sauce.

Charlotte de Pommes
(Apple Charlotte)

PEEL and core the apples and mince them coarsely. Cook them in the butter with the lemon zest, covered, for about 15 minutes, until the fruit is very soft. Remove the cover, and cook, stirring constantly to prevent scorching, until the moisture is reduced and the mixture is quite dry. Sweeten to taste with sugar and apricot jam.

Trim the crusts from a loaf of sandwich bread, sliced thin, and cut some of the slices into circles. Dip the circles one by one in clarified butter and line the bottom of a buttered charlotte mold (a shallow, round, straight-sided mold), overlapping the bread circles to make an attractive pattern. Line the sides of the mold with 1-inch strips of bread dipped in clarified butter, also overlapping.

Fill the mold with the cooked apple preparation, cover it with a buttered paper, and bake in a moderate oven (350°f.) for 40 minutes or more, until the bread is a fine golden brown. To serve, invert the charlotte in a heated serving dish. Serve with apricot sauce.

1 dozen tart cooking apples
3 tablespoons butter clarified
grated zest of ½ lemon
1 tablespoon sugar
1 tablespoon apricot jam
1 loaf sandwich bread

305

Sauce Abricot
(*Apricot Sauce*)

1 can apricots, 1 pound
1 can peaches, 1 pound
2 ¼ cups sugar

Force the fruits and their juice through a fine sieve, or purée them in an electric blender. Add the sugar, and cook for 1 hour, stirring from time to time to prevent scorching. Flavor to taste with a little Kirsch.

Charlotte à l'Américaine

6 tart cooking apples sliced
1 cup thinly sliced pineapple
1 cup sliced bananas
1 cup apricot sauce
½ teaspoon grated lemon rind
3 tablespoons clarified butter

Proceed as for *charlotte de pommes,* filling the mold with the raw fruit mixture. Bake the *charlotte* and invert it on a heated serving platter. Serve with more apricot sauce and with whipped cream.

Pouding de Gâteaux
(*Cake Pudding*)

2 tablespoons raisins
2 tablespoons mixed candied
  fruit
1 cup cake crumbs
2 tablespoons Kirsch
2 cups milk
2 tablespoons sugar
3 eggs

Mix the fruit, Kirsch, and crumbs together, and spread the mixture in the bottom of a buttered pudding mold. Scald the milk with a piece of vanilla bean, discard the bean, and add the sugar. Beat the eggs, gradually stir in the hot milk, and pour the custard over the crumb mixture in the mold. Set the mold in a pan of hot water and bake the pudding in a moderate oven (350°f.) for 45 minutes, until the custard sets and a knife inserted near the center comes out clean. Unmold on a warmed serving dish and serve warm, with *sauce sabayon.*

Sauce Sabayon

5 egg yolks
1 tablespoon sugar
CONTINUED

Combine the eggs yolks, sugar, and wine in the top of a double boiler and cook over hot but not boiling water, whisking constantly, until the custard coats the spoon. Add the Kirsch and serve hot or cold.

½ cup dry white wine
¼ cup Kirsch

Crème Meringuée
(*Meringue Pudding*)

SOAK the lady fingers in Kirsch, add the milk, sugar, and a pinch of salt, and force the mixture through a fine sieve. Beat the eggs and the egg yolks together and combine with the first mixture. Pour the batter into a well-buttered ring mold, set the mold in a pan of hot water, and bake the pudding in a moderately slow oven (325°f.) for about 45 minutes, until the custard is set and a knife inserted near the center comes out clean. Unmold the pudding onto a heat-proof serving dish.

Beat the egg whites stiff, and gradually beat in the powdered sugar. Fold the diced candied fruit, soaked in Kirsch and well drained, into one fourth of the meringue. Put this mixture into the center of the ring. Pile the remaining meringue on top of the ring, swirling it to make an attractive pattern. Bake in a hot oven (450°f.) for about 5 minutes, to brown the meringue topping. Serve with a custard sauce flavored with orange flower water.

½ pound lady fingers
½ cup Kirsch
2 cups scalded milk
¾ cup sugar
4 eggs
5 egg yolks
½ cup diced candied fruit
8 egg whites
1 pound powdered sugar

Pouding Grand Marnier
(*Grand Marnier Pudding*)

MELT the butter and stir in the flour and sugar. Do not allow this mixture to brown. Add the milk gradually, stirring constantly, and cook, stirring, until the sauce is very thick and smooth. Add the egg yolks, beaten with the Grand Marnier, and fold in the egg whites,

½ cup butter
½ cup sugar
1 cup cake flour
1½ cups scalded milk
5 eggs, separated
½ cup Grand Marnier

307

beaten stiff. Bake in a buttered pudding dish set in a pan of hot water for about 35 to 40 minutes in a moderate oven (350°f.). Unmold and serve with custard sauce flavored with Grand Marnier to taste.

Soufflé au Chocolat
(*Chocolate Soufflé*)

1 cup milk
¼ pound sweet chocolate
2½ tablespoons sugar
3 tablespoons flour
3 eggs
½ teaspoon vanilla extract
1 teaspoon butter

HEAT the chocolate and milk together, stirring until the chocolate melts. Remove the pan from the fire. Mix the sugar and flour in a bowl, add the egg yolks, and beat with a whisk until the mixture is very creamy. Slowly stir in the hot chocolate and milk. Return this mixture to the saucepan and cook, stirring, until the sauce is smooth and thick. Add the vanilla and butter. Fold in the egg whites, beaten stiff, and turn the mixture into a 1-quart soufflé dish, buttered and sprinkled with sugar. Bake in a moderate oven (350°f.) for from 20 to 30 minutes, until the soufflé is well puffed and browned. Serve at once. Serves 2–3.

Soufflé Vanille
(*Vanilla Soufflé*)

½ cup sugar
5 egg yolks
½ cup flour
2 cups milk
1 teaspoon butter
5 egg whites
vanilla bean

BEAT the egg yolks with the sugar until the mixture is light and fluffy, then beat in the flour. Scald the milk with a piece of vanilla bean and remove the bean. Pour the milk gradually into the egg mixture, and cook, stirring constantly, for a minute or two, until the mixture is smooth. Fold in the egg whites, beaten stiff, and turn the batter into a buttered and sugared soufflé dish. Bake the soufflé in a moderate oven

(350°f.) for from 30 to 40 minutes, until it is well puffed and browned. Sprinkle with confectioner's sugar and serve at once.

Soufflé au Kirsch
(*Kirsch Soufflé*)

Mix the sugar, flour, 1 whole egg, and 3 egg yolks. Scald the milk and stir it in gradually. Bring the mixture to the boil, stirring constantly, and cook for 2 minutes. Remove the pan from the fire and stir in the butter. Cool the batter and add the Kirsch. Fold in the 3 egg whites, beaten stiff. Bake in a buttered soufflé dish in a moderate oven (350°f.) for about 40 minutes until the soufflé is well puffed and browned.

½ cup powdered sugar
½ cup flour
4 eggs
2 cups milk
3 tablespoons Kirsch
1 tablespoon butter

Bananes Soufflées
(*Banana Soufflé*)

Cut the bananas in half lengthwise and lift out the fruit without breaking the skin. Reserve the skins. Put the pulp through a sieve. Stir the potato starch to a paste with the sugar, a pinch of salt, and the milk. Cook, stirring constantly, until the sauce thickens. Add the banana pulp, the Anisette, and the egg yolks, and boil up once. Pour the mixture into a bowl and cool it, stirring briskly. Fold in the egg whites, beaten stiff but not dry, and pile the mixture lightly in the banana skins. Sprinkle lightly with confectioner's sugar and bake in a moderate oven (350°f.) for about 10 to 15 minutes, until the soufflé is puffed and browned. Serve immediately.

6 bananas
1 tablespoon powdered sugar
1 tablespoon potato starch
½ cup milk
1 tablespoon Anisette
2 egg yolks
3 egg whites

Cold Puddings, Custards, Creams, Jellies

Riz Impératrice
(Molded Rice Pudding)

2 cups milk, scalded
½ cup Carolina rice
2 tablespoons sugar
3 tablespoons apricot jam
4 tablespoons mixed diced
   candied fruit
2 tablespoons Kirsch
2 cups milk
½ cup sugar
4 egg yolks
1 envelope gelatin
vanilla bean
strawberry gelatin

COMBINE the rice, scalded milk, sugar, a pinch of salt, and a piece of vanilla bean in the top of a double boiler, and cook over hot water for 1½ hours, stirring occasionally, until the rice is reduced to a thick cream. Cool slightly and add the jam and the candied fruit soaked in the Kirsch. Blend well.

While the rice is cooking, scald the second 2 cups of milk with a piece of vanilla bean. Add the sugar. Beat the egg yolks and warm them with a little of the sweetened milk. Return the egg yolks to the pan and stir in the gelatin, softened in ¼ cup water. Strain the custard, cool it, and combine it with the cooled rice. Pour the mixture into a mold filled with strawberry gelatin 1 inch high and chill it in the refrigerator for at least 2 hours, until it is very firm. Unmold the rice on a chilled serving platter and garnish to taste with whipped cream and fresh fruit.

Crème Caramel
(Caramel Custard)

2 cups milk
½ cup sugar
half a vanilla bean
4 egg yolks
2 eggs
½ cup sugar
½ cup water

SCALD the milk with the vanilla bean and dissolve in it the sugar and a pinch of salt. Beat the egg yolks and the eggs together and gradually add the strained scalded milk. Reserve the vanilla bean; it may be washed, dried, and used many times before it loses its flavor.

Cook the sugar and water in a small saucepan

until the syrup turns golden in color. Pour the syrup into a baking dish and tip the dish to coat it well with syrup.

Pour the custard into the baking dish, set the dish in a pan of hot water, and bake in a moderately hot oven (400°f.) for about 45 minutes, until a knife inserted near the center of the custard comes out clean. Cool the custard and invert the mold on a serving dish just before it is to be brought to the table.

Pots de Crème au Chocolat
(Chocolate Custard)

SCALD the milk with a piece of vanilla bean, add the chocolate, cut fine, and stir until the chocolate melts. Discard the vanilla bean. Beat the eggs, egg yolk, and sugar together, and gradually add the hot chocolate milk. Pour the custard mixture into small custard pots. Put the pots in a pan of hot, but not boiling water. Cover the pots with their own lids or, if they have no lids, cover the pan. Bake in a moderate oven (350°f.) for about 15 minutes, until the custard is set and a knife inserted near the center comes out dry. Do not allow the water in the pan to boil. Serve chilled.

2 cups milk
2½ ounces sweet chocolate
vanilla bean
2 eggs
2 egg yolks
2 tablespoons sugar

Crème à la Noix de Coco
(Coconut Cream)

PUT the milk and the shredded flesh of a fresh coconut in the top of a double boiler. Cook over hot water for 5 minutes, stirring constantly. Strain the milk through cheesecloth, pressing and twisting the cloth to extract as much of the liquid as possible. There should be 1 cup of

1 coconut
¾ cup sugar
¼ cup water
4 egg yolks
1 tablespoon rum or Kirsch

creamy liquid. If necessary, add a little milk to fill the cup. Boil the sugar and water together for 5 minutes. Combine the syrup with the coconut cream. Beat the egg yolks, warm them with a little of the cream mixture, and return all to the top of the double boiler. Cook, stirring constantly with a wooden spoon, until the cream coats the spoon. Pour the coconut cream into individual serving dishes and chill well before serving. Serves 4–5.

Crème Brulée
(*Burned Cream*)

6 eggs
¾ cup brown sugar or 6
  tablespoons white sugar
3 cups light cream
vanilla bean

BEAT the eggs and sugar with a pinch each of salt and freshly grated nutmeg until the mixture is light and creamy. Scald the cream with a piece of vanilla bean and stir it gradually into the egg mixture. Cook in the top of a double boiler over hot water, stirring constantly, until the mixture coats the spoon. Do not allow the custard to boil. Remove the pan from the hot water and set it in a pan of ice to cool, stirring frequently. Pour the custard into heat-proof serving cups and sprinkle it thickly with brown sugar, so that no custard shows. Brown the topping under the broiler, watching it carefully to prevent burning. Serve cold.

Charlotte Russe à la Vanille
(*Vanilla Charlotte Russe*)

lady fingers
2 cups milk
vanilla bean
  CONTINUED

PUT a round of paper in the bottom of a *charlotte* mold and cover it with lady fingers arranged in an attractive pattern. The lady fingers may be cut into triangles and arranged around a small round biscuit in the center like the petals of a flower. Line the sides of the mold with more lady fingers, upright and close together. Set the mold in a pan of ice.

Scald the milk with a piece of vanilla bean. Beat the egg yolks and sugar together and slowly add the hot milk. Return the mixture to the heat, and cook, stirring, until the custard coats a spoon. Soften the gelatin in ½ cup of cold water and dissolve it in the hot custard. Strain the custard into a cold bowl set in a pan of ice and stir it until it begins to thicken. Fold in cream, whipped.

Turn the gelatin cream into the prepared mold and chill it for 2 hours. To serve, unmold the *charlotte* on a serving platter and garnish the top with whipped cream forced through a pastry tube.

The gelatin custard may be flavored with orange or chocolate, or ½ cup candied fruit, cut fine and marinated in Kirsch.

4 egg yolks
⅔ cup sugar
2 envelopes gelatin
2 cups heavy cream

Crème aux Fraises Chantilly
(Strawberry Cream Custard)

COMBINE the first four ingredients in the top of a double boiler and cook over hot water, stirring from time to time, until the custard coats the spoon. Discard the vanilla bean. Cool the custard and fold in the cream, whipped stiff. Chill the mixture in the refrigerator.

Clean the berries and sprinkle them with the sugar and the Kirsch. Chill in the refrigerator for 1 hour.

Gently blend the two mixtures and refrigerate for 1 hour or more before serving.

4 egg yolks
2 tablespoons sugar
1½ cups milk
piece of vanilla bean
2 cups heavy cream
6 cups strawberries
½ cup Kirsch
½ cup powdered sugar

313

Oeufs à la Neige
(*Floating Island*)

2 cups milk
2 eggs, separated
2 tablespoons powdered sugar
½ teaspoon vanilla extract

BRING the milk to the boil in a shallow pan. Beat the egg whites stiff with 1 tablespoon of the sugar and a pinch of salt. With a dessert spoon, scoop out egg-shaped portions of meringue, and use a second spoon to slip the meringue eggs off into the hot milk. Poach the meringues for about 2 minutes, turning them once. Lift the firm "snow eggs" out of the milk and dry them on a towel.

Beat the egg yolks with the remaining sugar and gradually stir in the hot milk. Cook in the top of a double boiler over hot water, stirring constantly, until the mixture is thick enough to coat the spoon, but do not allow it to boil. Cool the custard and serve in individual glass dessert dishes, with the meringue eggs floating on top.

Bavarois au Chocolat
(*Chocolate Bavarian Cream*)

4 cups milk
vanilla bean
½ pound sweet chocolate
1 cup sugar
8 egg yolks
2 envelopes gelatin
2 cups heavy cream

SCALD the milk with a piece of vanilla bean and remove the bean. Add the chocolate, broken into small pieces, and stir until the chocolate melts. Beat the egg yolks and sugar together and warm the mixture with a little of the hot milk and chocolate. Return the mixture to the pan, and cook, stirring constantly with a wooden spoon, until the custard coats the spoon. Soak the gelatin in ¼ cup cold water and dissolve it in the hot custard. Strain the custard through a fine sieve into a cold bowl set in a pan of ice, and cool, stirring constantly, until the mixture thickens. Fold in the cream, whipped stiff, and turn the mixture into a mold dipped in ice water and drained. Chill for at least 2 hours, until the cream sets. To unmold, dip the mold quickly into very hot water, loosen the edges with a small knife, and invert on a chilled serving platter. Serve with more whipped cream, if desired.

Crème Danoise
(*Danish Cream*)

SCALD the milk and cream with a pinch of salt. Beat the egg yolks and the 3 tablespoons of sugar together and gradually stir in the hot milk. Return the mixture to the saucepan, and cook, stirring, until the custard coats the spoon. Do not allow it to boil. Soak the gelatin in the rum and dissolve it in the hot custard. Cool, stirring occasionally, until the cream is very thick and beginning to set, then pour it into a mold dipped in ice water. Chill for several hours or overnight.	1 cup milk 1 cup cream 3 tablespoons sugar 4 egg yolks 1 envelope gelatin ½ cup rum ½ cup water ½ cup sugar

Cook the water and sugar, stirring, until it turns a rich amber color. At once put the saucepan in a pan of ice and add 1 tablespoon water. Reserve the sauce.

Unmold the cream by loosening the edges with a knife and dipping the mold quickly into very hot water. Pour the caramel sauce over it. Serves 3–4.

Gelée d'Ananas
(*Pineapple Jelly*)

1 cup canned pineapple cubes	
SOAK the gelatin in the cold water for 5 minutes, and dissolve it in the boiling water. Add the re-	1 tablespoon granulated gelatin ¼ cup cold water CONTINUED

315

¼ cup sugar
1 tablespoon lemon juice
1¼ cups boiling water
½ cup hot pineapple juice
2 tablespoons Kirsch

maining ingredients, except for the pineapple, and stir well. Strain the mixture into a serving bowl and chill it until it begins to thicken. Fold in the pineapple cubes and return the jelly to the refrigerator to set. Serve very cold, with whipped cream, if desired.

Frozen Desserts

ICE CREAM is the most versatile and most beloved of desserts, alone or in combination with sweet sauces, fruits, or pastries. For all these uses, I can heartily recommend the excellent commercial ice creams now widely available.

Ice creams made at home in a churn freezer, whether it is turned by hand or by electric power, may surpass commercial ice creams in richness and flavor. The directions of the maker of the churn should be followed for best results.

Mousses are frozen without stirring, which makes them a good choice for the kitchen lacking a churn freezer.

Glace au Chocolat
(*Chocolate Ice Cream*)

¼ pound sweet chocolate
2 cups milk
½ cup sugar
4 egg yolks
1 cup heavy cream

BRING the milk to the boiling point with the chocolate, stirring until the chocolate is melted and the mixture well blended. Beat the egg yolks with the sugar in another pan. Stir in the hot chocolate milk and cook, stirring constantly, until the mixture coats the spoon. Cool the custard, stirring it occasionally, and fold in the heavy cream, whipped. Freeze in a churn freezer.

Glace à la Vanille
(*Vanilla Ice Cream*)

FOLLOW the recipe for *glace au chocolat,* above, omitting the chocolate. Flavor the cream with 1 teaspoon of vanilla extract, or boil the milk with a piece of vanilla bean.

Glace aux Fraises
(*Strawberry Ice Cream*)

MAKE vanilla ice cream, above. Just before freezing, stir in 1 quart of cleaned, sweetened, crushed strawberries, and 2 cups of heavy cream, whipped (instead of 1 cup).

Parfait au Café
(*Coffee Ice Cream*)

BRING the milk to a boil, add the coffee, and let the mixture infuse for 5 minutes. Beat the egg yolks with the sugar, and gradually stir in the hot milk and coffee. Cook in the top of a double boiler over hot water until the custard coats a spoon. Strain the custard into a bowl and cool it, stirring from time to time. Fold in the cream, whipped, and freeze in a churn freezer.

3 cups milk
5 tablespoons coffee beans
½ cup sugar
4 egg yolks
1 cup heavy cream

GRENADINE is a syrup made of pomegranates. It makes a delightfully colored and flavored ice.

Sorbet à la Grenadine
(*Grenadine Sherbet*)

BOIL the sugar and water together for 5 minutes. Add the grated yellow rind of the lemons, and let the mixture stand for 30 minutes. Strain

4 cups water
1 cup sugar
CONTINUED

317

2 lemons
1 cup grenadine

the syrup into a bowl, add the juice of the lemons and the grenadine, and freeze in a churn freezer.

Glace à l'Ananas
(*Pineapple Ice*)

1 can crushed pineapple
1 tablespoon sugar
1 tablespoon Kirsch

juice of ½ lemon

Mix all the ingredients and force them through a fine sieve, or purée in an electric blender. Freeze in a churn freezer.

Glace au Citron
(*Lemon Ice*)

2 cups water
1 cup sugar
2 lemons

Bring the sugar and water to a boil and remove the pan from the stove. To the hot syrup add the yellow zest of the lemons, being careful not to include any of the white pith (floating-knife vegetable peeler is a very useful tool for this task). Cover the pan, and let the syrup absorb the lemon flavor for 30 minutes. Add the juice of the lemons. Strain the mixture and freeze the ice in a churn freezer.

To make a lighter mixture, add a lightly beaten egg white before freezing.

Soufflé Glacé au Chocolat
(*Frozen Chocolate Soufflé*)

½ cup powdered sugar
6 egg yolks
3 cups heavy cream
¼ pound sweet chocolate

Combine the sugar and egg yolks in a metal mixing bowl and set the bowl in a pan of simmering water. Beat the mixture with a sauce whisk until the mixture is very fluffy and light and falls from the beater in a ribbon. Remove the bowl from the hot water and continue to whisk the mixture until it is cold. Soften the chocolate over hot water and cool it slightly before mixing it in. Blend well and fold in the cream, whipped stiff. Tie a band of paper around the edge of a soufflé dish to make a standing rim 2 inches tall. Pour the mixture into the dish and freeze it, without stirring, in a home freezer or in the coldest section of the refrigerator. To serve, remove the paper collar. The soufflé will stand above the edge of the dish, like a hot soufflé.

Mousse Glacée au Chocolat
(*Frozen Chocolate Mousse*)

TURN the mixture for *soufflé glacé au chocolat* into a *bombe* mold. Adjust the lid of the mold tightly and tie a strip of buttered cloth around the seam to prevent any salt water from leaking into the mold. Bury the mold in a mixture of 2 parts of ice to 1 part of rock salt for about 3 hours, until the mousse is firm. The mousse may also be frozen in a home freezer or in a refrigerator tray covered with aluminum foil. The flavoring may be varied to taste, with vanilla or coffee essence or liqueurs.

X

THE FORMAL BUFFET

THE FORMAL BUFFET

Never is the appearance of a dish more important than when it is to be presented on a buffet at a large formal reception. Here necessity has indeed been the mother of invention, for most of our elaborate cold preparations were created for just such occasions. The recipes for some of these decorative delicious dishes will be found under their categories.

A very wide variety of foods is suitable for the cold buffet, among them caviar, sea food cocktails, smoked fish, *pâtés,* salads of all sorts, fish and shellfish, *dindonneau froid nouvel-an,* galantine of chicken, *chaud-froid* of chicken, chicken in tarragon jelly, ox tongue, duckling Montmorency, Virginia ham, *foie gras* in port jelly, and *foie-gras mousse.* These cold dishes, which require little or no last-minute preparation, should be kept under refrigeration until serving time. If more than one platter of an aspic preparation is needed, the replacement should not be brought to the buffet until the last possible moment, so that it will appear at its best.

Hot foods afford a welcome contrast to the cold dishes on the buffet; they may be kept hot in, and served from, chafing dishes or similar equipment.

The menu-planner should take into consideration the different food habits and tastes that will undoubtedly be found in a large group, and should offer a choice of dishes that will suit all. The usual recipe for six will serve eight or more when more than one dish makes the course; for instance, three meat or poultry dishes will serve twenty-four guests at the buffet. The formal buffet should include a choice of such hors d'oeuvre as fish and *pâtés,* salad, cheese, and buttered rolls or small sandwiches. The sweet may consist of two or three kinds of cake or pastry and a fruit or cream dessert, again chosen with the varying tastes of the guests in mind.

INDEX

i

JOSEPH DONON

JOSEPH DONON was born in France on November 21, 1888. He came to the United States in 1912 as *chef de cuisine* for Henry Clay Frick. At the outbreak of World War I, he returned to France to serve in the army. Wounded and honorably discharged in 1917, he was awarded the Croix de Guerre with Palme and the Médaille Militaire. He is also an Officier of the Légion d'Honneur.

Returning to the United States after World War I, Donon became *chef de cuisine* for Mrs. Hamilton McKay Twombly and Miss Ruth Vanderbilt Twombly, serving them for thirty-eight years. He is a founder-member, and was for twenty-five years National General Secretary, of the American Culinary Federation, Inc., and has been Managing Editor of *Culinary Review,* the chef's national magazine. He is a founder-member and General Secretary of Les Amis d'Escoffier, and a founder-member and President of Les Amis d'Escoffier Society Foundation, Inc. Donon is also a member of the Advisory Commission on Hotel Technology, New York City Community College of Applied Arts and Sciences, and of the Advisory Committee on Culinary Art of the Food Trades Vocational High School, Board of Education, City of New York. For eighteen years he has been Chairman of the Annual Salon of Culinary Art and Exhibition of New York City, Inc.

Donon was, in 1950, the first recipient of the De Bands Annual Award, an "Oscar" presented each year to the person who has done most to advance the culinary profession in the United States. He and his wife now live in Middletown, Rhode Island.

THE TEXT OF THIS BOOK

IS SET IN GRANJON

a type named in compliment to Robert Granjon, type cutter and printer—Antwerp, Lyons, Rome, Paris—active from 1523 to 1590. The boldest and most original designer of his time, he was one of the first to practice the trade of type-founder apart from that of printer.

This type face was designed by George W. Jones, who based his drawings upon a type used by Claude Garamond (1510–61) in his beautiful French books, and more closely resembles Garamond's own than do any of the various modern types that bear his name.

This book was composed, printed, and bound by Kingsport Press, Inc., Kingsport, Tennessee. Paper Manufactured by S. D. Warren Company, Boston. Typography and binding designs by Warren Chappell.